WORTH DYING FOR

'An engagingly written, veritable page-turner. Whether the topic is ethnic identity, Japanese imperialism, Panamanian shipping law or the defeat of Nazism, flags speak volumes about our human condition'

– Lawrence Joffe, *Jewish Chronicle*

'In today's globalised and media savvy environment, the role of state and non-state symbols has become more important and in many cases more dangerous and evocative. This witty book brings to our attention this power, alongside the reality that we must not underestimate or misunderstand how the flags of our world came to be. A must read for anyone wishing to grasp the meanings behind today's international affairs.'

– Human Security Centre

WORTH DYING FOR
THE POWER AND POLITICS OF
FLAGS

TIM
MARSHALL

Elliott&Thompson

First published 2016 by
Elliott and Thompson Limited
27 John Street
London WC1N 2BX
www.eandtbooks.com

This paperback edition first published in 2017

ISBN: 978-1-78396-303-4

Picture credits:
Endpapers: alextrims/Shutterstock.com. Pages 12–13: Banaras Khan/AFP/
Getty Images; pages 42–3: Carl Court/AFP/Getty Images; pages 68–9:
Marcos del Mazo/Pacific Press/LightRocket via Getty Images; pages 112–13:
Khaled Desouki/AFP/Getty Images; pages 140–1: Handout/Alamy Stock
Photo; pages 162–3: Billy Wong/Alamy Stock Photo; pages 196–7: Jonathan
Torgovnik/Getty Images; pages 220–1: Jesse Kraft/Alamy Stock Photo;
pages 250–1: imageBROKER/Alamy Stock Photo.

15

A catalogue record for this book is available from
the British Library.

Typesetting: Marie Doherty
Printed by CPI Group (UK) Ltd, Croydon, CR0 4YY

MIX
Paper | Supporting
responsible forestry
FSC
www.fsc.org   FSC® C171272

CONTENTS

INTRODUCTION

*'I am no more than what you believe me to
be and I am all that you believe I can be.'*

The American flag 'in conversation'
with US Secretary of the Interior
Franklin K. Lane (Flag Day, 1914)

ON THE DAY OF 9/11, AFTER THE FLAMES HAD DIED
down and the dust had mostly settled, three FDNY fire-
fighters clambered onto the still-smoking wreckage of the World
Trade Center in New York City and raised the Stars and Stripes.

The event was not planned, there were no official pho-
tographers; the three men just felt that amid such death and
destruction they should do 'something good'. A local newspaper photographer called Tom Franklin captured the moment.
Later he commented that his picture 'said something to me
about the strength of the American people'.

How could a piece of coloured cloth say something so profound that the photo was reproduced not only across the USA
but in newspapers around the world? The flag's meaning comes
from the emotion it inspires. 'Old Glory', as the Americans

know it, speaks to them in ways that a non-American simply cannot share; but we can understand this, because many of us will have similar feelings about our own symbols of nationhood and belonging. You may have overtly positive, or indeed negative, opinions as to what you think your flag stands for, but the fact remains: that simple piece of cloth is the embodiment of the nation. A country's history, geography, people and values – all are symbolized in the cloth, its shape and the colours in which it is printed. It is invested with meaning, even if the meaning is different for different people.

What is clear is that these symbols have as much significance as they ever did, and in some cases more. We are seeing a resurgence of nationalism, and with it a resurgence of national symbols. Around the turn of the twenty-first century it had become fashionable in some intellectual circles to argue that the nation state would wither away in the age of globalization. That view completely missed the strength of identity still present in each nation.

Each of the world's flags is simultaneously unique and similar. They all say something – sometimes perhaps too much.

That was the case in October 2014 when the Serbian national football team hosted Albania at the Partizan Stadium in Belgrade. It was Albania's first visit to the Serbian capital since 1967. The intervening years had witnessed the Yugoslav Civil War, including the conflict with the ethnic Albanians in Kosovo. That ended in 1999 with the de facto partition of Serbia, following a three-month NATO bombing of Serb forces, towns and cities. Then, in 2008, Kosovo unilaterally declared itself an independent state. The move was supported by Albania and recognized by many countries – notably, Spain was one that did not. It understood that the sight of the Kosovar flag flying above the capital of an independent Kosovo might galvanize the Catalonian independence movement.

Fast-forward six years and tensions between Serbia and Kosovo, and by extension Albania, were still high. In the certain knowledge that they would be attacked, away fans had not been allowed to attend.

It was a slow-paced game, albeit with a highly charged atmosphere, punctuated by loud chants of 'Kill the Albanians' ringing out from the stands. Shortly before half time, fans and then some players began to notice that a remote-controlled drone was approaching slowly out of the night sky towards the halfway line on the pitch. It was later discovered to have been piloted by a thirty-three-year-old Albanian nationalist called Ismail Morinaj, who was hiding in a tower of the nearby Church of the Holy Archangel Gabriel, from where he could see the pitch.

As the drone came lower, a stunned silence began to descend around the stadium and then, as it hovered near to the centre circle, there was a sudden explosion of outrage. It was carrying an Albanian flag.

This wasn't merely the flag of the country, which alone would likely have caused problems. This flag bore the double-headed Albanian black eagle, the faces of two Albanian independence heroes from the early twentieth century and a map of 'Greater Albania', incorporating parts of Serbia, Macedonia, Greece and Montenegro. It was emblazoned with the word 'autochthonous', a reference to 'indigenous' populations. The message was that the Albanians, who consider themselves to be of ancient Illyrian origin from the fourth century BCE, were the real people of the region – and the Slavs, who only arrived in the sixth century CE, were not.

A Serbian defender, Stefan Mitrović, reached up and grabbed the flag. He later said he began folding it up 'as calmly as possible in order to give it to the fourth official' so that the game could continue. Two Albanian players snatched it from him, and that was that. Several players began fighting with each other, then a Serbian fan emerged from the stands and hit the Albanian captain over the head with a plastic chair. As more Serbs poured onto the pitch, the Serb team came to their senses and tried to protect the Albanian players as they ran for the tunnel, the match abandoned. Missiles rained down on them as the riot police fought fans in the stands.

The political fallout was dramatic. The Serbian police searched the Albanian team's dressing room and then accused the brother-in-law of the Albanian prime minister of operating the drone from the stands. The media in both countries went into nationalistic overdrive; Serbia's foreign minister, Ivica Dačić, said his country had been 'provoked' and that 'if someone from Serbia had unveiled a flag of Greater Serbia in Tirana or Pristina, it would already be on the agenda of the UN Security Council'. A few days later the planned visit of the Albanian prime minister to Serbia, the first in almost seventy years, was cancelled.

George Orwell's aphorism that football is 'war minus the shooting' was proved right and, given the volatility in the Balkans, the mix of football, politics and a flag could even have led to a real conflict.

Planting the US flag at the site of the Twin Towers did presage a war. Tom Franklin said that when he took his shot he had been aware of the similarities between it and another famous image from a previous conflict – the Second World War, when US Marines planted the American flag atop Iwo Jima. Many

Americans will have recognized the symmetry immediately and appreciated that both moments captured a stirring mix of powerful emotions: sadness, courage, heroism, defiance, collective perseverance and endeavour.

Both images, but perhaps more so the 9/11 photograph, also evoke the opening stanza of the American national anthem, 'The Star-Spangled Banner', particularly its final lines:

> *O say does that star-spangled banner yet wave*
> *O'er the land of the free and the home of the brave?*

At a moment of profound shock for the American people, the sight of their flag yet waving was, for many, reassuring. That the stars of the fifty states were held aloft by men in uniform may have spoken to the streak of militarism that tinges American culture, but to see the red, white and blue amid the awful grey devastation of Ground Zero will also have helped many ordinary citizens to cope with the other deeply disturbing images emerging from New York City that autumn day.

* * *

Where did these national symbols, to which we are so attached, come from? Flags are a relatively recent phenomenon in mankind's history. Standards and symbols painted on cloth predate flags and were used by the ancient Egyptians, the Assyrians and the Romans, but it was the invention of silk by the Chinese that allowed flags as we know them today to flourish and spread. Traditional cloth was too heavy to be held aloft, unfurled and fluttering in the wind, especially if painted; silk was much lighter and meant that banners could, for example, accompany armies onto battlefields.

The new fabric and custom spread along the Silk Route. The Arabs were the first to adopt it and the Europeans followed suit, having come into contact with them during the Crusades. It was likely these military campaigns, and the large Western armies involved, that confirmed the use of symbols of heraldry and armorial markings to help identify the participants. These heraldic bearings came to be linked with rank and lineage, particularly for royal dynasties, and this is one of the reasons why European flags evolved from being associated with battlefield standards and maritime signals to becoming symbols of the nation state.

Every nation is now represented by a flag, testament to Europe's influence on the modern world as its empires expanded and ideas spread around the globe. As Johann Wolfgang von Goethe told the designer of the Venezuelan flag, Francisco de Miranda: 'A country starts out from a name and a flag, and it then becomes them, just as a man fulfils his destiny.'

What does it mean to try to encapsulate a nation in a flag? It means trying to unite a population behind a homogeneous set of ideals, aims, history and beliefs – an almost impossible task. But when passions are aroused, when the banner of an enemy is flying high, that's when people flock to their own symbol. Flags have much to do with our traditional tribal tendencies and notions of identity – the idea of 'us versus them'. Much of the symbolism in flag design is based on that concept of conflict and opposition – as seen in the common theme of red for the blood of the people, for example. But in a modern world striving to reduce conflict and promote a greater sense of unity, peace and equality, where population movements have blurred those lines between 'us and them', what role do flags now play?

What is clear is that these symbols can still wield a great deal of power, communicating ideas quickly and drawing strongly on emotions. There are now more nation states than ever before, but non-state actors also use flags as a kind of visual sound bite to convey concepts ranging from the banality of cheap commercial goods to the depravity of religious and racial violence. This is something we've continually witnessed in recent history, from Hitler and the Nazi swastika – an image which even today evokes a powerful reaction – to the emergence of Islamic State (IS) and its emphasis on religious or prophetic symbols that can grab attention and, sometimes, garner support.

They go back to antiquity, and yet show no signs of going out of fashion. The most up-to-date consumer technology, the smart phone, can now provide you with the national flag emoji of your choice, and when there is a national tragedy, people from all over the globe will post messages along with the nation's emoji flag as a mark of solidarity.

This book could have told hundreds more stories than those found here; for example that of each of the 193 nation states, but that would have turned it into a reference work, and a very, very thick one at that. Instead, the stories recounted are those of some of the major national flags; some of the more obscure ones; and some that simply have the most interesting histories. In most cases the original meanings of the patterns, colours and symbols are important, but sometimes, for some people, those meanings have morphed into something else, and that is what the flag stands for now. The meaning is in the eye of the beholder.

We open with what is probably the most recognizable flag in the world: the Stars and Stripes, a visual representation that captures the American dream. Deeply revered by the vast majority of the population, it is the strongest example of how a symbol can come to define and unite a country. From the world's current empire we move to one of the past: the influence of the Union Jack extended to the furthest reaches of the globe, the flag representing the united front of a vast empire, but beneath the surface strong national identities persisted within the British Isles, and they haven't gone away, as shown by both the 2016 Brexit vote to leave the EU and continuing calls for Scottish independence.

The flag of the European Union also struggles to unify; in a continent with deeply rooted identities many Europeans are more attached to their national flags than ever. While some of these flags are based on Christian imagery, over the years the religious associations have mostly faded. Not so in the Arab nations to the south: their flags often feature powerful Islamic symbols and ideas that speak to the population. The symbolism is strong, but the nation states are weaker. The future may yet bring further change to the forms of these nations and their flags. A possible catalyst for this is the various terror cells operating in the region; the actions and influence of these organizations, ever present on our screens, are important to understand. Groups such as IS also use religious symbolism to great effect, instilling fear and creating global recognition.

Moving eastwards across Asia, we find an array of flags that reflect the sweeping movements of ideas, peoples and religions, in the twentieth century and well before. Many of these modern nation states have reached back to the roots of their ancient civilizations for their flags, often in response to a turning point in their history, in a fusion of old and new. In Africa, by contrast, we see the colours of a very modern conception of the continent, one that has thrown off the shackles of colonialism and faces the twenty-first century with increasing self-awareness. Latin America's revolutionaries kept closer cultural ties to the colonizers who shaped our world, and many of the continent's flags reflect the ideals of the nineteenth-century nation-builders.

Flags are powerful symbols, and there are plenty of other organizations that have used them to great effect – they may embody messages of fear, peace or solidarity, for example, becoming internationally recognizable in the shifting landscapes of identity and meaning.

We wave flags, we burn them, they fly outside parliaments and palaces, homes and showrooms. They represent the politics of high power and the power of the mob. Many have hidden histories that inform the present.

We appear to be in the midst of a resurgence of identity politics at the local, regional, national, ethnic and religious levels. Power shifts, old certainties fall away and at such times people reach for familiar symbols as ideological anchors in a turbulent, changing world. The reality of a nation does not necessarily live up to the ideals embodied in its flag; nevertheless the flag can, as Secretary of the Interior Franklin K. Lane 'quoted' the Stars and Stripes as saying, be 'all that you believe I can be'.

This is the emotion-charged emblem that is a flag. It has the power to evoke and embody sentiments so strong that sometimes people will even follow their coloured cloth into gunfire and die for what it symbolizes.

CHAPTER 1

THE STARS AND
THE STRIPES

---

*'There is not a thread in it but scorns
self-indulgence, weakness and rapacity.'*
Charles Evans Hughes, US
Secretary of State 1921–5

AMERICAN GOVT:
IS THE BIG TERRORIST
AGAINST THE MUSLIM
WORLD.
STOP
DRONE
ATTACKS. DRONE ATTACKS
IN PAKISTAN.
MAHAZ MULTAN.

Previous pages: Supporters of the banned organization Jamaat-ud-Dawa burn the Stars and Stripes in Multan, Pakistan, in May 2016, protesting against a US drone strike on Pakistani soil.

O SAY, CAN YOU SEE, BY THE DAWN'S EARLY LIGHT? IN the USA the answer is an emphatic yes. From dawn to dusk America is a riot of red, white and blue. The flag flies from government buildings, atop supermarkets and car showrooms, from the roof of the grandest mansion to the humblest white-picket-fenced homestead, and from the log cabin to the White House. In the morning it rises, hoisted onto a million flagpoles, as 'God's Own Country' sets about creating anew each day the most successful nation yet seen on earth.

This is the Star-Spangled Banner. The most recognizable, loved, hated, respected, feared and admired flag in the world.

The flag flies above well over 700 military bases in more than sixty countries around the globe, with over a quarter of a million US personnel serving overseas. To some of the people in these countries, the sight of the Stars and Stripes in this military context is a reminder that their security is partially dependent on the superpower. However, for America's detractors it is a symbol of overweening power and hubris. It represents the now out-of-date post-Second-World-War order, or even the flag of imperialism. Seen from outside a base in Poland, the flag is likely to give rise to a different emotion than when spotted in Iraq. A Japanese fishing fleet off the island of Taiwan will not question the right of an aircraft carrier flying the Stars and Stripes to plough the sea lanes in the way that a Chinese fleet would. Such is the disparity of emotion that some anti-Americans, particularly those on the European hard left, even depict it with swastikas instead of stars, displaying their own lack of historical knowledge, and spell America 'Amerika'. But this is alien to the countless people around the world who admire the USA and indeed call on Uncle Sam in times of need.

For Americans, the sight of their flag abroad is a reminder

of just how engaged they are in the world, of their history in various wars; criticism of their flag feeds into the perpetual debate in the USA about isolationism and engagement. President Bush entangled US military forces abroad in new wars, President Obama tried to get them out; he learnt the complexities of foreign policy, and ended up taking military action in more countries than his predecessor. As President Trump is now finding, for better or worse the power of America makes its presence on the international stage indispensable. A presidential decision not to act can have as many repercussions as that of intervening.

Americans revere their flag in a way few other peoples do. Its primary colours are their primary symbol of national identity, and at times the Stars and Stripes is considered an art form. The artist Jasper Johns has devoted much of his career to depicting it on canvas, in pencil, with bronze, and superimposing it on many other surfaces. For him it is not an icon to promote or denigrate, but the sheer power it projects and the emotion it arouses fascinates him as an artist. Andy Warhol also picked up the banner and took it forward, hinting at it in his visual commentary on America and Americana. For example, he took Neil Armstrong's photograph of Buzz Aldrin next to the flag on the moon, fused it with other photos from the epoch-making trip, and coloured it, including the flag, in pinks and blues. Warhol was not overtly political in his art, but he recognized not only an amazing moment in history, but also the time in which it took place. The psychedelic nature of the silkscreen paintings complemented the technological brilliance of the event at the end of the 1960s. The flag also featured on Bruce Springsteen's most successful album, *Born in the USA*; theories abounded as to the intentions behind the album artwork and what political message it conveyed. As Springsteen said in a *Rolling Stone* interview: 'The flag is a powerful image, and when you set that stuff loose, you don't know what's gonna be done with it.'

On the political front, the flag was used to tremendous effect in Ronald Reagan's seminal TV ad campaign of 1984, 'Morning in America'. Towards the end of the fifty-nine-second commercial, the voiceover delivers its killer line: 'It's morning again in America', and then Uncle Sam's future – young children – gaze in admiration as the Stars and Stripes goes up into a new day, a day of hope. The use of sunrise, the flag and an expectation of a bright future spoke to the collective consciousness of a nation still recovering from the Vietnam War and unsure of itself after the Carter presidency of 1977–81 in which Iran humiliated the USA during the Tehran Embassy hostage crisis.

From gazing at the flag from their front yard the children would have gone to school and recited: 'I pledge allegiance to the flag of the United States of America and to the Republic for which it stands, one nation under God, indivisible, with liberty and justice for all.' The Pledge of Allegiance, first published in 1892, spread slowly across the country and was useful in forging a national identity in the aftermath of the Civil War and during a period of high immigration. The flag was used to promote loyalty and unity in a fractured and diverse country; generations of Americans have since stood to attention, hand on heart, to acknowledge this symbol of the nation each morning. The Pledge became official when the National Flag Code was adopted at the National Flag Conference in 1923, by which time twenty-eight states had incorporated it into school ceremonies, and passed into law by Congress in 1942. In 1943 it became unconstitutional to require the Pledge be made, but it is a still a widespread practice and one almost unknown in other modern democracies.

All day these bits of painted cloth flutter in the breeze from sea to shining sea, with representations visible in every store, school, place of work and administration. And then at night, often with great ceremony and attention to strict guidelines, if 'Old Glory' is to be taken down it is done slowly, ensuring that no part of it touches the ground and that it is received 'by waiting hands and arms'. The Flag Code tells us: 'It is the universal custom to display the flag only from sunrise to sunset on buildings and on stationary flagstaffs in the open. However, when a patriotic effect is desired, the flag may be displayed twenty-four hours a day if properly illuminated during hours of darkness.' There are eight types of site where the flag is flown day and night under specific legal authority. These include Fort McHenry National Monument, Baltimore, the US Marine Corps Iwo Jima Memorial, Arlington, the White House, and at US Customs ports of entry.

For many Americans their flag is almost akin to a holy symbol. It is the representation of what they themselves describe as 'One nation under God', and American politicians have frequently paraphrased a saying of Jesus's, advancing the idea that America is 'a shining city upon a hill'. True or not, its flag is the subject of songs, poems, books and works of art. It represents its people's childhood, their dreams, their original rebellion against tyranny and now their freedoms. Its story is that of America itself, and the feelings Americans have for it represent the story of a nation. No other national flag comes close to equalling the recognition commanded by the US flag, nor the scale of negative and positive emotions it evokes.

This was highlighted after the 9/11 attacks when many

American politicians, and some TV news reporters and anchors began to wear a flag pin on their lapels. In the highly charged atmosphere of 2001 it quickly became either a badge of honour to show you cared, or, by not wearing one, grounds for suspicion of a lack of patriotism. It was of course a false dichotomy, but in the age of the febrile twenty-four-hour news cycle many people opted for safety first. Almost all members of staff in the George W. Bush administration wore them. The then Senator Obama briefly donned a flag pin after 9/11, then didn't, then, when challenged as to why during the 2008 presidential campaign, found it again and wore it almost every day.

It is ironic that many of these little metal symbols of emotion come from factories far away in East Asia. In 2010 the State Department was embarrassed to discover that its gift shop was selling USA flag pins in plastic bags marked 'Made In China'.

It took 183 years and several iterations for the flag to appear as we know it today. The current version with its fifty individual five-pointed stars, representing the fifty states of the Union, may not be the last. The prototypes for the flag emerged in the mid 1760s before the nation was born, and even now we hear the echo of those days in the modern conservative Tea Party; its members take their name from the original 'Sons of Liberty', who in 1773 threw 342 British chests of tea overboard in Boston Harbor in protest at unfair taxation. This event, which became known as the Boston Tea Party, consolidated the identification of Massachusetts as home of the 'Patriots' against what was increasingly being seen as an alien Britain. The Sons of Liberty had a flag with nine white and red horizontal stripes, and it is thought, but not proven, that the basic design of the Stars and Stripes was taken from this.

During the first skirmishes between the British and the

colonial militia in the American War of Independence, the rebel soldiers fought under a flag known as the Continental, or sometimes the Grand Union. It used thirteen alternating red and white stripes to symbolize the thirteen rebel colonies. On 4 July 1776, Congress declared independence from Great Britain and a year later passed the first of three major Flag Acts. The Marine Committee of the Second Continental Congress adopted a resolution which 'Resolved, that the flag of the United States be thirteen stripes, alternate red and white; that the union be thirteen stars, white in a blue field representing a new constellation.' Both thirteens represented the thirteen now independent colonies, which made up the brand-new (but then not so shiny) United States of America.

However, the Act did not designate what star pattern should be used or whether the stripes were to be vertical or horizontal, and to this day the flag is sometimes hung with the stripes vertical, as this is not considered wrong. Why the stars? That was not explained at the time, but a 1977 publication by the House of Representatives states that 'The star is a symbol of the heavens and the divine goal to which man has aspired from time immemorial.'

Nor was the symbolism of the colours of the flag explained. However, they match those of the Great Seal of the United States, the design of which Congress commissioned in 1776. The committee tasked to do this was told to come up with something that reflected the Founding Fathers' values. It chose red, white and blue, and the Great Seal was adopted in 1782. Upon presenting the seal to the Continental Congress, its secretary, Charles Thomson, said the colours 'are those used in the flag of the United States of America. White signifies purity and innocence. Red, hardiness & valour, and

Blue . . . signifies vigilance, perseverance & justice.' It is still used to authenticate some Federal documents, and appears on American passports.

You'd think that would be that, but as it is every American's flag, every American is free to interpret the colours as they wish. Some say the red is for the blood of the patriots who died in the War of Independence, some say it is for all those who have died fighting for the country. It is of course possible that red, white and blue came to mind in 1776 as they are the colours of the British flag, but that interpretation might not go down so well in the land of the now free.

The identity of the designer of the original flag is unclear. Legend has it that a seamstress called Betsy Ross, who made flags for the Pennsylvania navy, was responsible for the first version. That at least is what her grandson told a Historic Society meeting in Philadelphia in 1870. However, there also exists an invoice submitted to Congress by one Francis Hopkinson, who insisted that in return for designing the flag Congress owed him 'two casks of ale'. The jury is out.

Some years later a problem arose. In 1791 Vermont joined the Union, and then, the next year, so did Kentucky. This led to the Flag Act of 1794, which stipulated that for each new state that joined, another star and stripe would be added to the flag. It is this flag that would eventually become known as the Star-Spangled Banner, due to the poem that became America's national anthem – more of which later.

By 1818 the flag was becoming more stripy than a zebra, with eighteen states and Maine and Missouri already a twinkle in the Union's eye. So the Third Flag Act was passed, retaining the idea of an extra star for each new state, but returning to the original thirteen stripes of the original thirteen states. Congress still hadn't nailed down what pattern the stars should form, however, so there are numerous nineteenth-century versions of the flag still to be found in museums across the country. In 1912 President Taft passed an Act setting out exactly how the (by then) forty-eight-star flag should look, and that, apart from the addition of two more stars, is the one we see today.

Bar a star or forty, the flag of 1792 is pretty much the one for which the American lawyer and poet Francis Scott Key wrote his inspired ode in 1814, which became the national anthem, though not until 1931. The poem is the key to understanding how and why the flag captured the public's imagination; how a simple – even arbitrary – design created in the ferment of revolution could, over time, come to embody the highest values of the most powerful nation on earth.

The anthem arises from a conflict the British didn't start. They were fighting the French in the Napoleonic Wars and the conflict spilt over into the New World, because they occasionally plundered American shipping. President Madison took the opportunity to declare war on Britain in 1812. Sadly for Madison, Napoleon got it horribly wrong, lost the war he was fighting with most of Europe and was exiled in 1814, thus freeing up the might of the world's then superpower to have words with the country which would eventually take its place.

By 1814 Britain's troops had burnt the White House to the ground and its navy was sitting off the coast of Baltimore preparing to bombard Fort McHenry, the vital structure defending the city. Which it did. A lot. Just as the attack was about to commence, Francis Scott Key showed up, bobbing around in a boat alongside the might of the British navy, and asked for some prisoners to be released. He was eventually successful, but because he might have seen the British preparations for the assault, the Brits thought it wise to keep him on board for a few days while they demolished the fort.

Beginning at 06.30 on 13 September 1814, with Key on the deck of one of the warships, they launched the first of 1,500 bombs and 800 rockets at the structure. For much of the following twenty-five hours he peered through the smoke and the light thrown by the explosions to see if the huge American flag hoisted above the fort still flew, or if the bombardment had allowed the waiting British ground troops to storm in and raise their own.

The attack was a complete failure: the fort stood, and there were only four casualties on the American side. As Key looked on, the Stars and Stripes still billowed in the morning wind. He wrote the anthem there and then on the deck of a British warship: 'And the rockets' red glare, the bombs bursting in air, gave proof through the night that our flag was still there.' The first verse ended with a question, as he was still uncertain if the USA would prevail: 'O say does that star-spangled banner yet wave, O'er the land of the free and the home of the brave?' In the next few weeks the verses were printed and spread from Baltimore across the United States. Over the years the question mark seems to have become redundant in an increasingly confident American century.

The original flag that survived the shelling of Fort McHenry has been at the Smithsonian Institution's National Museum of American History since 1907. It now hangs in a low-oxygen, low-light, environmentally controlled chamber to help preserve it.

This is the design of the banner under which the Americans fought, as the Marines' Battle Hymn has it, 'From the halls of Montezuma to the shores of Tripoli'. This is the flag they flew as they created the American Empire, pushing ever further westwards across the continent, from the Appalachians, across the plains to the Rockies, and on to the Pacific.

It changed along the way, with extra stars added as new states joined the Union. Artillery units were the first in the military to use its basic design (with alternations) as a battle flag in the 1830s, then the infantry in 1842, and finally the cavalry in 1861. The cavalry had a Stars and Stripes guidon, which was a flag with a triangle cut out of the middle of the right-hand side, creating two points, and with the stars set in a clustered circle at the top of the hoist side. This was one of the designs carried by General Custer's Seventh Cavalry at the Battle of Little Big Horn in Montana in 1876.

Custer's men will have been familiar with another famous flag, the Gadsden, although even by that time it was already considered a relic of the colonial war. The Gadsden flag was designed by Brigadier General Christopher Gadsden (1724–1805) during the American Revolution and used as a battle flag by the Continental Marines. It has a yellow background featuring a coiled rattlesnake, beneath which are the words 'Don't Tread On Me'. This is not a request; it is a warning.

At the time the message was clear; the rattlesnake was found in some of the thirteen colonies and by the time of the Revolution was already associated with them. The motto 'Don't Tread On Me' was clearly a warning to the British and served to help rouse public opinion against being part of their empire.

Thereafter its use declined, despite a temporary uptick in the south during the Civil War. However, in the 1970s it was taken up again by activists in Libertarian circles as a symbol of individualism and mistrust of big government.

After 9/11 its popularity surged. The slogan hit a chord with a public stunned at being attacked in the homeland. Sales of the flag, and associated paraphernalia, grew steadily through the early part of this century and it began to feature on license plates and baseball caps.

Then, around 2010, supporters of the Tea Party and gun rights group took it up as a rallying call, but it also began to pick up other connotations. Extremists, opposed to the first black president, appropriated the flag and gradually, in some minds, it became associated with racism, helped by the fact that Gadsden had been a slave owner.

In 2014 the Equal Employment Opportunity Commission was asked to hear a case brought by a Postal Service worker that a co-worker's habit of frequently wearing a Gadsden flag cap to work was racial harassment. The Commission agreed the facts were enough for it to investigate but in a directive stopped short of deciding that the flag was a racist symbol and that wearing it constituted discrimination.

To those vehemently for or against the flag, ambiguity on the issue is not part of their world view. If you are on one side of the argument, you point to the part of the Commission's directive which states, 'It is clear that the Gadsden Flag originated in the Revolutionary War in a non-racial context.' On the other side the paragraph that leaps out at you is that the flag is 'sometimes interpreted to convey racially tinged messages in some contexts.'

To the rest of us the key words here are 'in some contexts'. As we will see later in the book, the British, especially the English, have been through similar arguments. There were periods late last century where, in context, flying the British flag was construed as potentially racist.

Flags can have 'multiple meanings'. You may mean one thing by flying one, but someone else may think you mean something entirely different. Proving intent, unless the symbol is overt, is difficult. Which brings us to the second most famous American flag.

During the American Civil War (1861–5), the North fought under flags featuring the Stars and Stripes, and it is from one of these that we get the nickname 'Old Glory'. A retired sea captain from the North, William Driver, had long given that name to the Stars and Stripes he flew on his ship. During the war he found himself in Nashville, Tennessee, where local armed Confederates demanded he hand over the flag, only to receive the reply, 'If you want my flag, you'll have to take it over my dead body.' The flag was then hidden until Union forces from the 6th Ohio Regiment took the city and were presented with it by Mr Driver. The 6th Ohio later adopted the motto 'Old Glory' and the tale spread around the country. Captain Driver is buried in Nashville and his grave is one of the few sites where the American flag can officially be flown twenty-four hours a day.

The North had their banner, but the armies of the Southern states also had theirs – in fact, there were several versions, and the one that has become the recognizable symbol of the south started off as the battle flag, rather than the official one of the Confederacy. It became known as the Confederate flag (and also as the Dixie flag or the Southern Cross) and had a red field with a blue diagonal cross with white stars on it. The Northern states won the war, and in its aftermath many Southerners continued to fly the Confederate flag at Civil War reunions, ceremonies and funerals. It commemorated the war dead, and celebrated a distinctly Southern culture. However, it also became associated with those in the South who had fought to defend slavery, and who, in the aftermath, ensured that the black population were subjected to numerous acts of racism designed to ensure they could not lift themselves from servitude. Among these were the notorious 'Jim Crow' laws, which effectively prevented many black people from voting. However, the Dixie flag, as the most overt symbol of this, only became nationally and then internationally recognized in the late 1940s. If you watch the epic 1915 blockbuster silent movie *The Birth of a Nation* by D. W. Griffith you will see, along with incessant racial stereotyping of black Americans, numerous scenes depicting massed ranks of the Klu Klux Klan, which was formed in the aftermath of the Civil War. However, in none of them is the Confederate flag seen, nor is it featured in the earlier Civil War battle scenes.

After the First World War there was a rapid growth in white supremacist groups, especially in the South, and gradually the Klan adopted the emblem. In 1948 the Confederate flag became the symbol of the States' Rights Democratic Party as it sought to shore up segregation against the fledgling civil rights movement. Article 4 of the constitution of what were nicknamed the 'Dixiecrats' stated: 'We stand for the segregation of the races.'

Despite this negative association, through the 1950s the flag also began to appear more and more as a cultural icon. To some it was simply a way of identifying heritage and regional pride, and representing the fact of the Civil War. It became widely used in advertising and popular culture. For example, the long-running *Dukes of Hazzard* TV series features two cousins riding around Georgia in a souped-up Dodge Charger, which was nicknamed the 'General Lee' after the famous Civil War hero. On its roof was the Confederate flag. This was not intended to suggest that the Dukes supported segregation, simply that they were 'good ol' boys' from the South.

However, given its political overtones and associations with the Klan, the flag has in some circumstances come to be considered as unfit to be flown in public places. In South Carolina in 2015 it was ceremoniously lowered and removed from the grounds of the capitol building following the murder of nine black churchgoers by a white man, Dylann Roof. Roof's online presence showed him spitting on the Stars and Stripes and waving the Confederate flag. After the ceremony President Obama tweeted: 'South Carolina taking down the Confederate flag – a signal of good will and healing and meaningful step towards a better future.'

Between 1865 and approximately the 1950s the Confederate flag had never seriously challenged the Stars and Stripes in popularity, but during the second half of the twentieth century it did grow into a reminder that not all the issues of the Civil War were in the past. However, by then its colours were firmly embedded in America's consciousness in the shape of the Stars and Stripes.

This flag has seen the Americans through two world wars, Korea, Vietnam, Iraq, Afghanistan and 9/11. It has also flown in the dust bowls of the Great Depression and during the civil rights movement. It has flown at hundreds of Olympic gold medal ceremonies as the country celebrates its continuing youth and vigour. It has flown at the top of Mount Everest and even been displayed on the Moon. Through all these struggles and victories, it has come to encapsulate so many of the values America holds dear, most importantly freedom and success. Small wonder that most Americans treat the flag with such respect, some to a degree outsiders can find strange.

The laws and codes of conduct surrounding the treatment of the American flag are staggering in their complexity, symbolism and number. It is in these laws that we glimpse the depth of feeling for what appears at times to be almost a sacred object, and we hear again and again the key words which press the emotional buttons of many Americans, such as 'allegiance', 'honour' and 'respect'. The rules about the flag would fill a book, but the few examples below, some of which are federal law under the Flag Code, tell us what patriotic Americans feel when they see, touch and think of their flag.

When the national anthem is played and the flag displayed, Americans not in uniform are supposed to stand to attention facing the flag with their right hand over their heart. Those in uniform should begin saluting the flag at the first note of the music, and hold the salute until the last note is played. That it is sung to a tune more suited either to a drunken karaoke night in downtime Tokyo, or perhaps the finale to a Verdi opera as a fat lady dies of consumption, is not the point. It is not the fault of the great American public that their anthem has an octane-fuelled octave and a half to it. It is regularly mangled at baseball, basketball and 'football' games by someone who won a Little League competition the year before and gets to destroy it by pitching their voice too high or too low. It is such a complex mix of chord changes that if you start wrong, you will finish wrong.

But back to the laws regarding the treatment of the symbol of the country. Things start to get serious – 'No disrespect should be shown to the flag of the United States of America; the flag should not be dipped to any person or thing.' 'When the flag is unfurled for display across a street, it should be hung vertically, with the stars arranged to the north or east. It must not touch the buildings, ground, trees or bushes' and so on for several pages, including, 'When the flag is used to cover a casket, it should be placed with the union at the head and over the left shoulder. The flag should not be lowered into the grave or allowed to touch the ground.' 'The flag should never be used for any advertising purposes.' 'The flag represents a living country and is itself considered a living thing. Therefore, the lapel flag pin, being a replica, should be worn on the left lapel near the heart.'

Although not all these rules are adhered to, notably that about advertising, the fact remains that the flag is a revered symbol. This reverence extends to folding it. I have seen this done several times at the funerals of American servicemen and women. On paper it reads oddly; if the flag were merely being put away in a drawer, the ritual might seem a bit much, but during a funeral ceremony, the slow, careful method of recovering and folding the flag, done in silence, can be quite moving. Belief in service to one's country is arguably more developed in the United States than in many other places, and the idea of sacrifice for a cause retains a hold on the collective psyche of the American military, especially the Marine Corps. When you attend the funeral of, or remembrance service for, a US Marine killed in combat you sense that it is a family affair.

That is why, while the detail of the flag-folding sounds over-dramatized in theory, in practice it can seem fitting: 'Straighten out the flag to full length and fold lengthwise once. Fold it lengthwise a second time to meet the open edge, making sure that the union of stars on the blue field remains outward in full view. A triangular fold is then started by bringing the striped corner of the folded edge to the open edge.' And so it continues until only the blue shows and the shape of the flag is now that of a cocked hat, emblematic of the tricorn worn by the Patriots during the American Revolution.

For the US Armed Forces, which oversee a flag-lowering and folding ceremony every evening or at funerals, each fold has a meaning. The first symbolizes life, the second the belief in eternal life, the third the belief in the resurrection of the body and so on through the fifth, which references naval officer Stephen Decatur's famous words about 'our country', 'right or wrong', to the eighth, 'a tribute to the one who entered into the valley of the shadow of death, that we might see the light of day'. In the end sequence the red and white stripes are finally wrapped into the blue and, according to the military, 'the light of day vanishes into the darkness of night'. Some of this could be considered problematic given its Christian undertones but, just as the Constitution does not stipulate which God the United States worships, the US military doesn't go into detail.

The Flag Code also guides Americans as to how to clean and mend the flag when necessary, but 'When a flag is so worn it is no longer fit to serve as a symbol of our country, it should be destroyed by burning in a dignified manner.' And therein lies a tale – nay, a funeral. The US Flag Code guidelines on the ceremony for burning the flag include the following advice:

> For individual citizens, small groups, or organizations, this should be done discreetly so the act of destruction is not perceived as a protest or desecration . . . an empty chair may be included as a 'Place of Honor' for those lovers of Old Glory who have passed on or are too infirm to attend.

Begin Ceremony. Include a chaplain or prayer per your tradition.

CEREMONY LEADER: 'We are gathered here to destroy these flags that have been deemed no longer service-able . . . These flags have inspired those who desired the taste of freedom and have represented hope to those oppressed by tyranny and terror . . . Know ye that these flags have served well and honorably. Their stars and stripes have been loosed to the winds of freedom and have basked in the light of liberty.'

This goes on at some length, concluding with everyone singing 'God Bless America'.

There are even more formal ceremonies. At these, before burning, at least six volunteers, called a 'Retirement Crew', stay behind to cut the flag into several pieces. Four hold a corner each, one cuts the flag and one receives the cut pieces. Again, there is an intricate ceremony concluding:

The flag is then burnt in a fire including redwood, 'to remind us of the red-blooded Americans who fought and died to build our nation under this flag. Oak for rugged strength that carried the flag across this nation and today reaches for the stars. Cedar to protect us from pestilence and corruption and preserve our American way of life' and 'walnut to remind us of the rich soil, the beautiful countryside and the fruitful brotherhood founded by our ancestors.'

Some patriotic Americans actually go to these lengths. It is similar to the Orthodox Jewish tradition of burying a damaged Torah scroll in a cemetery in order to show the 'words of God' absolute respect and is a reminder of how totemic the flag is to Americans.

Most Americans have probably not attended a ceremonial 'retirement' of their flag, and some will see it as a ritual too far. Nevertheless, that does not mean they would be relaxed about seeing their flag burnt, or otherwise desecrated, in anger. The burning of the American flag is a frequent occurrence in parts of the world, notably the Middle East, but it also occurs in the USA. Wherever it happens, the perpetrators are very aware of what they are doing and the emotions it will arouse. Even if they cannot articulate the meaning of their actions, they instinctively know that they are inflicting great insult, which is precisely why they do it. I've seen the flag burnt in Pakistan, Iraq, Egypt, Gaza, Iran and Syria. On all occasions there was something childlike about the inarticulate fury that accompanied it. Those doing the burning were obviously expressing their often-murderous feelings towards the USA, but I also felt that even in the act they subconsciously knew they were showing their frustration at their helplessness to do anything about the fact that the system they so hate is so successful. The participants were also from cultures which almost make a fetish of honour, and to so dishonour an 'enemy' brought great delight.

Seeing your country's flag burnt by people abroad can stir a different emotion than witnessing it being burnt in your own country by your fellow countrymen: in some ways the anger caused by this is even greater. A few years before his death the American singer Johnny Cash was introducing his song about the Stars and Stripes named 'Ragged Old Flag'. He told a packed auditorium, 'I thank God for all the freedoms we've got in this county. I cherish them. Even the rights to burn the flag, you know, I'm proud of those rights.' This surprised the Country and Western-loving audience, some of whom even began to boo before Cash asked for quiet and added, 'But I'll tell you what. We've also got a right to bear arms and if you burn my flag, I'll shoot you.'

It was an interesting take on the hierarchy of the First Amendment – 'Congress shall make no law respecting an establishment of religion, or prohibiting the free exercise thereof; or abridging the freedom of speech, or of the press; or the right of the people peaceably to assemble, and to petition the government for a redress of grievances.' And the Second – 'A well-regulated Militia being necessary to the security of a free State, the right of the people to keep and bear Arms shall not be infringed.'

In 1989 the Supreme Court used the First Amendment to interpret why it is not illegal in the United States to burn the national flag, as happens from time to time. It seems unlikely it would interpret the Second Amendment as allowing the response Mr Cash threatened. The ruling came at the end of a Supreme Court case, Texas v. Johnson, and was subsequently upheld (US v. Eichman, 1990). The ruling is interesting on many levels, not least because the court took the view that the flag was 'symbolic speech' – as such, burning it was stating a view and therefore was guarded by the First Amendment.

This followed years of flag-burning, especially during the Vietnam War. In 1968 Congress approved the Federal Flag Desecration Law, making it illegal to knowingly desecrate 'any flag of the United States by publicly mutilating, defacing, defiling, burning or trampling upon it'. Then, in 1984, a protestor against President Reagan's policies named Gregory Lee Johnson publicly burnt a flag in Dallas, Texas. The state arrested him for breaking a Texas state law and he was sentenced to a year in jail.

He appealed, citing the First Amendment, and the Supreme Court eventually ruled five to four in his favour. One of the judges, Justice Anthony Kennedy, reasoned as follows: 'Though symbols often are what we ourselves make of them, the flag is constant in expressing beliefs Americans share, beliefs in law and peace and that freedom which sustains the human spirit. The case here today forces recognition of the costs to which those beliefs commit us. It is poignant but fundamental that the flag protects those who hold it in contempt.'

This is a battle still being fought both in the United States and in other countries around the world. There is an unpassed bill still on the books in Congress called the 'Flag Protection Act of 2012' which, if made law in the future, could lead to prosecutions not just in the USA but abroad. The bill states that anyone who destroys or damages the American flag could suffer a 'fine of $100,000, imprisonment for up to 1 year, or both'. Anyone who steals a US flag belonging to the United States and then damages or destroys it could be liable to 'a fine of up to $250,000, imprisonment for up to 2 years, or both'. This paragraph also states that this law would be applicable 'within any lands reserved for the use of, or under the exclusive or concurrent jurisdiction of, the United States'. Arguably, had the Act been in force in the last decade, an Iraqi who burnt an American flag in Baghdad to protest the US invasion could have been prosecuted and sent to jail.

President Trump expressed his view when he was president-elect, tweeting 'Nobody should be allowed to burn the American flag – if they do, there must be consequences – perhaps loss of citizenship or year in jail!'. Given the reasons laid down by the Supreme Court, this tweet may have contradicted another he made in 2013 when he quoted George Washington: 'If the freedom of speech is taken away then dumb and silent we may be led, like sheep to the slaughter.'

Laws concerning flag desecration vary in different countries around the world, and the list of those where it is illegal is far from confined to repressive states. There does not appear to be a pattern or grouping for this, although in the modern democracies what laws remain on the books are rarely taken as seriously as in dictatorships. The UK, Australia, Belgium, Canada and Japan, for example, do not have laws prohibiting it, whereas Germany, Italy, Austria, Croatia, France, Mexico and New Zealand do. In Germany the law allows for a sentence of up to three years in prison, as it does in China. In France the maximum sentence is six months.

Back in the USA there is more work for lawyers who like to pose the question, 'What's red, white and blue – and made in China?' If the answer is the American flag then the lawyers can get to work. Several states have passed, or are enacting, laws that require all American flags sold to be produced in America. Minnesota has led the way, and now if a Minnesota shop sells a US flag made abroad the perpetrator of this new misdemeanour can be fined $1,000 and even thrown into jail for ninety days. It would make an interesting court case. The state law may contradict international trade deals signed at federal level.

Flags are big business in America, with 50 million sold there each year. Sales of foreign-made flags alone were worth $5.3 million in 2006; most were made in China, and despite the lawyers' efforts, it remains that way. The Chinese and others spotted the gap in the market following the 9/11 attacks in 2001. According to the US Census Bureau, quoted by the

Associated Press, on 12 September 2000 the Walmart chain sold 6,400 Stars and Stripes. One year later, the day after the Twin Towers attacks, they sold 88,000. In the wave of patriotism that swept the country in the following months, flag sales rose from coast to coast. Foreign suppliers were happy to meet the challenge. In 2000 sales of foreign-made American flags were worth about $750,000; in 2001 that figure rose to $51 million. Naturally demand slackened, but it is still well above pre-9/11 levels and now foreign-made flags account for about $5 million annually, a figure the state governors and American domestic flag-makers want to reduce.

In some countries, for example Sweden, exuberant flag-waving is considered unnecessary, almost uncouth. In others, such as the UK, there have been periods where ordinary people were nervous of flying the flag in case they were taken for right-wing extremists. But in the United States, for the majority of Americans it is not only as American as apple pie to take pride in the flag, but to make a public display of it.

How to reconcile this with the reality of America, where the American dream meets the nightmare of the projects, the prison system, the racism? The flag is still sometimes used to express the belief that there is something rotten in the state as well as something great. For example, in May 2016 anti-Donald Trump activists burnt the Stars and Stripes outside a Trump rally in Albuquerque, New Mexico, and several have been desecrated at 'Black Lives Matter' rallies. But to reconcile these different aspects is not so difficult: there are many positives to the American way of life. Like people everywhere, the flag's unique symbolism, its aspirations, speak to Americans, as national flags do to people everywhere; just because the country, the world, is not perfect, it doesn't mean you can't dream.

Of course it doesn't work for everyone. Once upon a time I used to deliver cars in America for people rich enough to pay a company to pay me to drive their vehicle several thousand miles if they moved home. On one occasion I was driving from Philadelphia to Texas, a mere 1,500 miles. I couldn't afford motels and so somewhere in Georgia I pulled into a service station to sleep for an hour and noticed a Creole man with his thumb out, trying to head south. He was a wild-looking guy, early thirties, unwashed, with red hair, ragged trousers and no shoes.

I slept, got a coffee and headed out to the highway. Several hours later, nearing Louisiana I pulled in again for another coffee. On the way out I noticed the same guy – thumb out, heading south. I did a quick calculation: the chances of him being picked up at the last pit stop, murdering his driver, disposing of the body, dumping the car and now setting up his next victim were slim.

We got on famously. By the time we entered Louisiana I had abandoned my plan to detour down to New Orleans and instead took a right and headed towards Texas and his home in Galveston, to which I was invited. We crossed the Gulf of Mexico on a ferry with dolphins racing ahead of us and leaping from the water. It was a beautiful moment on a beautiful day – and then we drove into the American nightmare.

Galveston is a racially divided oil town. My new friend lived on the wrong side of it. I had, and have subsequently, never experienced poverty in the First World quite like it. A run-down one-bedroom apartment which he shared with his sister – bare light bulbs, limited furniture and so many cockroaches the walls appeared to be moving. I stayed for a couple of days. One of them was the 4th of July. We went to a swimming pool where I was the only white person among several hundred black Americans. Wearing so few clothes only accentuated the difference in skin colour.

After my friend, along with some other older men, persuaded a few younger hot-headed guys not to repeatedly ask me 'What the fuck' I was doing in their pool, I asked one of my protectors if he would later be going to a July 4th party to celebrate Independence Day. He looked at me and then said slowly, 'What the fuck do I have to celebrate about this mother-fucking country?'

And yet. A few months later I was back in Philadelphia, at college, and talking with some new friends, two black Americans in their final year of study who were planning to join the US Marine Corps. 'Why?' I asked. 'Because,' replied one, 'I want to give something back to this great country which has given me so many opportunities.' As a white British youth in the early 1980s, this was not a sentiment I had ever heard from a young black British man.

Both sentiments, from Texas and Philadelphia, are valid, but the more widely held one is the latter. For all its faults America engenders in its population a sense of belonging, of liberty and of hope. To argue whether that is reality is not the point; it is *their* reality and, given the huddled masses still hoping to go to there, the idea of the red, white and blue of the Star-Spangled Banner still moves the human spirit.

For whatever reason, American ideals, captured in the emotionally charged history of the flag and divorced from the harsh reality of much of American history, speak to people and allow them, as Martin Luther King Jr said, to 'have a dream'.

CHAPTER 2

THE UNION AND THE JACK

'This blessed plot, this earth, this realm'
William Shakespeare, *King Richard II* (Act II, Scene 1)

Previous pages: A supporter of the right-wing British National Party waves a Union flag during a march past the Houses of Parliament in London, June 2013. Having been seen as a symbol of the Far Right in the 1970s and 1980s, the Union flag has subsequently been embraced by many – but not all – of the British people.

THE RED, WHITE AND BLUE – WHAT *DOES* IT MEAN TO you? The symbol of a modern, vibrant nation state confident in its identity? Or, to quote the actress Emma Thompson in early 2016 – 'a tiny little cloud-bolted, rainy corner of sort-of Europe, a cake-filled, misery-laden, grey old island'? The red, white and blue of the Union Jack might signify the glorious past of a still-powerful country, but then again it might give rise to the bitter nickname, as in parts of Ireland, for example, of the 'Butcher's Apron', symbolizing colonial oppression and a flag covered in blood. Perhaps it can stand for all these things simultaneously and much more besides: the 51st state? Cool Britannia?

As with any national flag, its beauty or otherwise is in the eye, imagination and politics of the beholder. However, more than most, the British flag, in its very union of symbols, can be divisive, even to parts of the very region it supposedly represents. Consider Shakespeare's celebration of 'this scepter'd isle' in *King Richard II*:

> . . . Against the envy of less happier lands
> This blessed plot, this earth, this realm
> This England.

At this point three of those 'less happier lands' might be Scotland, Northern Ireland and Wales, because for most of their inhabitants the words 'Britain' and 'England' are not interchangeable.

For England, the dominant partner in a union of four, this has not been an issue. For the others, particularly Scotland and Wales, it always has been. The shock of Brexit in the summer of 2016 has concentrated minds and many both within and without England no longer see the realm as so blessed. If this union is no longer part of the EU, some are prepared to unravel the Union Jack and instead merge their own flag with the twelve stars of Europe.

One occasion that encapsulated the English perspective was at Wembley Stadium on 30 July 1966, when England beat Germany to win the World Cup. If you study footage from the day you see that the stadium is a sea of red, white and blue, but almost every flag (apart from the German ones) is that of Britain, with just the occasional flag of England (the red Cross of St George on a white background) visible. Of course Britain was not playing that day, but to the English the British flag was synonymous with England. In the unlikely event that it had been Scotland playing in that World Cup final, there would not have been a single Union Jack flag flown but instead tens of thousands of Scottish Saltires (the white X-shaped Cross of St Andrew on a blue background) and other symbols of the Scottish nation.

To an extent some English people may have been subsuming their identity, putting their Britishness first and their Englishness second. To others, though, England meant Britain and Britain meant England. However, this idea seems not to be born of a thought-out and overtly practised superiority complex on the part of the English; it is more due to complacency and lack of understanding of the emotions of the other nationalities with whom they share their island. It was perhaps an inevitable consequence of the Act of Union between England (which had already fused itself with Wales) and Scotland in 1707 under Queen Anne.

The population of Scotland was about 1 million, the population of England and Wales was 5.5 million and the territory south of Scotland was becoming an economic powerhouse. Numerically it was never an equal relationship, and the divide has grown since the eighteenth century. Now, according to the Office of National Statistics, 84 per cent of the UK's 65 million people are English, 8.3 per cent Scottish, 4.8 per cent Welsh and 2.9 per cent Northern Irish. Most of us cannot help being influenced by such figures. However, just as all EU members are supposed to be equal, the 1707 Union was meant to be a coming-together of equals, too.

By 1707 there had already been a royal flag of Great Britain for a century. In 1603 James VI of Scotland and I of England had united the thrones of Scotland, Ireland and England but he kept the nations as separate states. He commissioned a new flag to depict his regal union on board ships, but it was not used as a national flag. The result was a mixture of the Scottish Saltire and the English flag. There were two problems with this. The red cross was imposed on top of the white saltire, so if you were so disposed, or Scottish, you might think that one flag was deemed more important. The other issue was that after Henry VIII had united England and Wales in the Laws in Wales Acts 1535–42, Wales was deemed a principality, not a state, and thus was not depicted on the flag whatsoever – not so much as a small fire-breathing dragon anywhere. The Welsh dragon dates back to at least the fifth century, when it was thought to be depicted in red or gold and may have been adopted as a symbol of power after the Romans left Britain. The oldest written reference to it as a Welsh symbol comes from *c.* 820 in the *Historia Brittonum*, possibly written by the historian Nennius. It refers to King Arthur, who, in legends written three centuries later by Geoffrey of Monmouth, is said to have had a father named Uther Pendragon (Dragon's Head). The Arthurian stories also feature a prophecy by Merlin about a long battle between a red dragon and a white dragon, which are taken as a reference to the struggle between Wales and England. So the symbol goes deep but, as stated, it never made it onto the flag of the United Kingdom. Constitutionally these issues may not matter, but emotionally, to this day, they do.

There's about as much clear documentation explaining why the English adopted the third-century St George as their patron saint as there is evidence for him slaying a dragon. However, it's thought that English Crusaders could have been using versions of his red cross on white for their pennants in the twelfth century, and that by the late thirteenth century it may have become widely adopted by English sailors. As for why his cross is red, that too is uncertain, although killing dragons was surely a messy affair and he may have got a spot or two of blood on his tunic.

Due to his exploits, St George has, in the heraldic traditions of coats of arms that developed in the eleventh and twelfth centuries, been identified with what came to be considered 'English values' – gallantry, honour, bravery – but as he was born in what is now Turkey and died in what is now Palestine, it's quite possible he never set foot upon the 'scepter'd isle', despite legend saying that he was at Glastonbury one year. Then again, he was never a Boy Scout either, but has become patriot saint of Scouts. Why he is further believed to be the saint who helps if you are suffering from syphilis is also lost to the mists of time.

St Andrew, meanwhile, became the patron saint of Scotland after the legendary King Angus saw a white X-shaped cross in a blue sky while fighting invading Saxons in the ninth century. The cross was taken to be that of St Andrew, who, legend has it, was crucified on an X-shaped cross. By 1286 it was well enough known for the government of Scotland to use it on seals.

By the time James joined the two thrones in 1603, the flags were symbols of the stark contrast between two entities who had been having a centuries-long quarrel. If the English were not marauding around in Scotland, then the Scots were busy raiding into England.

When the time came to design the new royal flag, it was obvious that there might be some tension. James authorized a proclamation beginning: 'Whereas, some differences hath arisen between Our subjects of South and North Britaine travelling by Seas, about the bearing of their Flagges', and went on to decree the fusion of the Cross of St George and the Saltire. When it became apparent that the English cross would be superimposed on the Scottish one, a group of eminent Scots asked the Earl of Mar to lobby the king to reconsider, because the design 'will breid some heit and miscontentment betwix your Majesties subjectis'. He didn't reconsider, and there did indeed follow some miscontentment between the subjectis. For some years after, many Scottish ships flew either the Saltire, or even, some evidence suggests, the new united flag but with the Cross of St Andrew atop the George Cross. To the modern eye this looks like a giant X crossing out the English symbol.

This fusion established the new design as the royal flag, until Oliver Cromwell came along and promptly abolished it in 1649, together with King Charles I, who was beheaded. Eleven years later, with the restoration of the monarchy, one of them made a comeback, and it wasn't the headless Charles.

Fast-forward to 1707, when various flag designs symbolizing the new official Kingdom of Britain were considered, including one with the Saltire taking prominence over the Cross of St George, which was described as a 'Scotts union flagg as said to be used by the Scotts'. Queen Anne and her Privy Council decided against it, and chose the first design that had been put to them, the one which featured the St George Cross in prime position, and which had already been flown from royal ships for a century.

This was the first Union flag and it would last until 1801 and the union of Great Britain and Ireland. Then the red saltire of St Patrick, representing Ireland, was added to the design to create the flag that we see today. The Irish themselves never embraced the red saltire, as nationalists felt it a British imposition. When Ireland became an independent country in 1922, the red saltire survived in the flag, partly as a representation of Northern Ireland's continued presence in the Union, and partly because it would have been horribly expensive to change everything.

The Cross of St Patrick is also why there are thin white stripes separating the red cross from the blue background. These contrasting lines are known as fimbriations – in the traditions of heraldry which informed the designs of some military and, later, national flags, certain coloured areas must be separated by 'metals' – white or silver, for example.

By this point you may have noticed that the terms British flag, Union flag and the popular Union Jack are being used interchangeably. That is because I have it on good authority that they can be, and that it is unnecessary to have stand-up rows in the pub about this, or resort to writing angry letters to the *Daily Telegraph* and *The Times*. Many a row has begun with the words, 'It can only be called the Union Jack when it is flying from the jack of a ship', but rarely has it concluded decisively. So, for the definitive answer I turned to Graham Bartram, author of *British Flags and Emblems* and leading vexillologist at Britain's Flag Institute, which in turn is a world authority in vexillology – the study of flags. Given that Graham personally designed the flag of Tristan da Cunha and helped with the flag of Bosnia, he is a better source than the man with the red face down the pub, and unlike your pub friend he's prepared to accept that the contradictory evidence is what proves the rule.

As Graham, and the Flag Institute, has it, the word 'jack' was being used by 1600 for a small flag flying from a small mast. Within thirty years it had become common practice to fly the Union flag from a particular mast, which was now called a 'jack'. We know that it was called the Union flag by then as King Charles refers to it in a 1634 proclamation, insisting that it should not be flown from any vessel other than those in the navy ('on pain of Our high displeasure'). There is evidence that it became known as the Jack flag, and then as the Union Jack.

So far, so 'Jack only aboard ship', but there was no formal ruling on this and the term Union Jack passed into common usage for the flag wherever it was displayed. There is a 1902 pronouncement from the Admiralty declaring that it could be called either the Union Jack or the Union flag. Six years later the Earl of Crewe, in a reply to a parliamentary question, stated: 'The Union Jack should be regarded as the national flag.' And that, you might think, is that. Except neither the Admiralty nor Parliament (without due process) had the authority to make such statements and regard them as final.

Besides, as the Flag Institute notes, by 1913 someone at the Admiralty hadn't read the 1902 memo and referred in writing to the 'Union flag', adding in a footnote: 'A Jack is a Flag to be flown only on the "Jack" Staff.' The authoritative Reeds Nautical Almanac used to solemnly declare that it was the Union Jack only when it was a 'small flag flown from the jackstaff', but the last time it dipped a toe into these turbulent waters was in 1993, since when it has preferred not to mention the subject.

In 1933 the then Home Secretary, Sir John Gilmour, proclaimed that 'The Union flag is the national flag and may properly be flown by any British subject on land.' However, his saying it was so did not make it so, and to date no law has been passed enshrining the Union Jack/flag as the flag of the UK. It has become so through custom and practice, which, although unusual, is partially due to the UK's lack of a codified constitution. As for the Jack/flag debate, unless evidence is uncovered to the contrary, then what should be the last word (but probably won't be) goes to the Flag Institute's booklet titled *Union Flag or Union Jack?* From page two:

> Among those who are informed about the matter, it is generally accepted that either name may be used . . . There is apparently a movement in some quarters, including, it has been suggested, in some Government departments and the media, including the BBC, to seek to exclude the name 'Union Jack' on the grounds of incorrectness. We might also ask, then, what happens to the colour and personality of the flag when a politician or a newsreader wishes to appeal to the history and the power of the standard, in a speech or an article, or a piece of editorial reflection. Or what happens when the public audience for that speech or article fail to understand, or just don't like, the reference to the Union Flag rather than the populist Jack . . . It is certainly the considered view of the Flag Institute that both terms are correct; and that either may be used.

This appears to be the Flag Institute's way of saying 'get over yourselves'.

Whatever you wish to call it, this is the multicoloured, fimbriated, complex and yet clear flag that travelled all around the world. It was flown at Waterloo, Trafalgar, Balaclava, Rorke's Drift, on the Somme, at Gallipoli, on the beaches of Normandy and on to Goose Green in the Falkland Islands, Basra in Iraq and Camp Bastion in Afghanistan. It also flew over grandiose official buildings in capital cities around the globe, and in the backwaters of obscure regions in India, Malaya, Burma, Kenya, Sudan, Australia, Belize and so many other places where the map was coloured pink and the sun never set on the British Empire. Until eventually it did.

Before that, though, across the world the sight of the flag of Great Britain was the representation of an island nation with an astonishing story. The flag stood for British sea power, empire, scientific progress and exploration. Simultaneously, to some it represented the evils of colonialism, and a player in a game of great power rivalry. It has also represented regiments of many colours and creeds who have fought with and for the UK.

How it is seen now depends on whom you ask. In the Palestinian territories, for example, the Union Jack is negatively associated with the British role in dividing Mandate Palestine between Jews and Arabs. However, in India, it's not so clear cut. There is certainly a degree of contention, considering the history of British colonial rule, replete with oppression, economic exploitation and resultant famines – and there are some who are keen to emphasize the negative impact of colonialism in India, particularly those in authority. But that is not the only sentiment, and my experience is of a residual warmth towards the British flag and what it stands for. A recurring joke

I have heard from ordinary people while travelling in India is 'If you British would just come back, things would work better'. It is not meant to be taken seriously but as a comment on the somewhat chaotic organizational skills of the modern civil service occasionally on display in India. Perhaps the lack of a more widespread animosity to the colonialists is symbolic of an increasingly confident India, with the fastest growing major economy in the world, looking to a future in which the Brits and their flag are of diminished importance.

These days, the Union Jack is to be seen around the world in two forms. One: commercially, on a billion T-shirts, album covers, mugs and thousands of products emblazoned with the symbol of the venerable home of the Mother of Parliaments, the Industrial Revolution and one of the greatest empires ever seen, but also of a new cool twenty-first-century Britannia. The other form is the same way as always: on flags. Britain's colonial legacy means the Union Jack still flutters in the breeze of many a nation state, but when it does so it is usually in the canton, or top left-hand-corner, of a flag which remembers the past but looks to its own future.

The symbol of the UK is still present in the flag of Fiji, for example, although the country is in the process of changing its flag. Prime Minister Bainimarama has said it is 'time to dispense with the colonial symbols', stating that there is a 'need to replace the symbols on our existing flag that are out of date and no longer relevant, including some anchored to our colonial past. The new flag should reflect Fiji's position in the world today as a modern and truly independent nation state.' It seems that other Commonwealth countries agree; just four of the fifty-three members (Fiji, Tuvalu, Australia and New Zealand) still retain the Union Jack in their flags.

Australia and New Zealand periodically ask themselves if they can be bothered with going to the trouble of designing a new, non-Union Jack flag, but so far answer in the negative. In the 2016 New Zealand referendum, 56 per cent of voters chose to keep the existing version and rejected a rather natty dark-blue flag featuring a striking silver-white fern branch. It seems that public opinion is on the side of the Union Jack; to many it represents their ties, past and present, with the UK. Perhaps that's due to the lasting effects of British colonial rule, with the majority of the population, around 69 per cent, being of European descent, mostly British and Irish. The indigenous Maori form around 15 per cent of the population. It seems likely that given time and changing ethnic demographics, one day the flag may be replaced, but for the next decade or so the Union flag's position on it appears safe.

The Union Jack features in a few more flags around the world: the island of Niue, which is administered by New Zealand, and the British protectorates of Bermuda, Anguilla, the Cayman Islands and Montserrat feature the Union Jack in the canton of their flags, as do those of Ontario and Manitoba in Canada. British Columbia breaks this tradition and has the Union Jack across the top third of the flag, with the sun rising above the waves of the Pacific in the bottom two-thirds. Newfoundland and Labrador uses a modified version of the British flag in its left half.

One of its less well-known appearances is on the flag of Hawaii. The Hawaiian flag was, and remains, a hybrid in the style of the American flag's stripes, but with the British flag in the top left-hand corner, a design that reflects its relative proximity to the USA but also its traditional relationship with Britain. Hawaii was never a British colony, but the British emblem persists in its flag despite an unfortunate 'misunderstanding' in 1842 by one Lord George Paulet. He was a British Navy commander with a large degree of initiative and confidence in his abilities, but a lack of access to a phone or Twitter account, or indeed any other form of electronic communication. Had that been different he might not have unilaterally taken control of Hawaii on behalf of the British Crown even as the British Crown was preparing to acknowledge that Hawaii was not subordinate to the UK.

Relations between Honolulu and London were cordial and trade brisk, and so when, in 1816, King Kamehameha I wanted a national flag designed, he approved the one which came back bearing the current symbols. His first son, King Kamehameha II, maintained it, and his second son, King Kamehameha III, saw no reason to change things. It was win/win. However, in 1842 Paulet had worked himself up into a lather over some presumed injustices against British subjects living on the islands. From aboard the warship HMS *Carysfort* in Honolulu harbour he issued a series of demands to His Majesty King Kamehameha and warned: 'Sir: I have the honour to notify you that Her Britannic Majesty's ship *Carysfort*, under my command, will be prepared to make an immediate attack upon this town at 4 p.m. tomorrow (Saturday) in the event of the demands now forwarded by me to the King of these islands not being complied with by this time.'

With an hour to go before bombardment would commence, the king wisely decided that discretion was the better part of valour and Paulet duly hoisted the British flag on all the islands of Hawaii. And there it stayed for a whole five months until Paulet's superior, Rear Admiral Thomas, showed up, tore a strip off him, apologized to the king, hauled down the flags and acknowledged the restoration of Hawaiian sovereignty. 'No harm done,' said the king, or words to that effect, and despite that little local difficulty, and the UK's formal acknowledgment of Hawaiian sovereignty the following year, the design remained (with a slight alteration in 1845). It is the only US state flag to incorporate the Union Jack, and so even today the British flag flies over a little piece of the Republic that is the United States of America.

Of course not everyone was so magnanimous, especially most of those countries which had not only tasted versions of gunboat diplomacy but also colonialism of somewhat more longevity. Pakistan, India, South Africa, Kenya, Nigeria, Burma and so many others ditched the red, white and blue upon becoming nation states and made their own statements of sovereignty through colour, design and symbolism.

And so here we are now, a twenty-first-century Britain, with one of the oldest nation-state flags in the world, which cannot escape its glorious but bloody past, and with the people it represents constantly asking themselves about their modern identity both at home and abroad.

At a political level the Union flag still represents a major power in the world, albeit one which is losing its voice in the EU. The military that fights under it is massively diminished, but in comparative terms is easily among the strongest in Europe. Economically the flag still represents one of the largest economies in the world and, as an expression of 'soft power', the continuing success of its scientific and cultural exports.

The Union Jack no longer stands for an empire, although it will always have imperial connotations; even so it is still treated with respect, if not reverence, by most of those it represents. Many Brits do not know one end of their flag from the other, which is a mark not of disrespect but of an amiable cultural trait – and explains why from time to time it is flown upside down, despite this being a sign of distress.

The correct way is to have the wider of the white stripes, separating the red from the blue, at the top left-hand side of the flag. But people are to be forgiven if they are standing outside Buckingham Palace on a royal wedding day and forget to check the status of the Union flag handkerchief or some such they may be waving. It is a little more serious at international events, although even the British government have got this wrong before, including at a trade signing deal with China in Downing Street, thus proving that even at the top levels many Brits don't know the top from the bottom of their flag. And in 2016, as Britain plunged into the EU negotiations ahead of its In/Out referendum, the flag could be seen hanging upside down outside the EU headquarters in Brussels. It's not known if this was accidental, the French having a laugh, or the Brits signifying distress.

How should it be treated? The British flag should be 'hoisted briskly', but 'lowered ceremoniously'. It should not be handled in a manner so as to permit it to be easily torn, soiled or damaged. However, it is not against the law to burn or otherwise destroy the flag. In contrast to the tradition in the USA and some other countries, the British flag is allowed to touch the ground. In the 1980 footage of one of the ceremonies when the British flag was lowered for the last time in Rhodesia, as it became Zimbabwe, you see it being allowed to drop all the way into the African dust; the symbolism surely did not escape those present. On Remembrance Sunday the flag, and others including the Queen's, are draped on the ground. This is known as vailing and is a mark of respect.

Then there are the government-approved regulations as to how to fly the national flag, or indeed any flag, most of which are either unknown to the public or are cheerfully ignored. According to the 2012, more liberalized regulations, you may fly a flag if it is 'maintained in a condition that does not impair the overall visual appearance of the site' upon which it is displayed, and of course if you have permission to so do from the owner of the site – this includes the local highway authority. There are three categories of flag: those 'which can be flown without consent of the local planning authority', those 'which do not need consent provided they comply with further restrictions' and 'flags which require consent'. In the event of your being unsure you are advised to 'contact your local planning authority, who can provide detailed advice'. When they say 'detailed' advice, they really mean it.

For example, you do not need consent to fly the flag of any other country, even that of France. The UN flag is fine; in fact, you are at liberty to fly the flag of any international organization of which the UK is a member. So flying the International Monetary Fund flag is OK, but you need to check if you want to display that of the International Association for Bear Research and Management, as the UK is not listed as a member, nor does the IABRM feature in the government's list of permissible flags. Furthermore, flags of 'any island, county, district, borough, burgh, parish, city, town or village within the United Kingdom' are all fine, as are the flags of the Ridings of Yorkshire – indeed any historic county within the United Kingdom, and more. What you can't do is attach advertising to the flag.

Some flags, however, must comply with several other restrictions regarding size, lettering, number, location and duration of display. For example, since 2012 you can design a flag representing yourself, with your name on it, and are at liberty to fly this from a vertical flagpole on the roof of your house. However, only one flag thus situated is permitted at any one time. If you have a flag flying from a projecting flagpole, you cannot have another flying from a vertical flagpole on your roof without permission. Fortunately, you can have a flag flying both from the rooftop and in your grounds without having to ask permission. This last ruling is subject to certain other restrictions which I won't go into, but which your local planning authority would be glad to discuss with you in great detail. Flag 'You', or others in this category, can be of any size except 'where a flag is flown within an area of outstanding natural beauty, area of special control, the Broads, conservation area or a National Park'.

The British military have their own rules and restrictions regarding the flying of flags, which are equally detailed and more closely adhered to. For example, the Union Jack flies at the masthead of a ship when the Sovereign or an Admiral of the Fleet is present (though Royal Navy ships and submarines will always fly the White Ensign flag). In the unlikely event of a court martial taking place on board, it would also be flown, but from the yardarm. In the seventeenth century navy ships flying the flag were exempt from paying harbour duties, which encouraged commercial vessels to fly it in order to avoid taxes. Charles I's insistence that only naval ships could fly the Union Jack still applies today.

The UK is made of many things, but summed up in one symbol. As Graham Bartram puts it, 'A flag is the one object which represents your entire national identity. If I asked a hundred people how they would express Britain in one object, or to bring along a single object which represented the UK, ninety-nine would bring along the Union Flag, and one might bring a teapot.'

If you can get past the relatively few self-hating Westerners in the UK and their media cheerleaders, you still find a residual respect and sometimes deep admiration for the Union flag, but the level of these emotions varies in different parts of the country. Among England's myriad ethnic minorities, the British flag appears to be more attractive than the English version; polling suggests that this is because it is considered to be more inclusive of everyone, whereas the English flag, to some, signifies 'whiteness'.

A YouGov/British Future poll ('This Sceptred Isle: 2012') threw up some fascinating insights into the differences. The unifying factor was the monarchy: 84 per cent of English respondents associated the flag with the monarchy, as did 82 per cent of Welsh and 80 per cent of Scots. The British military was also associated with the flag for 80 per cent of English, 77 per cent of Welsh and 70 per cent of Scots. However, when we move to the words 'pride' and 'patriotism' the divide is more accentuated: 80 per cent of English respondents associated the flag with pride and patriotism, but that dropped to 68 per cent of Welsh and just 56 per cent of Scots. Overall, a majority of Britons hold mostly favourable views of their flag, but the divide is present again when it is connected with negative traits. For example, just 15 per cent of English people looked at the flag and connected it with racism and extremism; 25 per cent of Scots polled felt this way. The figures don't prove that the English see themselves in the Union flag more than the other nations and are more attached to it, but they do suggest it. They also indicate that the centuries-old difficulties between the nations of the UK are more keenly felt outside England.

Nowhere is that more true than in Northern Ireland, an issue now brought back into focus amid the Brexit crisis. Even in 2016 there are still districts in which religious and political affiliations are publicly symbolized not just by the flag that is flown, but also by the colour of the pavement kerbs. There are Protestant parts of Belfast, for example, where you turn a corner and the kerbs are red, white and blue in support of the Union, and Catholic districts where they are green, white and orange to represent Ireland's tricolour, although this is less common these days. Most of the city's population don't bother to get out the paintbrushes, but the colours on display do represent an ongoing battle for identity through symbolism of which everyone who lives there is aware.

The green of the Irish tricolour signifies Ireland's Catholics, the Republican cause and revolution, orange represents Ireland's Protestants, and the white separating the two colours hope for peace between them. Orange, the colour of Protestantism, is linked to the Battle of the Boyne of 1690. William of Orange, the Protestant King of England, Scotland and Ireland, defeated the forces of the deposed Roman Catholic King James II at the River Boyne, near Drogheda in Ireland. This consolidated English – and Protestant – domination of Ireland, a victory still celebrated by some Protestant 'Orangemen' each 12 July, mainly in Northern Ireland. During the Orange Order marches the British flag is prominent, and at bonfires on the evening of the 12th it is not unusual for the Irish flag to be burnt. Burning the flag of another nation is not the norm anywhere else in the UK, and that it takes place at all speaks of the emotions of the politics of Northern Ireland.

The flying of flags from government buildings is an especially sensitive issue. In December 2012 Belfast City Council decided to limit the number of days when the Union flag would fly from the City Hall in order to 'acknowledge that we live in a shared society'. Loyalists, who are mostly of Protestant heritage, saw this as a symbolic dilution of British sovereignty. Protests began immediately and lasted for months, occasionally descending into rioting. In 2015 the Irish tricolour appeared above the Parliament Building at Stormont for ten minutes. Loyalist politicians declared themselves 'deeply offended', and an unsuccessful police investigation began which involved seven detectives working for at least four months to find those responsible. A shadowy pro-Irish independence group, the '1916 Societies', said it raised the flag as a symbolic gesture to assert 'that British rule is based on conquest, is without legitimacy, and usurps the sovereign will of the people'. The group's name harks back to the 1916 Easter Rebellion against British rule in Ireland, which resulted in up to 500 deaths.

The Irish tricolour came into popular use in 1848 and was inspired partly by the republican revolutions across Europe that year. Its use spread after it was unfurled by the nationalist Thomas Francis Meagher at a meeting in Waterford on 7 March 1848. In a speech he expressed the hope that 'The white in the center signifies a lasting truce between the "Orange" and the "Green", and I trust that beneath its folds the hands of the Irish Protestant and the Irish Catholic may be clasped in generous and heroic brotherhood.' It's a work still in progress, as displayed on Belfast's pavements. The year 2016 was no different. The 100th anniversary of the Easter Rising in Dublin led to heightened tension and incidents in the Irish Republic, Northern Ireland and parts of Scotland.

This volatile and very visible sensitivity over the British flag in Northern Ireland may have contributed to the decline in its use throughout the UK during the late 1970s and 1980s. It is impossible to prove, but once the armed violence of what were called The Troubles in Northern Ireland exploded onto TV screens, the wider population may have become more educated about the problematic shared history of the islands and its symbols. What is widely accepted is that at about the same time both the British and English flags began to be appropriated by the extreme Far Right in England. Both, but especially the British flag, featured prominently at the extreme right-wing National Front Party marches and in their literature and discourse. The NF, complete with flag lapel badges, began to try to recruit supporters outside English football grounds and inside pubs. Gradually an association grew between the flags and fascism.

The British had never really gone in for saluting their flag, or flying it at schools; there was no daily pledge of allegiance, and such rules as there are in handling it were unknown to almost everyone and still are. However, it was the symbol of the nation, and mostly respected as such. Then it began to fall out of fashion, and the English flag was almost a no-go area for those nervous of being associated with the Far Right. There was an unspoken assumption in England that prominent displays of either flag, outside state events, might symbolize an aggressive mindset supporting the dominant white culture of the pre-mass-immigration era.

To some it undoubtedly did. In the mid 1980s I took a bus from Oxford train station bound for Oxford United football club, which was due to play Leeds United. The bus, packed with Leeds supporters, passed a group of young black men in their late teens. From the top deck came the chant 'There's no black in the Union Jack! Send the bastards back!' It was routine, albeit to be reviled. It was shocking, but it wasn't surprising.

Had there been black in the Union flag, they would simply have come up with something else equally moronic and offensive, but it was interesting that they had seized upon the flag as a weapon of division.

Attitudes towards the flag of St George began to change in the mid 1990s. Many observers, this one included, believe that the tipping point was the 1996 European Football Championship Finals, during which England played Scotland at Wembley Stadium in London. This was at a time when Tony Blair's Labour Party, which would take power in 1997, was already talking about granting devolution to Scotland. There had been a rise in Scottish and Welsh nationalism in the late 1980s and 1990s, although it was less tied to right-wing sentiment. Now devolution was in the air at exactly the same time as there was a massive merchandising campaign aimed at the English to coincide with their hosting of the finals. Thirty years on from 1966, there was more awareness that the flag of England was not the Union Jack, and that as the Union flag included the Scottish Saltire, waving it about at an England v. Scotland match was not appropriate. England won 2–0.

Twenty years later still, England sports fans are now comfortable wearing a replica shirt bearing the Cross of St George and waving the English flag. In 2010, the black British rap star Dizzee Rascal was confident enough to front England's official World Cup song in an England shirt with his name on the back while singing 'Come and have a go if you think you're hard enough'.

The devolution of powers to Scotland, Wales and Northern Ireland has helped give rise to a greater awareness of Englishness, amid talk of such issues as English taxpayers subsidizing Scottish welfare. The divide between the countries has also been widened by the result of the 2016 referendum, in which a clear majority of Scots voted to remain in the EU, only to see the weight of the English and Welsh votes tip the balance the other way. This has again awoken the issue of Scottish independence, which, were it to become a reality, would in turn open the question of what flag would represent what remains of the UK. For example, the Welsh, hitherto unrepresented on the Union Jack, could well feel it's time for the Welsh dragon to have equal status with the Cross of St George.

Both the English and British flags have been rescued from the clutches of the Far Right over time by a thousand small incidents, the sort you sometimes don't even notice. As long ago as 1992 the black British Olympic sprinter Linford Christie began to celebrate winning a race by catching a British flag thrown to him from the crowd and draping it around him as he acknowledged the applause. It is now routine for British athletes of whatever colour to do this, and is rarely commented on. In one recent incident when it was, it was given short shrift. Multiple gold medal winner Mo Farah is Somali-born but is now British. After yet another victory he was asked by a reporter if he'd rather be flying the colours of the country of his birth: 'Look, mate,' he replied, 'this is my country.' There, in one image and in one sentence, was the possibility for the Union Jack to acknowledge the past, but also to look to the future, go forward and be what it is supposed to be – a symbol of unity.

CHAPTER 3

THE CROSS AND
THE CRUSADES

'It is with such baubles that men are led.'

Napoleon

Previous pages: Demonstrators in Madrid, Spain, cover a European Union flag in red paint, protesting the EU's deal with Turkey to manage the flow of refugees into the continent, March 2016. Tensions within and between nations resulting from migration have tested the unity and resolve of Europe's leaders and peoples in recent years.

THE FLAG OF THE EUROPEAN UNION IS, AND AT THE same time is not, the European flag. In fact it's not definite that it's actually even a flag.

When is a flag not a flag? In the early days of what became the EU, member states, especially the UK, feared that it might replace their nation-state flags and so officially it is 'an emblem that is eligible to be reproduced on rectangular pieces of fabric'. It is a sort of half-flag, a Schrödinger's flag.

But the EU flag, which 'represents' only twenty-eight countries, is also that of the Council of Europe, which has forty-seven member states including Turkey and Russia (the only missing European country is Belarus). So, it is a flag. But whereas the EU has a combined population of 508 million, that of the Council of Europe is 820 million, so while the Council of Europe could claim to have the one true flag, it's a bit of a stretch for the EU.

Numerous emails to the great and the good of Brussels asking for clarification on this subject only elicit directions to an agreement 'published in the Official Journal of the European Union (OJ C 271, 8.9.2012, p. 5)', which is not only written in a strange tongue known only to bureaucrats, but even when translated mostly does not correlate with any known language. However, be assured: 'The flag/emblem does not supersede national flags. It is rather symbolic to demonstrate adherence to the wider community of the European countries and identification with common values and principles.'

Whatever the truth, the emblem/flag/half-flag now reflects an idea, an ideal and a reality. The idea was to create a symbol with which Europeans would identify; the ideal was of a peaceful, prosperous, unified continent; and the reality is that, measured against much of European history, there have been times since the Second World War when this has been the case. For those to whom the flag still signifies an achievable dream, the fight is on for it to continue to have meaning in the lives of Europeans.

The blue background and circle of twelve stars, which now flies from Council of Europe buildings in every European country bar one, dates back to 1955. That year the Council, which was founded in 1949 to bring together the recently warring European 'tribes', finally agreed on a design after rejecting a number of submissions. The other colours had been taken: red for the Soviets, green for Islam, white for surrender, black for mourning, light blue for the UN etc., so dark blue it was. The circle of stars was the idea of Arsène Heitz, who worked for the Council's postal service in Strasbourg and who had submitted dozens of designs.

Originally there were to be fifteen stars for the fifteen Council members; however, one of the stars represented the Saarland, then a part of France but previously part of Germany. As Paul Levy, who was then Head of Information and who actually drew up the final design, explains: 'The Germans were against fifteen because that would suggest a politically independent entity. They proposed fourteen. That was unacceptable to the Saarland. The French proposed thirteen, an Italian said, "Yes, but thirteen is unlucky." So they adopted twelve to be symbolic of everyone.'

Only once this had been agreed, and the flag made its appearance in 1955, were symbolic meanings heaped upon the design. It was noted that twelve is a symbol of perfection, that there were twelve Apostles of Jesus, twelve months in the year, twelve signs of the Zodiac, and so on. It was even pointed out that there was a similarity with the description of the Virgin of the Apocalypse in the Book of Revelations, 12:1: 'And there appeared a great wonder in heaven; a woman clothed with the sun, and the moon under her feet, and upon her head a crown of twelve stars.'

Naturally, in the internet age this has become a conspiracy theory promulgated by the hard of thinking, which involves an alleged devious scheme by Catholic Europe to dominate everyone. Dig deep enough, say for about two minutes, and eventually you reach extraterrestrials and shape-shifting lizard people, but not the fact that when the Council of Europe signed off on the flag Turkey was, and still is, a member.

Still, as internet warriors are not weighed down by facts, I offer further proof as to why you really shouldn't waste your time believing in this particular theory when there are so many other, even more idiotic, ones with which to while away your life. To believe that the Council/EU flag is a symbol of an Illuminati/lizards/Catholic/etc. conspiracy you'd have to be convinced that two of the world's dullest organizations, which creak with boredom, devised a plan so devilishly fiendish that surely only Dr Evil from the *Austin Powers* films could have hatched it while on a time-travelling mission from his underground lair. This dullness, by the way, is a very good thing, especially when compared to 1939–45. It is supposed to be boring.

Given that it had taken several years to sort out a flag for the Council, when the European Community (later to become the EU) decided in 1985 it wanted one as well it just pressed copy and paste and adopted the twelve stars. The two organizations share similar ideals – promoting democracy and human rights – but the former never embraced the ideals of union the latter has always harboured. For example, Russia, a member of the forty-eight-state Council, has never considered diluting its sovereignty with a political union headquartered in Brussels.

The question is often asked: 'What is Europe?' and the answer is: 'Depends who you ask.' It is a geographical area, but again the definition of that depends on perspective. The majority of Turkey is in Asia, but some people regard it as part of Europe. East of the Urals is in Asia; but is Siberia in Europe, if Russia is European? What about Georgia? Iceland? Definitions are flexible, as was seen in the 2016 Eurovision Song Contest in which Australia came second.

The Council and the EU may share the same flag, representing two entities, but the Council members outside the EU are comfortable with it designating, for their purposes, a non-law-making multinational organization. EU members see the flag, when flown for the EU, as a representation of a law-making, sovereign-power-diluting, political coming-together, but endlessly argue about the depth and breadth of that togetherness.

Anyway, after 1985 for the EU it was symbolic 'job done' with the flag – now for the unity bit. At its core the raison d'être of the EU is to get France and Germany to hug one another so closely that they can't get a hand free with which to thump lumps out of each other. It has been extraordinarily successful in this, but the ideological dream of creating a European state to match a European flag? Less so.

Until this decade it was not unusual to hear the argument that the moves towards 'ever closer union' would result in the homogenization of European culture. Apparently the Europeans might even all end up being dominated by French cuisine. In reality, the homogenization has been of the kind we see almost everywhere, that of McWorld. Man is born free, but everywhere he is in fast-food chains. However, I bring you news from beyond the River Elbe: the East European dumpling is alive and well. National and regional variety flourishes and pesky human nature continues to confound politicians. As de Gaulle said of France in the 1960s, 'How can you govern a country with 246 different types of cheese?'

The people of the nations of Europe have stubbornly resisted becoming one, not because they don't like each other but because they like themselves. There appears to be a yearning for authenticity. This is in part reflected in the continuing power of the national flag in each country. The relatively new concept of European identity finds itself battling with national identities and symbols that have been forged over centuries.

In this new Age of Uncertainty some people are reaching back to the old symbols and the old groupings. The Nordic states are increasingly looking to each other for solidarity, and regarding themselves as a regional bloc. This runs counter to the ideology of the EU that sought an end to factions within the continent, striving for an ever closer union.

In central Europe we find another challenge to this concept in the shape of the Visegrad Group, consisting of the Czech Republic, Slovakia, Hungary and Poland. Its website informs us that the four countries 'have always been part of a single civilization sharing cultural and intellectual values and common roots in diverse religious traditions, which they wish to preserve and further strengthen'. They have shown this unity in defying both the EU and Germany, taking a very strong shared position in rejecting their proposals for distributing the wave of refugees and migrants in recent years.

Flags, and the importance nation states and peoples attach to them, give the lie to the famous theory of the American thinker Francis Fukuyama in his *The End of History and the*

Last Man, published in 1992. Dr Fukuyama argued that the fall of the Berlin Wall was not 'just the end of the Cold War but the end of history as such: that is, the end point of mankind's ideological evolution and the universalization of Western liberal democracy as the final form of human government'. This damaging idea continues to influence generations of foreign-policy thinkers who appear oblivious to the patterns of history and the political direction of Russia, the Middle East, China, swathes of Central Asia and elsewhere. It is damaging because it causes some people to assume that such a thing as the end of history is possible, and that mankind's 'ideological evolution' must end in liberal democracy. This is as wrong as the Marxist theory of the inevitability of the 'law of history' leading to a Communist utopia.

The problem with Dr Fukuyama's and Dr Marx's theories are that they come into contact with real people. In Dr Fukuyama's case they have helped foster the complacent idea that what the liberal democracies have is inevitable and everlasting. It is precisely because liberal democracy is so rare, and so delicate, that enormous care needs to be taken in governing it, and that includes listening to the people who live in these havens. The British and American establishments each got a shock in 2016 in the EU and Presidential votes. Each may have learned that sneering at 'deplorables' is perhaps less helpful than trying to understand them.

For several decades the EU has subsumed national identities beneath a blanket of prosperity, but, for better or worse, they never went away. Now they are resurfacing and look likely to grow stronger for the foreseeable future as Europeans continue to debate the levels of dilution of sovereignty they will accept. Flags as the idea of nationhood will play their role.

The diverse kingdoms of Europe were relatively late to the flag scene, but once they got the idea there was no holding them back. As previously mentioned, it's thought that the Chinese first used designs we would now recognize as flags as early as 1,500 BCE. After the invention of silk it was possible to attach a light, relatively large piece of dyed cloth sideways to a staff and travel long distances with it. The custom spread to the Arabs, and by the time of the death of the Prophet Mohammed (632 CE), flags were the norm. There are a few examples of embryonic flag-like emblems appearing on the periphery of Europe at this point, but the custom was not widespread across the continent.

In the sixth century CE the Byzantine armies were flying a piece of red cloth from their vexilloids (a square piece of cloth fixed to the top of a staff); the practice spread to Hungary and Central Europe, and the Vikings were certainly by this time flying triangular versions from their ships. It's clear that 'flags' were catching on, particularly in warfare. In the Bayeux Tapestry, made in 1077 about the events of 1066, you can see a flag in the Viking style immediately behind William the Conqueror, and another has a cross on it. This dates the practice to before the terrible encounter between Europe and the Arab regions during the Crusades, but it seems likely that European flags, especially those with the Christian cross on them, grew out of the Crusades.

During the First Crusade (1096–9), the different armies from different parts of Europe realized they needed to distinguish themselves from each other for purposes of waging war. Naturally, given the circumstances, the Christian cross was used, but in varying colours and shapes. One colour with a particularly shaped cross would signify the forces of that region, say the Franks; another might only be that of an individual count or prince. These symbols would develop into a fully fledged system of heraldry with coats of arms, and it was within this that an entire complicated catalogue of rules governing flags took form: what shape, what colour, when and where they should be flown, in what order, and so on. This system became an important way of identifying or displaying rank and lineage, particularly in regard to royal houses.

There is thus an easy path in tracing the what and the why of the French flag, and it is worth following. We start with the blue of St Martin's cloak, going all the way back to the fourth century, move on to the red of Charlemagne in the eighth, and reach the white of Joan of Arc in the fifteenth. But that does not tell the whole story, with its twist and turns, of the route to the iconic flag of the Fifth Republic, and the detail within that broad brush sweep is fascinating.

St Martin was a conscripted Roman soldier from what is now Hungary who converted to Christianity, pulled off the odd miracle or two, became Bishop of Tours and is best known for cutting a rather expensive blue lamb's wool cloak in two in order to give half to a beggar. After his death (not from cold), his burial place in France became a shrine and, a few decades later, one King Clovis (466–511) had him disinterred. And there was the cloak!

Clovis was the leader who first united the Frankish tribes into what became an embryonic France. Given his devotion to St Martin, it became the custom to carry the saint's cloak into battle tied to a staff, alongside other flags, as it had become associated with victory. When not out and about it was kept in a tent-like oratory which eventually became known as a chapel, derived from the Latin word *capella*, or cloak. It is thought the symbol of the fleur-de-lis, traditionally associated with French kings from around the thirteenth century, may also have originated with Clovis, as a sign of his divine right to rule.

The blue cloak of St Martin became a blue flag, which continued to be carried into battle all the way up to the Battle of Poitiers in 1356, when the English gave the French such a beating that they lost faith in the blue. By this time they were also carrying the red of Charlemagne, but this was curtailed following another catastrophic defeat at the hands of the English, this time at Agincourt in 1415. Nevertheless, the blue and the red were established as recognized symbols, as was the royal-blue banner of France first used in the twelfth century.

White then became popular due to Joan of Arc, who flew the colour during the Siege of Orléans, which stopped the English in their tracks in 1429. The best description we have of it is in her own words, recorded during her trial for heresy a few months before she was executed:

'I had a banner of which the field was sprinkled with lilies . . . it was white, of the white cloth called "boc-cassin"; there was written above it, I believe, "Jesus Maria"; it was fringed with silk.'

She was then asked, 'The words "Jesus Maria", were they written above, below, or on the side?'

'At the side I believe.'

'Which did you care for most, your banner or your sword?'

'Better, forty times better, my banner than my sword!'

Flags of these three colours were often (though not exclusively) flown for the next 350 years, usually as single colours, occasionally as a tricolour. White may have been the most popular, but no version was yet officially that of the nation state.

By the time we reach the French Revolution in 1789, the colours of Paris had been red and blue for several centuries, and the Paris militia wore in their hats blue and red silk-ribbon cockades, which were an important kind of political 'badge' recognized throughout the city. To this was added white for purity (and in the tradition of Joan of Arc), and by the end of the year these were the official cockades and were effectively regarded as displaying the joint national colours.

Sailors in the French navy then defied their mostly aristocratic senior officers and demanded the right to fly the new flags to mark the new era. In a speech at the National Assembly in 1790, the Comte de Mirabeau denounced 'as seditious conspirators those who would speak of maintaining old prejudices . . . No, my fellow deputies, these tricolors will sail the seas; earn the respect of all countries, and strike terror in the hearts of conspirators and tyrants!' He got his way and a variety of red, white and blue flags appeared in different designs. Gradually these began to be used on land, and in 1812 the French army officially adopted the three vertical stripes; hence we can occasionally spot the Tricolor in paintings of Napoleon's ill-fated invasion of Russia.

Its general use, and official standing, waxed and waned during the following tumultuous years of the royal restoration, Napoleon and the revolution of 1830. Then, as a constitutional monarchy, it was decreed that 'The French nation again takes up its colours.' From then on, during the Third, Fourth and Fifth Republics, the standard Tricolor we see today (with minor alternations) has been the flag of France. During the Second World War the flag of Marshal Pétain, who headed the collaborationist

Vichy regime, displayed the motif of a double-bladed axe – the *Francisque* – which harked back to the embryonic French state forged by the Franks. In response, General de Gaulle's Free French flag featured the cross of Lorraine, but both kept the famous blue, white and red – the colours which came to stand for liberty, equality and fraternity.

These days, if you say 'the Tricolor' it is often assumed you mean the French flag, as it has a global reach and has transcended the representation of a nation to also represent the three principles above. Opinions differ as to how to accomplish those principles – indeed, they differ as to what the words mean – but, as a symbol, the French red, white and blue embodies the aspirations of hundreds of millions of people and is a global icon. In the wake of the 2015 coordinated terrorist attacks in Paris, this symbol appeared on social media websites around the world. People attached it their accounts, not just to signal solidarity with France, but with the idea of freedom in mind, which, despite its mixed, indeed chequered history, France still engenders.

To its east, across the Rhine, we find another tricolour with roots many centuries old, but in a relativity new country: Germany, with its black, red and gold flag.

The first time these colours came together as a national flag was as recently as 1919, upon the formation of the Weimar Republic. Before (and indeed after) that, the formula was black, white and red, the colours of the first flag flown after the federal states unified to become Germany in 1871. These had long been colours associated with the Germanic regions. Writing sixty years after the Battle of Tannenberg (1410), the Polish chronicler Jan Długosz recorded the banners captured from the defeated Teutonic Knights, a Germanic order that had grown out of the Crusades, which hung in the Wawel Cathedral of Kraków until 1603. Of the fifty-six flags noted, most were red or white, the next most popular colour being black. The red was partially the influence of Charlemagne, the first Holy Roman Emperor, who united much of Europe, including the Germanic lands.

Later, the Holy Roman Empire adopted a gold heraldic shield with a black eagle; and when it was disbanded in 1806, the popularity of the colours lived on in the German regions. In 1813, as people began to agitate for German unification, Prussia's Lützow Free Corps, which had been formed to fight Napoleon, took black and red with gold fringes as its uniform. At the same time an influential Students' Association was formed, with members coming from all the German regions. It adopted black, red and gold in the belief that these were pan-German colours representing all the German-speaking peoples, whether they were from what is now the Czech Republic, Germany, Italy, Austria or elsewhere. For some, this represented the aspiration of moving towards both unification and democracy.

By 1830 the French had reinstated their Tricolor, and this influenced many Germans (though far from all) to adopt black, red and gold as theirs and use it as their 'national' symbol. By 1867 there was a prototype Germany in the shape of the North German Federation, but it was prevented from using those colours as its national symbol by the impressive, and immovable, force of Otto von Bismarck. As he was from Prussia, whose flag was black and white, he demanded the new flag be black, red and white. The Iron Chancellor almost always got what he wanted. When German unification was completed in 1871, these became the official colours of the flag of the Second

Empire. It lasted almost four decades, but could not survive the trauma of Germany losing the First World War. In came the Weimar Republic and the black, red and gold of the previous century, with, for some, its connection to democracy. However, that could not withstand the rise of Adolf Hitler and the Nazi Party, which rejected the colours of the republic and instead reverted back to those of the empire.

Shortly after the Nazis took power in 1933, a decree was issued: two flags would now fly – a black, red and white tricolour, and the swastika, which was the flag of the Nazi Party; they were to be flown from all official buildings and German ships. Two years later, and by now firmly in control of the state, Hitler ruled that the sole flag of Germany would be the swastika. This was passed into law by the Nuremberg Flag Laws of September 1935 and may have been partly prompted by an incident in New York City that had caused a diplomatic row between Germany and the USA.

In late July of that year, several hundred Communist Anti-Nazi demonstrators were on a pier in New York harbour as the German liner the SS *Bremen* was about to leave. Dozens fought their way past ranks of police officers, boarded the ship, tore down the swastika flag and threw it into the Hudson River. Tensions were running high at the time. The 'Germantown' neighbourhood in the Upper East Side was split with a minority of ethnically German Americans supporting Hitler, while many others, including refugees from Nazi Germany, opposed them in league with the unions. The Upper East Side would go on to become the headquarters of the notorious Nazi-supporting German American Bund.

A regional newspaper, the *Sunday Spartanburg Herald*, noted at the time, possibly wryly, that 'when the German emblem was tossed into the Hudson River, it floated and was recovered. It might have gone to the bottom and Hitler might have claimed damages.' Nevertheless, the German chargé d'affaires protested to the US State Department but was told that the insult was to the Nazi Party and not the nation. Eight weeks later the Nuremberg Flag Laws changed that possibility and the Party flag became the state flag.

This most notorious of symbols, supposed to be the emblem of a 1,000-year-old Reich, was only a national flag for a decade (1935–45) but has a history going back thousands of years. The swastika, or hooked cross, has been found by archaeologists in Asia, Africa and Europe. The image was used in 'proto-writing' towards the end of the Stone Age, 12,000 years ago, but precisely what it represented is, to date, a mystery.

The most visually compelling theory for its origins is that of the late, great American astronomer Carl Sagan. In his book *Comet*, Sagan points to an ancient Chinese manuscript known as the 'Book of Silk', dating from around 2,200 years ago. It depicts the sightings of comets and in one drawing you can clearly see the tail of the comet in the shape of what we now call the swastika. Sagan's theory was that rapid rotation formed 'curved streamers, as you can easily see in the pattern formed by a rotary garden sprinkler [which give] . . . the usual representation of the swastika'. If correct, it is not a great leap to believe that mankind had seen this shape in the skies since before recorded history and naturally enough attributed a meaning to it.

In parts of Asia it is still used as a religious symbol. For example, the flag of the Jain religion in India has a swastika in its central white horizontal band, which represents the four states of existence. For Hindus a right-hand swastika is one of the 108 symbols of the god Vishnu, among other things, and is found in many temples as well as in art and decoration.

It is in ancient India that we find the most frequent use of the swastika and it is from there that it made its way to Nazi Germany. Adolf Hitler was obsessed with ideas of racial purity and that the Germanic peoples were descended from the Aryan 'race', which had migrated from the Indus Valley region. He believed the Aryans were the master race, despite the fact that the term Ayran originally referred to a root language and not ethnicity.

In 1920s Germany the hooked cross was known as the *Hakenkreuz* and nationalist writers using pseudoscience suggested it was a uniquely Aryan symbol. Writing in *Mein Kampf* (1925), Hitler recalled that in 1920, the year the Nazis adopted the swastika, he was aware that the Party required a 'symbol of its own struggle' and that it needed to be as 'effective as a large poster'.

He utterly rejected the black, red and gold flag of the Weimar Republic but was taken by the traditional German colours of red, white and black. Party members had submitted various designs, many of which included the swastika somewhere on the field. Hitler admitted that one of these was similar to the flag that emerged, but claimed credit for the design which was adopted: 'I myself, meanwhile, after innumerable attempts, had laid down a final form; a flag with a red background, a white disk, and a black swastika in the middle. After long trials I also found a definite proportion between the size of the flag and the size of the white disk, as well as the shape and thickness of the swastika.' He also spelt out the meaning of his design: 'The red expressed the social thought underlying the movement. White the national thought. And the swastika signified the mission allotted to us – the struggle for the victory of Aryan mankind.'

In his reference to a 'mission allotted to us' we hear Hitler's mystical train of thought. Although the Nazis are not popularly known for an interest in the metaphysical world, many members were caught up in ideas of mysticism and the power of symbols. In their design of the swastika they found something that appeared to have an almost enigmatic pull on the masses, albeit one that eventually pulled them, and tens of millions of others, towards destruction.

That is the context in which the Western world sees this ancient symbol, which is why in several countries, including Germany, it is banned. It is also why it, and variations deliberately echoing it, are still used by the extreme Right. In the USA, for example, the image lives on propagated by gangs such as the Aryan Brotherhood, which recruit in prisons and also operates as a crime syndicate.

Even those without the education to know the details are aware of its power to shock instantly and induce the hurt and anger they seek to inflict. However, as a classic ancient symbol it has survived the abuse of the Nazi years and remains in other parts of the world intact and without negative connotations. In regions where the Buddhist, Hindu and Jain religions are dominant, such as Japan, Vietnam and China it is not unusual to see it – the emblem of the Falun Gong movement in China, for example, features a Dharma Wheel with a swastika in the centre. In India it is one of the 108 symbols of the Hindi god Vishnu and can be found in decorations for celebrations, on cakes, and sometimes is even drawn on the hood of new cars to bring luck.

However, in a different culture and in the aftermath of the horrors of the Second World War, with the total surrender of

Germany, it was utterly unthinkable that the flag could still be used. Europe sought to rebuild itself, and Germany its reputation. Part of the healing process was the banning of the swastika and the reintroduction of the black, red and gold of ancient and recent history. Both West and East Germany readopted the flag of the democratic Weimar Republic as both claimed to be the one true democratic Germany. The flags were identical until 1959, when the East Germans added a Communist-inspired coat of arms consisting of wheat, a hammer and a pair of dividers to represent the peasants, the workers and the intellectuals.

The two Germanys had sent a joint team to the Olympic Games of 1956 and as their flags were identical there had been no flag issue; but now there was. Happily, it was settled with the compromise that the joint team would march under the black, red and gold but with the Olympic rings on the red, which is what happened in 1960 and 1964. In 1968 separate teams were entered but each complied with the compromise agreed earlier, and after that each used their national flag. After the fall of the Berlin Wall in 1989 and German reunification the following year, the problem was solved.

Many East Germans made their feelings plain in the heady days when the Wall came down by cutting out the coat of arms from the flag. They drew inspiration from the Hungarians, who in 1956 had done the same during their uprising against Soviet occupation. The Romanians followed suit in late 1989.

The recently reunified Germans took a while to warm to their newly reintroduced colours, but this was due to a suspicion of flag-waving born of the experience of the Nazi years. By the 2006 World Cup, which they hosted, the German people were more confident about what is now one of the Continent's most successful democratic countries. The black, red and gold was waved all the way to the semi-finals. The flags were more than decoration: they were a symbol of a nation aware of the twists and turns of its history and confident for the future. For this generation of young Germans the war was a long time ago, and even the fall of the Wall is history. They are familiar with that history, but are no longer as hung up on it as their parents and grandparents. The slowly rising nationalism seen in response to the immigrant crisis is of a different kind to the murderous hysterics of the pre-war years and much of it does not indulge in wrapping itself in the flag. We have decades to go before the Germans view the war years as no longer relevant to today, but the shadow cast by Hitler has been slowly shortening, and during those years Germany has been building democratic institutions strong and admired enough to allow a return of the black, red and gold into popular culture.

Time for a break. Which brings us to the flag of Italy. We must do lunch.

Let's start with an avocado, mozzarella and tomato salad. If you're not fond of avocado, no problem Sir/Madam, we can do you one with basil. Either way, you're having a *tricolore* salad in the colours of the Italian flag.

I cannot see this gorgeous, clean, vibrant green, white and red flag without thinking of food. That it shouts 'Pizza! Pasta!' from a million restaurants around the world is testament to the correlation between the flag and the cuisine of the country. Chinese restaurants tend not to have the red flag and hammer and sickle flying outside to entice you in, and spotting the flag of Tunisia doesn't make you think of heading home to whip up the national dish of couscous.

A few more seconds thinking about what the colours conjure up and I'm on my Piaggio-designed Vespa scooter

(1967 model) heading for the San Siro Stadium to see the AC Milan–Inter Milan derby. If there are a few of us, we'll take the Fiat 500, but the designated driver can only have a very small glass of Montepulciano and that's your lot.

None of this is to belittle Italy's national symbol; it is more to underline what a fantastically successful projection of soft power the flag is via the quality of the country's products. In this there is a unifying factor in a state which has always struggled to feel truly united and which has seen the rise of separatist movements and aggravated divisions between the north and the south.

Until the end of the eighteenth century, the peoples of the Apennine Peninsula and the surrounding regions and islands had a rich history of flag-making, representing the city states and kingdoms. But in the spring of 1796 Napoleon crossed the Alps and threw the old order of small, absolutist states into chaos. French troops entered Lombardy, of which Milan is the capital, and it became the Transpadane Republic. The Milanese militia at the time wore a green and white uniform, and when it was transformed into the National Guard of the Repubblica Transpadana red was added. The Legione Lombarda was also using the same colours. In October that year Napoleon wrote to Paris that 'les couleurs nationales qu'ils ont adoptées sont le vert, le blanc et le rouge' ('the national colours they adopted were green, white and red').

French troops also overthrew the old regime in neighbouring Modena, which was briefly renamed the Cispadane Republic. A newly created militia called itself the Italian Legion and it too took green, white and red for its uniforms; these were also the colours of the Republic's horizontal tricolour flag, which had red at the top, white in the middle and green at the bottom.

In 1797 the two merged to form the Cisalpine Republic and in 1798 took the tricolour as a national flag in the vertical design we now know as the flag of Italy. It was without doubt influenced by the French flag. The new 'state' under French domination became the Italian Republic and then the Italian Kingdom. The demise of Napoleon led to a hiatus in the coming-together of Italy, but the idea, and the colours of national unity, had been formed.

During the 1800s the tricolour became more widespread throughout the peninsula. The Risorgimento, or resurgence of nationalism, became unstoppable and was led by men such as Giuseppe Mazzini and Giuseppe Garibaldi, who both fought under its colours. In 1861 the Italian state was born, Victor Emmanuel II was proclaimed King of Italy and there was no question as to the colours of the flag; however his coat of arms of the House of Savoy was added and there it stayed until 1946.

Benito Mussolini had the usual fascistic obsession with symbols but he left the flag alone. It was only changed when Italy became a Republic after the Second World War and the Savoy arms were removed. The flag is flown proudly by the state institutions, but the public does not always share that pride in the institutions. Italy remains a nation of regions; many people seem to identify more on a local level, and regional flags are sometimes a more common sight. But the country does come together at times – most notably when the national football team, the Azzurri, takes the field, and then the spectators are unmistakably, unequivocally united under their *tricolore*.

Some people attribute various values to the three colours of the otherwise plain flag: red, the usual blood spilt for independence, green for the verdant landscape and white for the Alps. None of it is official, and none has a historical trail, but, as always, the meaning is in the eye of the beholder, and this writer beholds avocado, mozzarella cheese (buffalo, naturally) and tomatoes. *Salute!*

And *skål!* as we head from the sunny south to the Nordic north – to Scandinavia and Finland.

Here we find one of the few obvious groupings of flags in Europe – the Scandinavian Cross. There are other groupings – for example, the horizontal tricolour is found in neighbouring countries beginning in the Netherlands, through Germany, Austria and all the way down to Bulgaria – but there is little linking these flags as a particular set, and tricolours are common across the globe. The Scandinavian Cross, however, is instantly recognizable and of the same shape, albeit either in blue or red, on the flags of Norway, Denmark, Sweden, Finland and Iceland. In all cases the cross is positioned slightly towards the hoist (on the flagstaff) and the right-hand 'arm' of the cross is elongated.

It is a little ironic that the symbol has survived for so long given that this is now the least religious part of Western Europe, while countries with high levels of church attendance, such as Spain and Italy, do not display the Christian symbol.

The five Scandinavian Cross flags are all based on the Danish flag, with its white cross on a red field. This is known as the Dannebrog and is considered to be the world's oldest national flag, having been the recognized symbol of the country since the early 1200s (even if officially it is dated much later). There is a legend, known to all Danes, that the origins of the flag date to a battle against the pagan Estonians in 1219. King Valdemar II was having a difficult time of it, so the bishops accompanying the troops went in for a spot of praying and on cue God threw down from the sky the Dannebrog. Valdemar caught it before it touched the ground, and inspired by this miracle the Danish army went on to achieve a famous victory. Historical proof of the event is at best sketchy, but it is a tale told down the centuries and is as likely as, say, that of England's King Arthur and the Round Table, and as such of equal value in establishing the psychological 'truths' that bind a nation together.

The very same banner went on to have all sorts of adventures. It was captured by one of the German states in 1500, only to be rescued in 1559 and later taken back to Denmark, where, alas, over a century it crumbled to dust. Allegedly.

It was far from the last Danish flag to disappear. In 2006 the Dannebrog became that year's most-burnt flag. In September 2005 the *Jyllands-Posten* newspaper had published twelve cartoons of the Prophet Mohammed, including one showing him wearing a turban shaped as a bomb with a burning fuse. Many Muslims considered this offensive, not just because of the manner of the drawings but because most interpretations of Islamic law forbid depictions of the Prophet.

At the time it caused a small row in Denmark. Several months later a delegation of the offended travelled around the Middle East publicizing the cartoons in a successful bid to ensure that many more people were offended. This resulted in demonstrations in which dozens of people were killed across the Muslim world and the Danish and Norwegian Embassies in Damascus were burnt, along with hundreds of Danish flags.

You could argue that this was all a little unfair on Denmark given that the government had not published the cartoons, but it was even more unfair on the good people of Switzerland and Savoy. Many of the flags that were burnt were home-made and, quite understandably, those making them didn't always concentrate very hard on where to place the white Christian cross on their red backgrounds or study its proportions. Frequently it was centred instead of being towards the hoist. This resulted in numerous flags of Switzerland and Savoy going up in flames accompanied by chants of 'Death to Denmark!' The general lack of understanding of Europe was on display, mirroring Europe's paucity of understanding of the Middle East.

The Dannebrog now hangs from the ceilings of butchers' shops emblazoned on ham and packets of bacon, on beer bottles, cheeses – in fact almost anything you can sell. The Danes are hugely proud of their flag and yet usually quite relaxed about what it is displayed on. There is an exception: its use by the Far Right is causing ripples of discomfort, and the population at large does not want it hijacked for their purposes. However, having been part of their lives for so many centuries, for now it remains patriotic but not overtly nationalistic. Its commercial use is as ubiquitous as its personal use, flying, as it does, from the homes of many ordinary citizens. 'Made in Denmark' is a symbol of the good life, and the Dannebrog is part of the good Danish life.

Up the road, across the Øresund Bridge, the Swedes are a bit sniffy about this. In Sweden use of the national flag is nowhere near as widespread and, as in the UK, had to be rescued from the extreme right-wing elements in the country. Because so few ordinary people flew the Swedish flag or used it for commercial purposes, in the 1990s its appearance outside of officialdom became associated with neo-Nazis. It has subsequently been reappropriated, but its use is still a sensitive issue and it remains one of the 'less-waved' flags of Europe. The Swedes made an exception in the Euro 2016 football championships, where almost to a man and woman they 'flew' the flag on shirts and hats. However, back home they are also aware that nationalist parties, such as the Swedish Democrats, are increasingly displaying it and a Far Right magazine is called *Blue-Yellow Questions*, so it is again becoming . . . problematic.

The popular view of Sweden is that it is a haven of cultural ultra-liberalism and third-way economic policies. This view is at least two decades out of date and belongs to the Sweden of Abba, not the Sweden of mass immigration. Since the 1990s the market has been slowly allowed into the state. Welfare and education spending are significantly down, and some schools have even been privatized. Strict police and intelligence surveil-lance laws have been passed by several successive governments. Ethnic enclaves are common in the urban areas and unemploy-ment is high, especially among non-white Swedes. According to figures from the Organisation for Economic Co-operation and Development, one-fifth of Swedes were born outside the country or have at least one parent who was. This is the back-ground to the debate about the flag and its place in society as Sweden adjusts to its new circumstances.

The flag borrowed the design of the cross on the Dannebrog but coloured it yellow against a blue field. Research suggests that as early as the 1400s the Swedes were using a gold cross on blue as their national symbol, and blue and yellow became the official colours of the Swedish royal family.

Norway's flag, dating from 1821, also takes the Dannebrog's cross design, as the country was ruled by Denmark from 1388 until 1814, when it was ceded to Sweden. The red and blue colours were inspired by the French Revolution and their Tricolor, but also reflect the country's relationship with Denmark and Sweden. The Swedish king allowed its use on land but not at sea in order to restrict a possible growth in its popularity and thus foster Norwegian nationalism. It took until 1898 for Norway to be granted this right, and both the delay and necessity to campaign for it actually hastened the separation of Norway from Sweden in 1905.

The Norwegians are now fiercely proud of their flag, country, currency and nationhood. That, and offshore oil and gas, which boost the world's largest sovereign wealth fund, go a long way to explaining why it chose to remain outside the EU.

Finland, meanwhile, was also under Swedish rule, from approximately 1150 right through to 1809, when Sweden was defeated by Russia in the Finnish War. It was then occupied by Russian troops, but whereas the previous masters had insisted that Swedish was the official language of Finland and that the administration of the country would be run from Sweden, the Russians allowed a greater deal of autonomy.

These new (relative) freedoms encouraged Finnish nationalism and in late December 1917, with Russia in chaos after its revolution, Lenin recognized a unilateral declaration of independence made by Finland on 6 December. A national flag was now required, and there were two main candidates. On the day of the independence declaration what was known as the 'Lion Flag' flew over the Finnish senate; this had a red field with a gold lion. However, by this time a blue and white flag had become popular and was flown as the Finnish colours from many boats. The blue and white had been championed by the Finnish poet, writer and historian Zachris Topelius as early as 1862. He said the blue stood for the plentiful lakes of Finland, while the white was for the abundant snow.

Parliament began a heated debate on the merits of the different flags, but an even more heated disagreement then broke out in the shape of the Finnish Civil War of 1918. Lenin may have written a thesis on the right of self-determination for Finland, and thus agreed to independence, but there were limits to his open-spiritedness and he wanted to define this self-determination as being guided by Moscow and Communist in nature. He encouraged several military units to break from Finland's Civil Guard and form the 'Red Guard'. In the five months of fighting that followed, what became known as the 'White Army' defeated the 'Red Guard'. This made the decision on a flag somewhat straightforward. Red had gone out of fashion. The following year the Republic of Finland proudly flew its flag of the white field and blue Scandinavian Cross.

Finally, across the Norwegian Sea and out into the Atlantic lies Iceland. It may be almost 1,000 miles out from the European mainland, but its culture and history put it in the Scandinavian region. The red Scandinavian Cross, with white fimbriations, on the blue field of its flag, expresses several things: its Christian heritage, its connections to the Nordic peoples, its domination by first Norway and then Denmark from 1380 to 1944, and the close relationship it has with Norway, from where many of the Icelanders' ancestors came.

The five flags of the Nordics are an aberration in European flag culture; nowhere else is there so obvious a grouping insofar as the moment you see one of them you know the region it is from, even if not necessarily the exact country. The use of the cross is far from the norm in the rest of Europe; in addition to Switzerland, Greece, Malta and Slovakia all feature a cross in their flags, but all are different shapes from that of the Nordics.

However, there are other symbolic references to Christianity on Europe's flags. For example, the green on the Portuguese flag is a nod to the green cross of Aziz used by a Portuguese order of chivalry, which dates all the way back to the Knights Templar and the Crusades. The red is from another heraldic group, the Order of Christ. In 1911, after Portugal became a republic, a commission was appointed to consider the colours of the new flag and there was no doubting the strength of feeling when it came to red. It had to be there because 'it is the combative, hot, virile colour par excellence. It is the colour of conquest and laughter. A singing, ardent, joyful colour . . . It reminds us of blood and incites us to victory.'

More interesting, arguably, is that the coat of arms in the centre of the flag is set on an armillary sphere. This was an instrument used for navigation and is symbolic of the Age of Discovery, when Portuguese sailors were at the forefront of opening up new trade routes to what were, for the Europeans, undiscovered lands. The coat of arms is based on a design that dates back to 1139, and it is also deeply Christian. It features five white dots on five blue shields – a reference to the Battle of Ourique, fought in Portugal in 1139, in which Alfonso I defeated five Moorish kings 'In the name of the five stigmata of Christ'. Hence five dots and five shields.

The flag is even referred to in Portugal's national anthem:

> *Unfurl the unconquerable flag*
> *In the bright light of your sky!*
> *Cry out all Europe and the whole world*
> *That Portugal has not perished.*
> *Your happy land is kissed*
> *By the Ocean that murmurs with love.*
> *And your conquering arm*
> *Has given new worlds to the world!*

Austria's red-white-red horizontal stripes are also Christian in origin and entail another of the founding myths so beloved by nation builders, and often by their populations. As the story goes, Duke Leopold V of Austria was so busy hacking away in a battle during the Siege of Acre (1189–91) in the Third Crusade that his surcoat (the long, sleeveless, often white, tunic worn over armour) became completely splattered in blood. After a hard day's crusading, he removed his belt to reveal a white band where the blood had not reached. True or not, within a few decades Emperor Henry VI was handing out red and white shields to knights for acts of exceptional bravery, and by 1230 the colours were associated with the region. However, it wasn't until after the Second World War that the simple red-white-red design without a symbol became the official flag of the state.

According to the Pew Research Center in Washington, approximately one-sixth of the world's national flags contain a Christian symbol. If so, by my reckoning that is roughly thirty-two flags, of which, depending on criteria, almost two-thirds are in Europe. Most Europeans are not overtly aware of the symbols: we see the flag of Sweden, not the Christian cross on a flag. However, with people's increasing awareness of history, and now the rise of Islam in Europe, these symbols are likely to be increasingly used by the Far Right to try to define the Continent as what they think it is, and in opposition to what they think it is not. Particularly considering the religious symbolism often on display in flags of Islamic countries, where most people are well aware of the meanings being conveyed. Turkey's President Erdogan has accused the EU of not wanting Turkey to join because it's a 'Muslim-majority country', despite officially being a secular state; perhaps religion will still prove a key sticking point, and the crescent and star, derived from that of the Ottoman Empire, too stark a reminder of a conflict that has existed for centuries.

Apart from the examples mentioned above, there is not a great deal of other obvious religious iconography in the European flags; this is due in part to the surge of republicanism which swept away various royal dynasties and their heraldic emblems.

The Dutch flag used to be orange, white and blue, representing the Protestant Prince William of Orange, also known as William the Taciturn. He led the revolt against Catholic Spain at the beginning of the Eighty Years' War, which resulted firstly in the independence of some of the Dutch provinces and eventually all of them, forming the Dutch Republic. Known as the Prince's flag, this tricolour became an early symbol of independence from Spain. The royal colours were the natural choice for the flag, but by the mid seventeenth century the orange had been changed to red as the orange dye faded quickly and was not easily spotted out at sea. So the Dutch royal family adopted red, white and blue, but on right royal occasions the tricolour is flown with an orange pennant fixed to the top.

The colour still dominates the country, especially when the national football team is playing and most people wear orange shirts in honour of the Oranje, as they are nicknamed. Red, white and blue are the official national colours – indeed, during the German occupation in the Second World War some people would hang out their washing in red, white and blue patterns – but there's no doubting which colour is the one most associated with the Dutch, both by themselves and other people. This is a rarity: what is regarded as the national colour does not feature on the national flag.

The Russian tricolour is also interesting . . . up to a point. It has none of the iconography of the hammer and sickle of the Soviet Union and is, in fact, simply a reversion to the old pre-Communist-era flag. The white-blue-red horizontal stripes are popularly thought to have been introduced by Peter the Great, who travelled widely in Europe in the late 1600s and, allegedly, was taken by the Dutch tricolour, which he used as the template for the national flag.

After his death it had a bit of competition. In 1858 Alexander II decided he wanted a black-yellow-white flag, and given that he was Emperor there were a good many made and used, but they do not appear to have supplanted the original. In 1881 a young man named Ignacy Hryniewiecki blew him up in a bomb attack in St Petersburg and, other than in a few modern-day fringe royalist and extreme right-wing groups, that was the last we saw of the black, yellow and white. The white-blue-red flew unchallenged until the Bolsheviks started to introduce the early version of their Red Flag in 1917.

The red Soviet hammer and sickle flag, another twentieth-century emblem that flew above the graves of tens of millions, has never had quite the same connection with evil in the Western mind as its Nazi counterpart, despite being the symbol of a system that killed so many civilians in so many countries, especially Russia and China, where millions starved to death. There are still admirers of the hammer and sickle who see in it a symbol of hope.

Mental gymnastics are required to overlook the gulag and the terror and say that 'on balance' Communism was a good thing but even now, with the archives opened, there are still many who cannot accept that a faith they have held for a lifetime may have contributed to mass murder. Few people would argue that 'on balance' the Nazis, with their full employment and autobahns, were good for Germany, but when it comes to the hammer and sickle, that's when the mental gymnastics take over. The ideas behind the flags may be part of the explanation.

The Nazis were quite open about the symbolism of their flag: it represented what they believed about superior races, strength, weakness and purity, views which were crushed amid the wreckage of Europe. But the hammer and sickle, in the symbolism if not in the practice of Communism, represents the idea of international solidarity, unity between the urban proletariat and peasantry, and the dignity of labour, even as the lyrics of 'The Red Flag' have it: 'It gives the hope of peace at last'. So its defenders can either close their eyes and ears to the vast crimes committed, or they can argue that what the flag stands for remains true even if in practice those ideals were betrayed. As the Soviet anthem stated:

> United forever in friendship and labour,
> Our mighty republics will ever endure.
> The Great Soviet Union will live through the ages.
> The dream of a people their fortress secure.
>
> Long live our Soviet motherland,
> Built by the people's mighty hand.
> Long live our people, united and free.
> Strong in our friendship tried by fire.
> Long may our crimson flag inspire,
> Shining in glory for all men to see.

Although it symbolizes Communism, the Red Flag, with hammer and sickle, did not exist during the lifetime of its founder, Karl Marx (1818–83). Its gradual use began when the Bolsheviks came to power in Russia. As is the way in revolutions, symbolism was considered of prime importance: the symbols of the ancien régime were destroyed and replaced with those befitting the new era. Red was already considered a revolutionary colour, especially following its use during the Paris Commune uprising and subsequent socialist government of 1871, and as with most flags it became associated with the blood of those who had given their all for the cause.

The Bolshevik leader, Vladimir Lenin, approved the design of a red flag with a hammer and sickle, and a five-pointed red star above them to signify the unity of purpose shared by the peasants and the industrial workers. It also shows that the proletariat will be guided by the Communist Party. The Russians, by the way, say 'sickle and hammer'– *serp i molot* – but somehow this was reversed in popular Western parlance.

For the first few years after the revolution, the hammer and sickle were surrounded by a wreath of grain, but when the flag was officially adopted in November 1923 that had gone and the design was very similar to the one we now know. There was a slight change to the shape of the sickle and the length of the hammer, and in 1980 the red was brightened, but apart from that the flag of 1923 is the one that flew above the Kremlin until December 1991, and which to this day still represents Communism around the globe. At state level a version of it still flies in China, but there the Party has almost stopped even pretending it is Communist. Instead it embraces a ruthless capitalist dictatorship but uses the machinery and symbolism of the Party to control the people.

Some of the countries that suffered under the Soviet Union – in essence the Russian Empire – ban the hammer and sickle, as it represents to them cruelty, torture, impoverishment, colonialism and totalitarianism. Many of those who lived under the tyranny committed under these symbols shudder at the memory of the flag. However, there are other countries that never endured its rule where, to some young people, the ideals still hold true. To them, the red and the work tools remain a useful shorthand to signal class-consciousness, rebellion and egalitarianism. It might look somewhat dated, but rebellious youth are not likely to gather under a modern banner depicting, say, a white keyboard and a fluorescent high-vis jacket.

It no longer flies particularly high in Russia, though, because, in essence, Communism lost the Cold War, Levis beat Lenin, and NATO faced down the Warsaw Pact. The flag can still be seen during demonstrations, but it is mostly flown by the less well-off elderly, pining for a time of state planning and greatness. It is not about to make a comeback.

The Russian tricolour flies throughout the Russian republics, and now also in the parts of Georgia and Ukraine effectively seized by Moscow. The annexing of Crimea was hugely popular in Russia, and we may not yet have seen the full extent of where Mr Putin will attempt to plant the national colours.

The influence of Russia has also ensured that the red, white and blue, in whatever order, became symbolic of pan-Slavic unity as the various Slavic people sought to overthrow Austro-Hungarian or Ottoman domination. The Slavs emerged as a loose ethnic group around 1,500 years ago, in territories stretching from parts of the Czech Republic to beyond the Urals, and from the Baltic Sea down to Macedonia. They speak languages that can be traced back to a proto-Slavic tongue. Through place, language and religion they have all been influenced by Russia, and it is that influence we see in their flags, such as those of Serbia, Slovakia, the Czech Republic and Slovenia.

Two of the latter examples, Serbia and Slovenia, were among the six republics that constituted Yugoslavia. When the Kingdom of Serbs, Croats and Slovenes was proclaimed in

1918, it took the Slavic colours but in a blue-white-red horizontal version, and upon being renamed Yugoslavia added a red five-pointed star to the flag. The break-up of Yugoslavia in the early 1990s required six (eventually seven) new flags. Serbia, Slovenia and Croatia all went for variations on red, white and blue; Montenegro readopted a red flag with a double-headed eagle dating from the late nineteenth century, and Macedonia looked somewhat further back for inspiration.

There is nothing quite like the Macedonian flag elsewhere in Europe. It has an eye-catching yellow sun with eight rays on a red background. Upon independence in 1991, the first flag designed was similar to the one we now see, but with a smaller sun symbol with sixteen rays. The original design is known as the Vergina Sun, which appears in art from antiquity as a sixteen-, twelve- or eight-pointed star but most frequently with sixteen rays, and this was the one chosen for the Macedonian flag.

However, that symbol was used in the fourth century BCE by Alexander the Great and his father Philip II of Macedon, historical figures whom both Macedonia and Greece claim as their own. Given that Greece insists that Alexander and Philip were Greek, and more importantly that the Greek region known as Macedonia has nothing to do with neighbouring, er, Macedonia, Athens took extreme umbrage at the use of what it claims as a Greek symbol.

This is not a trivial quarrel between archaeologists, but an ongoing territorial dispute. There remain people in Macedonia (the country) who claim Macedonia (in Greece) as part of a greater state, with Thessalonica as its capital. Fearing that this was just part of Macedonian claims to the Greek region, Greece imposed an economic blockade and began calling in favours from friendly countries at the UN and in the EU, and even registered a complaint with the World Intellectual Property Organization. It worked. In 1995 not only was the flag redesigned to feature an eight-rayed sun, but at the UN and in the EU the country was referred to as the 'Former Yugoslav Republic of Macedonia' (FYROM), thus addressing Greek concerns about a nation state having the same name as one of its regions. However, many individual countries did recognize it as the Republic of Macedonia, much to the irritation of the Greeks.

It took several years for the old flag to disappear from public use, and no one in the country calls it the FYROM. Official views on the dispute could be found upon landing in the capital's airport at Skopje, which since 2006 has been named . . . Alexander the Great Airport. On your way out to find a cab, you could see an imposing statue in the arrivals hall featuring . . . Alexander the Great (on a horse, to boot), and you could then drive into town along . . . Alexander the Great Highway.

The issues have not gone away: the 2015–6 refugee crisis at the Greek-Macedonian border inflamed tensions, and Greece has been standing in the way of Macedonian accession talks to enter NATO – another example of the politics of the nation state trumping those of the pan-European ideal. However, the two sides began to negotiate an official name change, albeit in the face of mass demonstrations against this in both countries. A deal was cut in 2018 and the FYROM was officially named North Macedonia in a ceremony in February 2019, although again there were mass riots in Greece the month before. The Macedonians renamed their airport 'Skopje International', the road into town became 'The Friendship Highway', and Greece dropped its opposition to Macedonia joining NATO. At least these questions of identity have been solved through diplomacy, whereas the flags of the last two states to be carved out of Yugoslavia were born out of war.

Kosovo is the simpler of the two. It was a region within the Yugoslav Republic of Serbia and then became part of Serbia when Yugoslavia was dissolved. The majority of the population are ethnic Albanian and Muslim and there are people in the region who believe that it, and parts of Macedonia, belong to 'Greater Albania'.

In 1999 NATO bombed Serbia into submission during the Kosovo War and forced its troops to leave the province. Tens of thousands of Kosovo's Serbs then faced the revenge of the majority population following waves of ethnic cleansing and were themselves forced to flee.

In 2008 Kosovo unilaterally declared independence, a move now accepted by a majority of UN and EU states but not all, and certainly not by Serbia. Its flag has a blue field with the outline of the country's borders in yellow in the middle. There are six white stars above this representing Kosovo's different ethnic communities. The stars are a nice touch, an effort at reaching out and forging unity, but so far that is a project which has hardly progressed since the war in 1999.

Bosnia-Herzegovina, on the other hand, was ruled for centuries by the Ottomans and then the Austro-Hungarian Empire before becoming part of Yugoslavia. To the alarm of its Bosnian Serb minority, it decided to secede from Serb-dominated Yugoslavia in 1992. The worst of the Yugoslav wars quickly broke out and became a three-way fight between Bosniaks (as the Bosnian Muslims came to be called), Bosnian Croats and Bosnian Serbs, with Croatia and Serbia backing their respective ethnicities.

During the three years of fighting, the Bosnian government used as its flag a design taken from a dynasty which had ruled

Bosnia and Dalmatia in the fourteenth century. It was a blue shield on a white background with six yellow fleurs-de-lis. It was supposed to be neutral, but became associated mostly with the Muslim side of the conflict. In his influential and controversial book *Clash of Civilizations* (1996), Samuel Huntington relates how, during the siege of Sarajevo, some Muslim residents of the Bosnian capital would hang the flag alongside those of Saudi Arabia and Turkey, to reflect gratitude for their diplomatic stance on the war and their humanitarian assistance. At the war's end in 1995 there was clearly the need for a new flag.

The parliament in Sarajevo could not agree on a design (nor much else), bitterly riven as it was by the mass slaughter of the war years. So in 1998 the United Nations High Representative, Carlos Westendorp, imposed the current flag, which is devoid of religious or historical symbols. It has a mostly blue background with a central yellow triangle, which represents the shape of the country and whose points are a reminder of the three main population groups. The blue and yellow consciously echo the flag of the EU. To the hoist side of the triangle are nine white stars, the colour of peace.

At the press conference to unveil the design, Mr Westendorp's press officer, Duncan Bullivant, was informed by one reporter that it looked like the label on a box of cornflakes. Mr Bullivant, aware that these things are subjective, did not pursue the matter but instead explained why the stars at the top and bottom of the flag were cut off at the edges: 'I'm informed by the technical experts who designed it that the stars are infinite and what is represented on the flag is a continuation rather than a finite number. If you understand that, you're a better man or woman than I am.' He also said: 'This flag is a flag of the future; it represents unity, not division. It is a flag that belongs in Europe.'

It is also a flag that may one day join those within the EU family, should that family survive. Bosnia applied for membership in 2016, but it is likely to be a decade before its accession. In those years the European Union will change. The aftershocks of the British EU referendum will continue and what the Union will look like in the mid 2020s is unclear. The Union has been plunged into a prolonged debate about what it is and what it should be. There are governments who believe that the answer to the question is 'More Europe', and there are those who believe, as does this author, that that risks actually accelerating the break-up of the Union in its current form. Within each of the countries there are groups actively seeking to break the Union. The refugee crisis has also exacerbated the strain on the Union; with the EU initially unprepared for the sheer volume of immigrants arriving, many countries took matters into their own hands, tightening their borders – in some cases actually erecting physical barriers – arguing about the numbers each country would accept, with some Eastern European countries, such as Hungary, resisting EU attempts to share the burden across the continent. These fractures further challenge the EU, as people seek to protect their own national identities from the perceived threat of increased migration.

In 2010 most Europeans asked to name an extreme right-wing anti-immigrant party from a country other than their own may have come up with one – the French Front National. Now parties such as Golden Dawn in Greece, the AFD in Germany, Jobbik in Hungary and many others are known across the continent. No matter that Golden Dawn fly flags with overt Nazi symbols or that you can trace the heritage of Jobbik to the Hungarian fascists of the 1930s, the twin pressures of the 2008 crash coinciding with mass immigration has opened the way for the re-emergence of the right into the mainstream.

In 2014 about 700,000 migrants and refugees crossed into Europe, most by sea via the Mediterranean. Many thousands, who were fleeing war and poverty in the Middle East and Africa, drowned on the way over. The next year that figure almost doubled – Germany alone had almost half a million applications for asylum in 2015. In 2016 the figures dropped slightly to the low hundreds of thousands due to an EU deal with Turkey, but in 2017 people kept coming and there are few reasons to believe the flow can be stopped.

The Europeans are told by the mainstream politicians that the continent needs immigrants due to a falling birth rate, but large sections of the electorates are not listening and point to the pressures being put on housing, medical care, schools, welfare and the equally thorny issue of culture. The governments tried at first allow the EU to deal with the crisis, which failed miserably. The extreme-right parties have grown accordingly, often drawing on symbols of nationalism, leading to some of the mainstream tacking to the right. The German government at first welcomed 1 million refugees/migrants and came up with a plan for them to be distributed across the twenty-eight EU countries. They hadn't factored in that many EU countries would say no thank you. The cohesion of the Union fractured under the pressure.

Where once the over-riding symbolism of the EU flag meant a common European home, to some people it now means different things. Many in Bosnia might still see it as a flag of hope, something to help bring them into a region of prosperity and peace, but to some in Greece it might be a flag of economic and political oppression. To right-wingers it is a symbol of a system which is changing the culture of the continent. The French and German governments both continue to see it as the glue that holds them together. They are desperate to ensure that no matter what the shape of the Union is in a decade's time, they have not come unstuck.

The certainties of the intellectuals behind the embryonic European project of the 1950s are no longer as widely held. Where once the EU flag fluttered, it now falters, unsure of which way the wind is blowing. To its south, though, the uncertainty is even greater.

CHAPTER 4

COLOURS OF ARABIA

'White are our acts, black our battles,
green our fields, and red our swords.'

Safi al-Din-al-Hilli (1278–1349)

Previous pages: Egyptian demonstrators hold the flags of Arab nations in Tahrir Square, Cairo, in May 2011. The protest called for national unity after attacks on Egyptian churches, part of the wave of civil unrest that followed the overthrow of Hosni Mubarak's government in January 2011. It also expressed solidarity with Palestinians marking the 'Nakba' or 'catastrophe' of the displacement that occurred when Israel was established in 1948.

I F THE ARABS ARE A NATION, THEN THEY ARE A NATION of many flags. That so many of the flags share the same colours speaks of Arab kindred, but at the same time their diversity tells us this conceptual nation is divided in many ways. Some of the modern nation states do not have deep roots, and over the next decade we may well see new flags fluttering in the gale-force winds sweeping Arabia.

There are twenty-two countries in the Middle East and North Africa that could be described as Arabic and they have a combined population of more than 300 million people. They stretch from Morocco on the shores of the Atlantic Ocean, across to Egypt on the Mediterranean Sea, and eastward and southward to Kuwait, Oman and the Arabian Sea. Within this region there are many different ethnic, religious and linguistic communities, including Kurds, Berbers, Druze and Chaldeans, but the two dominating factors are language and religion. The vast majority of these 300 million people speak a version of Arabic and belong to a branch of the Islamic faith.

This explains why the flag of the pan-Arab movement, which sought to overthrow Turkish rule in the Middle East during the First World War, was designed with the colours white, black, green and red, all of which have significance in Islam. Pan-Arabism as a political idea failed, even if there remain believers in the cause. We still see the idea in the colours of many Arab nation states, notably Syria, Jordan, Yemen, Oman, the UAE, Kuwait, Iraq and the would-be nation state of Palestine. These colours also inform many of the flags of the non-Arab countries further east which came under Islamic rule, for example Iran and Afghanistan.

These colours were combined in the flag designed and raised by the leader of the Arab Revolt of 1916, Sharif Hussein of Hejaz, who hoped to unite the myriad Arab tribes under one banner and win independence from Ottoman rule. Some historians argue that the British Diplomat Mark Sykes actually designed the flag; either way, it's clear there was British involvement, and Arab unity served British interests in the region at the time.

The flag was intended to represent a huge Arab nation in which, hitherto, there were only the flags of tribes and Islamic dynasties. The Arab Revolt flag has three horizontal stripes: black at the top, green in the middle and white at the bottom. The left-hand third of the flag has a red triangle pointing to the right. As the Islamic star and crescent were present in the Ottoman flag, including them would not have signified a break with the past; instead the European tricolour was used as the basic design and incorporated deeply Islamic and Arabic symbolic colours.

The white is for the Umayyad dynasty, which ruled from Damascus between 661 and 750 CE and extended the Islamic Empire all the way to Portugal in the west and Samarkand in the east. The Umayyads are said to have chosen white as their colour as a reminder of the Prophet's first major battle at Badr. In 750 the Umayyads were overthrown by the second great Sunni Islam dynasty, the Abbasids, who chose black to distinguish the new era from the old, and as a sign of mourning for the death of relatives of the Prophet Mohammed (570–632) at the Battle of Karbala. The black also symbolizes the main banner said to have been flown by the Prophet; in addition, in pre-Islamic times black was probably the colour of the headdress worn when tribes went into battle, which gives it further significance. The green represents the Shia Islam Fatimid dynasty of 909–1171, which was founded in North Africa; but green is also more widely regarded as the colour of Islam because it is said to have been the favourite colour of the Prophet: tradition has it that he wore a green cloak, and that green flags were flown by his followers during the conquest of Mecca. To this day you still see many minarets around the world lit up at night in green. The symbolism of the red is less clear, but many scholars believe it was included in the Arab Revolt flag because it was the colour of Sharif Hussein's tribe, the Hashemites.

As with almost all other examples around the world, these four colour associations acquire their meaning in the eye of the beholder and thus become real even if the minutiae of their origins are unknown. As Mina Al-Oraibi, a leading Arab journalist, told me in an interview for this book, 'The flag of 1916 is known to most Arabs, and they identify with it. The history of the colours is generally known, if not all the detail, but in the most immediate thinking of Arabs, the link is to pan-Arabism.'

When Sharif Hussein came up with the idea of the Flag of Revolt he had other designs in mind as well. One of his sons became (briefly) King of the Hejaz, and of the two others, one became King of Jordan and the other King of Syria and Iraq; the original thinking was that the flags were to be identical except that the Jordanian would have one star, the Iraqi two and the Syrian three.

Hussein was the last Hashemite Emir of Mecca and King of the Hejaz, a region in the west of what is now Saudi Arabia which includes Mecca and Medina. He claimed direct descent from the Prophet Mohammed and his dynasty had held power in an unbroken chain for 700 years. At the height of his ambition he envisaged a vast Arab state stretching from Aleppo in the north of Syria all the way down to the port of Aden in Yemen on the Arabian Sea.

To achieve this, he teamed up with Captain T. E. Lawrence of Arabia fame and successfully took on the Ottoman Turks. He then expected the Brits to help his cause, but realpolitik was always going to countermand whatever agreements he thought he and Lawrence had come to. Hussein had one idea, the British and French had another. He began to call himself King of the Arab Countries; the British, however, would only recognize him as King of the Hejaz. What they knew, and he didn't, was that in 1916 the French and British had concocted the Sykes-Picot Agreement and, instead of helping pan-Arab unity and Arab independence, they had secretly agreed to divide the regions up between themselves – but not before they had used the Arab tribes to help them defeat the Ottoman Empire. Hussein's world was about to collapse around him, and with it the prospect of one flag for one nation.

He first refused to accept the 1919 Treaty of Versailles, and then would not sign the Anglo-Hashemite Treaty on Iraq which was due to be ratified in 1924. Both treaties would have codified elements of the Sykes-Picot Agreement relating to the Arab regions, which was anathema to the ambitions of Hussein and indeed most Arabs. Had he kept the British on side in those years, the borders of the Middle East might look very different now. In the event, Arab neighbours, with alternative ideas about who controlled what, sensed a weakened king and made their move.

Those neighbours were the Al Saud tribe led by Abdul-Aziz bin Saud of the Al-Sauds, who commanded the Wahhabi army in the Najd region to the east of the peninsula. He'd sat out the Arab Revolt, had already conquered what would prove to be the massively oil-rich regions bordering the Gulf, and now looked westward. As long as the British backed Hussein,

Abdul-Aziz would not dare take him on, but by 1924 London had tired of the Hashemite leader and his dreams of pan-Arabism. Support was withdrawn and the die was cast. Lawrence would later write that Hussein was 'a tragic figure, in his way: brave, obstinate, hopelessly out of date'.

Abdul-Aziz engineered a series of complaints against Hussein, for example claiming that he was preventing tribes from Najd from making pilgrimages to Mecca. His forces invaded and within weeks captured Mecca. With the army of Abdul-Aziz at the city gates, Hussein abdicated, went into exile in Cyprus, and by the end of 1925, Abdul-Aziz had taken the whole of the Hejaz. Some of his more radically ambitious supporters wanted to carry on into Transjordan, Iraq and Kuwait, but Abdul-Aziz played a better international power game than had Hussein and knew this would bring him into direct competition with the British. In 1927 he did a deal with London and proclaimed the Kingdom of Hejaz and Nejd. Just five years later, in 1932, he announced a new country: the two kingdoms would be united as the Kingdom of Saudi Arabia.

New country – new flag. But, given the 'difficulties' between the Hashemites and the Saudis, the house that Saud built could hardly use anything resembling the Flag of Revolt; instead it needed quite the opposite. So the Saudis made a statement in green. By 1932 it's thought that the Wahhabis had, for at least 100 years, featured the *shahada*, or proclamation of faith, on green flags. So the template was plain green with *La ʿilaha ʿilla-llah muhammadun rasulu-llah*, or 'There is no god but God: Muhammad is the Messenger of God' written across it in white calligraphy. In 1902 Abdul-Aziz had added a sword to the design to symbolize the House of Saud. He liked it so much that he kept it as the flag for the newly unified kingdom, even if it contained no reference to the Kingdom of Hejaz.

A book published in 1934 called *National Flags* by E. H. Baxter states that 'this flag is said to have been designed about 100 years ago by the grandfather of the present King', and according to the CRW Flags website: 'That it was in use in 1911 is evident from the contemporary photograph reproduced between pp. 190 and 191 in Robert Lacey's book *The Kingdom*'. Abdul-Aziz tinkered with the design: sometimes there were two swords, sometimes a white vertical stripe at the hoist, but by 1938 the version we see today, which became official in 1973, had more or less been agreed upon. The main difference is that now the sword is less curved.

The Saudi flag is made so that the *shahada* reads correctly, from right to left, when seen from either side and the sword always points in the same direction as the script. It is one of the few flags that is never lowered to half-mast, as this would be considered blasphemous. In a similar vein, it is rare to see it displayed on clothing, such as T-shirts or shorts, and there can be a particular problem with it being displayed in advertising. In 1994 McDonald's managed to offend many Muslims ahead of that year's World Cup Finals by printing all the flags of the participating countries on its take-away bags. Saudi Arabia pointed out that it was not perhaps in the best possible taste for one of its sacred tenets to be crumpled up and thrown in a rubbish bin. Hundreds of thousands of bags were subsequently withdrawn.

In the run-up to the 2002 World Cup Finals, FIFA wanted to license a football bearing the flags of all the countries playing that year. The Saudis complained on the grounds that they didn't want a picture of their flag hoofed around on global television, especially as it bears the *shahada*. And in 2007, with the best intentions, the US military dropped a load of footballs from a helicopter on Afghanistan, over a village in Khost Province, in order to give the children something to play with. Alas, some of them were adorned with the Saudi flag. Any games being played were soon abandoned in favour of a demonstration against the Americans' insensitivity. The result? An apology from the US military, and a lesson learnt. There have also been complaints about British pub landlords flying the Saudi flag during sporting events: the way around this is to use the official emblem of the country – a palm tree with two crossed swords.

But flying the flag? Not a problem – in fact the bigger the better, indeed the taller the better. The world's tallest unsupported flagpole resides in Saudi Arabia's second city, Jeddah, in King Abdullah Square, which is as large as you might have imagined and then a bit bigger. Think of four football pitches arranged in a square, then put a 170-metre-high flagpole in the middle and on top of that a flag which is 49 metres long and 33 metres wide. The flag weighs 570 kilos, or about the same as five baby elephants. The Jeddah flagpole took the record in 2014 from one in Dushanbe in Tajikistan (165 metres), which itself beat the one in Azerbaijan (162 metres), which took over from the 160-metre flagpole in North Korea, which positively towered over the 133-metre one in Turkmenistan. This is a race to the top which has not yet finished.

The flagtastic Saudi leadership attempts to be the pioneer of global Islam. However, even in the 1930s, the Saudi leadership was more concerned with expanding the power of the Sauds and their fundamentalist Wahhabi version of Islam than they were with the rest of the Arabs. To this day there remains a degree of resentment in other parts of the Arab world that the Saudi regime lays claim to being the Custodian of the Two Holy

Mosques – Mecca and Medina. Riyadh's legitimacy springs from conquest, and Saudi Arabia's official version of Islam is shared neither by Shia nor most Sunni Muslims. Wahhabi Islam rejects tolerance and insists on the political enforcement of its religious beliefs at all levels. This ideology has influenced both Al Qaeda and Islamic State (IS), and has come back to bite the Saudi state. Strictly speaking, Wahhabis do not accept the principle of the nation state; however, Saudi Arabia is built on a dual power structure – the House of Saud and the Wahhabi clerics. The two had cut a deal in the eighteenth century, which to this day is, loosely speaking: 'You do the politics, we'll do the religion.' As long as the state does not curtail the power of the clerics, most of the Wahhabi elite will not seek to overthrow it. What they failed to factor in, though, was that their ideas about the nation state would help create terrorist revolutionaries such as Osama bin Laden and many others.

In the decades during which European colonialism was coming to an end, few of the new Muslim-majority nation states followed the Saudi example of using the *shahada* on their flags, and only a handful went for green as the dominant colour. The leaders of the new Arab states were not known for their piety, and while some were practising Muslims, most were also infused with the somewhat contradictory ideology of socialism, notably those in the Ba'ath Party which ended up running Syria and Iraq. Given their proclivity towards a strong state, the leaders could hardly make the dominant colour of Islam that of their own country.

By the time the new kingdom of Saudi Arabia was proclaimed, Jordan already had its flag, based on Sharif Hussein's pan-Arab design, including the star inside the red triangle of the Hashemites. This star is seven-pointed; it is associated with the seven hills upon which the capital, Amman, is built, and the first seven verses of the Koran in the opening *Surah*, which are about God, humanity, national spirit, humility, social justice, virtue and aspirations. That red triangle continues to signify the Hashemite dynasty, as Sharif Hussein's descendants are still on the throne in Jordan; but given that about half of Jordan's population is now Palestinian, the depth of loyalty to the crown is an unknown quantity. The Jordanian flag was originally supposed to encompass the territory of Palestine as well, thus the Palestinian flag is now identical to Jordan's, minus the star. By the 1930s the flags of Iraq and Syria, although not yet independent from the British and French, were also based on the Revolt flag.

Some states followed the Ottomans, however, and adopted variations of the star and the crescent on a variety of backgrounds, as these motifs had become associated with Islam, despite predating Islam by several centuries. It is known that the city of Byzantium (later Constantinople, and now Istanbul) adopted the crescent moon as its symbol. When this happened is unclear, but legend has it that a brilliantly waxing moon was shining on the night the city won a decisive battle in 339 BCE. At the time, the crescent moon was the symbol of the Goddess Artemis. The Romans, who centuries later conquered Byzantium, knew Artemis as Diana, and so carried on the tradition of using the crescent as the symbol of the city and also used it on the flag. When the Turkic peoples conquered what was by then Constantinople in 1453, they maintained the symbol, added it to their flags, and it began to become associated with the Muslim world. According to tradition, the founder of the Ottoman Empire, Osman I, had a dream in which the crescent moon stretched across the entire world.

Originally the Ottoman Empire flew the crescent on a green flag, but this was changed to red in 1793, and legend has it that in the modern flag of Turkey the crescent and star are reflected in a pool of the blood of Turkish soldiers. It is popularly thought that the points of the star represent the Five Pillars of Islam – faith, prayer, charity, fasting and pilgrimage – but it is doubtful that this was the original intention as when it was introduced in 1793 the star had eight points, only being reduced to five in the mid 1840s.

In the twenty-first century the Islamic crescent in the Turkish flag seems, to many people, to have become more noticeable. There is no getting away from the argument about whether Turkey is European or not, and interestingly, as Europe becomes less Christian, the debate as to whether its culture is based on Judaic-Christian values becomes louder. This all plays into the migration/refugee crisis and the seemingly end-less argument over Turkish accession to the European Union. You can make a forceful argument that religion and the EU are nothing to do with each other, and indeed a country's reli-gion is not part of the entry criteria; nevertheless, religion has entered the discourse. Rightly or wrongly, to some people in Europe the sight of the crescent stirs the collective memory of ancient battles, and of the Ottoman Empire's high western watermark at the gates of Vienna in 1683.

The Turkish crescent and star flies proudly outside NATO headquarters on the outskirts of Brussels, and yet there are those who cannot envisage it alongside the EU member states at the EU headquarters a few miles downtown. Of course NATO is a military alliance spanning half of the globe, and the EU is a political and (arguably) cultural grouping. Even so, both are also values-based. Turkey's ancient symbol, invoking Islam, is, more than three centuries after the Battle of Vienna, part of a very modern political battle destined to be waged for the next few decades.

The Turkish flag also featured heavily during, and in the aftermath of, the failed coup attempt in mid-July 2016. The authorities sent out a message on social media calling people onto the streets to oppose the coup, and the mosques then issued the 'Sela' prayer from the loudspeakers in their minarets. This prayer is normally used for funerals, but is also sometimes understood as a call to gather people together. They responded in huge numbers, many waving the Turkish flag as they approached the units responsible for the coup. It was also used to cover some of the bodies of those killed in the ensuing violence, and then again, en masse, after the coup had been defeated, when hundreds of thousands of people rallied in support of President Erdogan, and/or to show their defiance and opposition to the renegade military action. The gatherings were a sea of red and white, with men and women waving the crescent and star, wrapping themselves in the national colours, or carrying huge flags, sometimes hundreds of feet long, through the crowds. During the night red flares, of the type used by football fans, added to the riot of colour. Not everyone was supporting the President, but the use of the national flag as a unifying symbol suggested that if the people could agree on one thing, it was that they were against the military coups that have plagued their country for many years. The failed coup and the subsequent crackdown on dissent, has only weakened Turkey's liberal democratic credentials and strengthened Erdogan's Islamist supporters.

Algeria and Tunisia are among the countries whose flags are also influenced by the Ottoman era. They could have gone with versions of the Arab Flag of Revolt, but the pull of 'Arabia' is not as strong in North Africa as it is in the Arabian peninsula. There remains a strong North African identity and culture across the region, even if the Arab invasions did result in making them majority Muslim and Arabic-speaking societies. In the Algerian flag the 'horns' of the crescent are much longer than usual, as Algerians believe this brings luck. The Tunisian flag is similar to the Turkish version (a red crescent and star in a white circle, on a red field), so much so that in 2014 government supporters in Egypt protesting about Turkey's backing of the Muslim Brotherhood would on occasion burn the Tunisian flag by mistake.

All these Arabic Muslim colours and symbols have spread as far as did Islam, and seeped deep into non-Arabic cultures. Iran is a good example. Its flag even has Arabic script on it, while at the same time it is also deeply Persian and revolutionary. The Iranian flag is a simple tricolour: three horizontal bands, green at the top, white in the middle and red at the bottom. It dates from 1980, the year after the Islamic revolution overthrew the Shah of Iran and brought the religious fundamentalists led by Ayatollah Ruhollah Khomeini to power. The green signifies several things in Iranian culture, including happiness and vitality. Green is also, as we've noted, the colour traditionally linked to Islam, and in the fiercely Shia Islamic Republic of Iran it can also be seen as a recognition of the Shia Fatimid dynasty. White is the traditional colour of freedom, and in Iran the colour red is associated with martyrdom, bravery, fire and love.

The colours, and what they stand for, are interesting enough, but the motif in the centre of the flag is what makes Iran's flag exceptional. The Islamic Republic needed to signify a break with the era of the Shah, but at the same time reassure an ancient culture that this was not Year Zero. Iran's traditional culture did survive the terror that followed (and continues), but on issues that challenged the clerics' absolute power, such as women's dress, the iron fist of Khomeini's version of Islamism came down hard.

The Republic's design solution was to use the colours of the pre-revolution flag, but lose the Lion and Sun emblem in the centre, a motif which dated back to at least the fifteenth century, and according to some scholars much earlier. The Lion and Sun were originally astrological symbols but they had become associated with royalty, and as such they had to go.

The new design was drawn up by Hamid Nadimi, an Associate Professor in Architecture at the Shahid Beheshti University in Tehran. He knew which emotional buttons to press and he pressed them with a brilliantly stylized construction. Nadimi was well versed in history, culture and religion. He hit upon the idea of a motif for the centre of the flag which drew on all three and would find favour among the new leaders. To the outsider the motif in the centre of the Iranian flag is an unrecognizable symbol. To the Iranian eye it is redolent of a *laleh* – a tulip.

When you first visit Tehran it takes a while before you begin to realize how ubiquitous this shape is in the capital. Once you see it, you spot it everywhere, especially as a journalist, as nine times out of ten (or, in my case, four times out of four) the 'tourist authorities' will insist you stay in the Laleh Hotel, formerly the InterContinental but renamed after the revolution. It can safely be assumed that the intelligence-gathering facilities are first-class at the Laleh, much superior to the ones available at a hotel you might book for yourself.

The tulip and Iranian culture are intertwined, and there are a number of things with which Iranians associate it – death, martyrdom, eternal love and, recently, even opposition to the ayatollahs. The flower blooms in spring, which also heralds Nowruz, the Persian new year, and for more than 3,000 years the two have been linked. Each spring during the celebrations Iranians sing, 'This spring be your good luck, the tulip fields be your joy'.

As so often in these matters, legend plays a role. In this story a sixth-century prince named Farhad hears that the love of his life, Shirin, has been killed and so promptly jumps off a cliff. However, as in the case of a Capulet and a Montague several centuries later, Shirin was in fact alive and well and the victim of a vicious rumour spread by a love rival. The story was so tragic that in the very place where the prince fell tulips began to grow, nourished by his blood.

In the same era, the great Shia Muslim hero Hussein, grandson of the Prophet Mohammed, was martyred in battle against the Umayyad Dynasty near Karbala in what is now Iraq. And which flower sprang from Hussein's blood? You guessed right, and the tulip is now a symbol of Shia martyrdom. Hussein is said to have taken on an army of several thousand men despite being accompanied by only seventy-two followers and members of his family. The moral of that story might be 'choose your battles wisely', but Hussein's group believed that only the Prophet Mohammed's family could lead the new religion of Islam, and that it was better to die fighting for justice than to live with injustice. This tenet of the Shia faith was at the root of the great schism between Sunni and Shia Muslims and self-sacrifice has been central to the Shiite sect ever since. During the Iran–Iraq war of 1980–8, when the Iranian government urged its young men into battles in which hundreds of thousands died, the tulip appeared on the posters and billboards honouring the martyrs, and one of the battle cries was 'every soil is Karbala'. This, then, was the atmosphere in which Nadimi designed the new flag.

Running the length of the top of the red stripe, and the bottom of the green stripe, is the stylized Arabic inscription *Allahu Akbar*. It is repeated twenty-two times in honour of the 22nd day of the month of Bahman in the Iranian calendar. This was the day in 1979 when, with the country in uproar and millions on the streets, national state radio crackled into life with the words, 'From Tehran, the voice of the Islamic Republic of Iran'. The red tulip in the centre of the white band is a complex symbol, or set of symbols. It comprises four crescents and a central stem which can be read as a geometrically symmetric form of the word Allah, but also as symbolizing the Five Pillars of Islam. The stem is also a sword standing for the strength of the nation. Ayatollah Khomeini liked all this symbolism, so it was no surprise when, after his death in 1989, the faithful decorated his tomb with seventy-two stained-glass tulips, the number harking back to the martyred Hussein's difficult last day.

However, the tulip is meaningful for all Iranians, not just those who support the revolution, and so it was not a surprise that in 2009, when opposition protests broke out against the re-election of President Mahmoud Ahmadinejad, some demonstrators used the flower as a symbol of defiance. I remember one particularly violent day leaving the Laleh Hotel and walking down through Laleh Park to cover the demonstrations. I watched as young people, some holding *lalehs*, were battered by plain-clothes security men riding on the back of motorbikes which would roar up onto the pavements to chase them down.

After an exchange of views with some of the riot police, I was later treated by a doctor, who, through research for this book, I now know may have been at the Laleh Hospital.

It is rare for a religious motif to be so brilliantly utilized in so many aspects of a people's life; and in bringing together the history, religion, myths, legends and even poetry of the nation, it marks the Iranian flag as an exceptional example of how a symbol can speak volumes.

Most countries do not use religious imagery on their flags for several reasons, chief among them being that if the state is not founded on faith, or has multiple popular faiths, a religious flag could be more divisive than unifying. This explains the Lebanese flag. The country is made up of a patchwork quilt of ethnicities and religions which occasionally comes undone. If the Sunnis, Shia, Druze, Alawites, Catholics, Maronites and others who make up the 4.5 million population each had representation on the flag it might look a bit of a mess. Many Lebanese (only half-jokingly) also like to think of themselves as Phoenicians and not Arabs, and so it was not surprising when they did not take up the pan-Arab colours upon independence in 1943. Instead the new state took as its symbol the cedar tree, which is linked with Lebanon as far back as the time of King Solomon 3,000 years ago. The Book of Hosea (14:5–6) contains one of the Bible's numerous references connecting them: 'I will be like the dew to Israel; he will blossom like the lily; he will take root like the cedars of Lebanon'.

The Iraqis and Egyptians had no such qualms about their Arab and Islamic connections. Both borrowed from the 1916 red, black, green and white flag of the Arab Revolt, with the Egyptians using their revolution of 1952 to renew its power by calling it the Arab Liberation Flag. Now the black also stood for the experience of colonial oppression, the red for the sacrifice required to rid the Arabs of the colonialists, and white for the peace and bright future of an independent Egypt. The pan-Arab dream had not yet died, however, and when Egypt and Syria joined together in the short-lived experiment of the United Arab Republic of 1958, their flag was the red, white and black tricolour, but with two green five-pointed stars to symbolize the two countries, and Islam, and as a nod back to the Arab Revolt flag.

In 1972 Egypt tried again, this time forming the Federation of Arab Republics with Syria and Libya. Now the stars were replaced by the Hawk of Quraish, which represents the tribe the Prophet Mohammed led. This too failed, and in 1984 Egypt reverted to the flag we know today but with a stylized gold eagle on the white band, the 'Eagle of Saladin' (Salah al-Din), the great Islamic warrior who made it as far as Cairo and built the citadel there in 1176. The symbol of an eagle was found on its western wall and so is assumed, but not proven, to have been his personal motif. It can be found on flags, seals and official documents throughout the Middle East, for example on the emblem of the Palestinian Authority.

There are a thousand and one fascinating things about Saladin's life, not least of which is that the Arabs' greatest warrior hero was, according to most experts, a Kurd. However, he is far more revered in Arabic Muslim culture than in Kurdish as he did little for Kurdish national identity. This is why an eagle does not feature in most of the Kurdish flags that are flown in the Kurdish regions of Iran, Iraq, Turkey and Syria. It does appear in the coat of arms of the Kurdish Regional Government in Iraq and in other regions, but it is not considered to be the Eagle of Saladin.

During the 2011 Egyptian uprising, which helped the army to overthrow President Mubarak, the flag of Egypt was everywhere as all sides claimed to be acting for the good of the nation. In subsequent uprisings and demonstrations countless flags have been flown by numerous factions, but there has not been a threat to the national flag, nor has there ever truly been a revolution as Egypt has returned to what it has long been: a military dictatorship/democracy hybrid. This is one of many reasons why the term 'Arab Spring' was always a foolish one to use when trying to understand what was going on in Egypt and indeed the rest of the region.

Iraq meanwhile, as noted earlier, had originally gone for black, white and green with two stars representing Arabs and Kurds, and a version of the Flag of Revolt's red triangle because members of the royal Hashemite family were in charge. However, once the Hashemites were overthrown in a 1958 coup, Iraq became a republic and the Hashemite red triangle disappeared. In 1963 the socialist-inspired Ba'ath Party took over, changed the flag to a red, white and black horizontal tricolour, and included three stars in the white band in anticipation of ever-closer union with Egypt and Syria. The union never happened, and by 1991 the two Arab brother nations were supporting the American-led war against Saddam Hussein's Iraq following its invasion of Kuwait. By this time Syria's Ba'ath Party had massively fallen out with Iraq's version and the Egyptians were firm allies of the USA. Nation-state rivalries trumped pan-Arab nationalism, and all the Arab countries were alarmed that Iraq had unilaterally crossed a fellow Arab state's border.

Saddam used those epoch-making days to add the words *Allahu Akbar* to the flag in his own handwriting. After his overthrow in 2003, his script was removed (as were the stars a few years later); the words remain, however they are now displayed in the classic decorative Kufic style. Mina Al-Oraibi, an Iraqi writer, finds this problematic:

> The Iraqi flag has been politicized over the last few decades. Adding *Allahu Akbar* was part of Saddam's attempt to make the 1991 war one about 'defending Islam'. Many Iraqis resented this addition, as they knew it was Saddam's way of manipulating religion for his own political ends. Surprisingly, after the 2003 war the Iraqi political class decided to remove the three stars of the Iraqi flag and keep the *Allahu Akbar*. This made many Iraqis unhappy, as they see their identity based on a nation state, not a religion. The Iraqi flag means much to me as a symbol of Iraq, however it is more a symbol of the troubles Iraq has faced and the political manipulation of religion, rather than the unifying symbol that it should be.

It is also the case that the Arabic script on the flag does not make the Iraqi Kurds feel comfortable, given that it is not their language, nor does the Islamic call endear Iraq's Christians to it, especially at a time when they are being forced from the country in tens of thousands.

Iraq's Muslim identity is also fractured. The national army goes into battle against IS flying the state flag, but alongside it are the flags of numerous militia, mostly Shia, sometimes Sunni, who are fighting for the aims of the Shia and the Sunni of Iraq, not those of a united nation state. For example, the Badr Organization (previously Badr Brigades) is a Shia militia originally formed in exile in Iran. It retains close links with Tehran and some of its battle flags are similar to those of Iran's Revolutionary Guard and of the Iranian-backed Lebanese Shia Hezbollah forces. Other banners flown feature the Shia martyr Hussein ibn Ali.

According to the Pew Research Center, a third of the 193 member states of the United Nations have national flags which include religious symbols. Of these sixty-four states about half have a Christian symbol, and twenty-one of them a sign associated with Islam. Unsurprisingly, Israel is the only country to use symbols of Judaism.

Despite it being relatively modern, the exact origins of Israel's flag are unclear. Certainly one of the founders of modern Zionism, Theodor Herzl, wrote in 1896: 'We have no flag, and we need one. If we desire to lead many men, we must raise a symbol above their heads. I would suggest a white flag, with seven golden stars.' That idea never flew, and by then there were already prototypes of the flag we know today on display at political meetings in Palestine, the USA and in Europe. Within a few years versions of it had become the accepted symbol of Zionism. However, upon the establishment of the State of Israel in May 1948, there was still no agreement on what the national flag should be. The Shield of David (also known as the Star of David), the Menorah and the Lion of Judah all had their supporters.

Five months later, in October, having asked the public to submit designs, the government approved that of Richard Ariel, which was similar to the Zionist flag of the nineteenth century. The blue and white represents the Jewish prayer shawl, the *tallit*, while the Shield of David is a recognized symbol of Judaism, albeit a relatively modern one, only becoming strongly associated with the faith in the Middle Ages. The Menorah became the official seal of the state, and the Lion of Judah the symbol of Jerusalem.

The Israeli flag sits, sometimes uncomfortably, in the middle of a huge arc of countries that display Islamic symbols, which are found in the Asia-Pacific region, the Middle East, North Africa – with one, Comoros, being situated in the Indian Ocean below the Sahara. Unsurprisingly, the regions correspond to the spread of Islam, and they include places as diverse as Malaysia, Uzbekistan, Pakistan and Libya.

For several decades the Libyan flag was unusual in that it was a simple green field with no script or motif. This was in the era of Colonel Gaddafi and his 'Great Socialist People's Libyan Arab Jamahiriya', in which he fancied himself as 'Dean of the Arab leaders', a philosopher and a literary giant. The green, of course, represented Islam, but also his 'Green Book'. This was a collection of ramblings by a man who increasingly looked unhinged as the years passed but continued to insist that Libyans be guided by such bons mots as 'Women, like men, are human beings. This is an incontestable truth . . . Women are different from men in form because they are females, just as all females in the kingdom of plants and animals differ from the male of their species . . . According to gynaecologists women, unlike men, menstruate each month.'

Such pearls of wisdom could not save him during the 2011 revolution and NATO bombing campaign, which resulted in his death at the hands of a mob in the desert. As the uprising had spread across the country, many protestors began to fly the old flag of independence, with its red, black and green horizontal stripes and white crescent and star in the centre. It quickly became the symbol of defiance, and after Gaddafi's death was adopted as the official flag of the country, which itself was renamed Libya.

This original flag was that of the Kingdom of Libya, which had broken free from Italy in 1947 and became an independent state in 1951. The basis was the flag of the religious Senussi dynasty of the Cyrenaica region in the east of the country next to Egypt, a black flag with the star and crescent on it. The red band was added to represent the blood of the people but also because it was the colour of the southern region of Fezzan, and green because that was the traditional colour of the Tripolitania region in the west bordering Tunisia. In 1951 the colours sym-bolized the coming-together of three distinct regions which had hitherto not been ruled as a single independent entity. In 2011 they again depicted the three regions, but this time there was little to hold them together.

Tripoli is so named because of the Greek word for three towns, *tripolis*, which were Oea, Sabrata and Leptis Magna – hence the region becoming known as Tripolitania. When the Greeks later settled the area 400 miles east along the coast they built a town called Cyrene, which in turn led that area to be known as Cyrenaica. They did not identify the two regions and Fezzan as a single geographic, political or ethnic entity, nor did the Romans see it that way when they took over. Then came the Arabs, then the Ottomans and finally, in the twentieth century, the Italians, who at first named the region 'Italian North Africa', then split it into two colonies – Italian Tripolitania and Italian Cyrenaica. In 1934 they resurrected a term used by the Greeks 2,000 years previously for all of North Africa except Egypt – Libya. After the Second World War Tripolitania and Cyrenaica were administered by the British and the French ruled in Fezzan, until 1951, when the Italians gave up all claims on the region and the nation state of Libya was born. The populations of all three regions were told, 'you're all in this together'.

The fifty-five years of statehood, more than half of them under a dictatorship, have not forged a nation and the three colours on the flag once again symbolize division. At the time of writing there appears little short-to-medium-term possibility of Libya succeeding as a unified state. The flag of IS has appeared in several towns along the coast, and although this is attracting the attention of what passes for a government in Tripoli (and that of governments on the other side of the Mediterranean), it adds to the instability of what at times edges towards failed state status. The future may be a mirror of the past, although a loose federal arrangement could emerge.

So, the Arab nation? If language binds Arabs together, the idea has a foundation, albeit one with many dialects. If it denotes a people then the idea falters, given that the Arabs are many peoples. What instead has grown steadily since the mid 1970s is political Islam. Given that many strands of Islamic thought do not recognize the divides between politics, religion and borders, flags such as that of IS (discussed in Chapter 5) are therefore at least pan-Arab and at most global. However, although religion will often beat other cards, for example nationalism or political philosophy, the sheer brutality and utopian ideas of violent Islamist groups will probably ensure their eventual demise, but that will be a struggle lasting generations. In the summer of 2016, Tunisia's main Islamist party, Ennahda (which voluntarily relinquished power after an election), recognized the separation of mosque and state, claiming: 'We are leaving political Islam and entering democratic Islam.' If the party means what it says, then 'democratic Islam' is an experiment, and one in opposition to the IS/Al Qaeda worldview. The Turkish model of a Muslim fully democratic secular nation state appears to be struggling; the Tunisian model will be worth following. Tunisia rejected the pan-Arab colours for its flag, and its mostly homogeneous North African population is now working out which bits of the political Islam, which originated well to its east, it will use and which it will discard.

The Egyptian diplomat and intellectual Tahseen Bashir is credited with coming up with the phrase 'Tribes with flags' to describe the Arabs in the 1960s. He went on to say that the only real nation state in the region was his own. That may reflect the old Cairo-centric worldview of many of his countrymen, which itself is reflected in the Egyptian saying, '*Masr Om Al Dunya*' – 'Cairo is the mother of the world'. His quote might also be disliked by some Arabs, who resent the fact that it has been picked up and used by the outside world. However, what Bashir was getting at was that the ethnic and cultural coherence of a bonded nation state requires more than lines drawn in the sand by colonialists and a few national flags as symbols of something which might not exist in the minds of all people living within those lines. Some of the flags are in danger of being lowered and then covered by the sands now swirling dangerously from the Mediterranean to the Arabian-Persian Sea.

Federalism may yet be the fate of Iraq, Syria and Yemen: new flags to symbolize new federal realities, or even new flags for new nation states. If so, some will use the green, white and black with which the Arabs are so familiar, but they are also likely to feature red, as a lot of blood will be spilt drawing the new lines, and the depiction of martyrdom is unlikely to fade from their culture.

The Stars and the Stripes

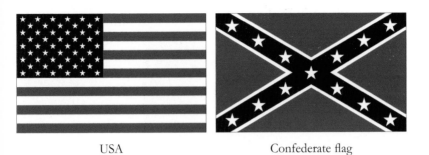

USA

Confederate flag

The Union and the Jack

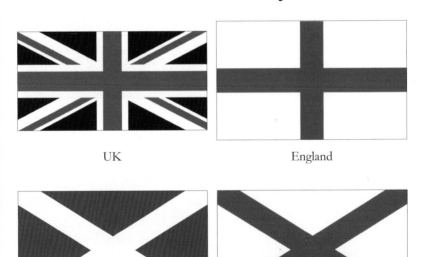

UK

England

Scotland

St Patrick's Saltire

Wales

Ireland

Fiji

Australia

New Zealand

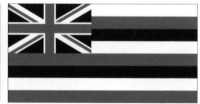

Hawaii

The Cross and the Crusades

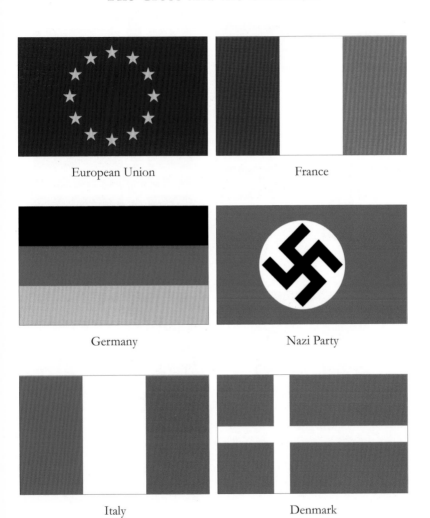

European Union

France

Germany

Nazi Party

Italy

Denmark

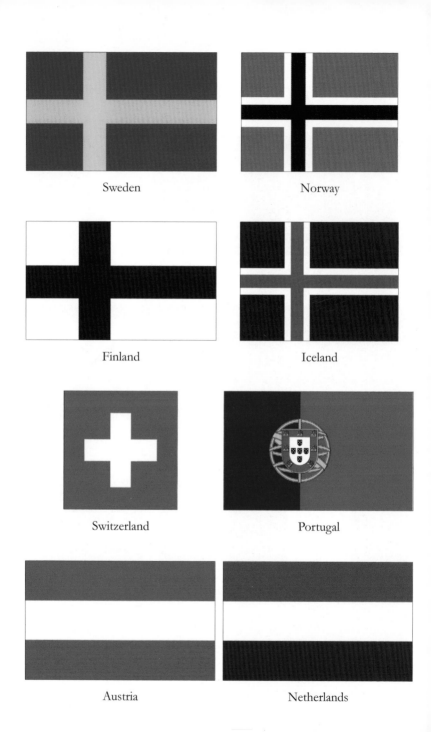

Sweden

Norway

Finland

Iceland

Switzerland

Portugal

Austria

Netherlands

Russia

Soviet Union

Serbia

Slovenia

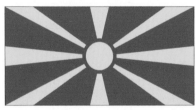

Macedonia

Kosovo

Bosnia-Herzegovina

Colours of Arabia

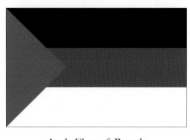

Arab Flag of Revolt

Saudi Arabia

Jordan

Turkey

Algeria

Tunisia

Iran

Lebanon

Egypt

Iraq

Israel

Libya

Flags of Fear

Islamic State

Jabhat al-Nusra

Hezbollah

Hamas

Hamas logo, and alternative flag

Fatah

Al-Aqsa
Martyrs' Brigades

Izz ad-Din al-
Qassam Brigades

East of Eden

Turkmenistan

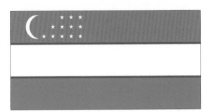

Uzbekistan

Kazakhstan

Kyrgyzstan

Afghanistan

Pakistan

India

Nepal

China

Taiwan

South Korea

North Korea

Japan

Japanese military flag

Flags of Freedom

Ethiopia

UNIA

Jamaica

Rastafari (and, previously, Ethiopia)

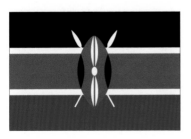

Ghana

Kenya

Mozambique

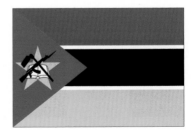

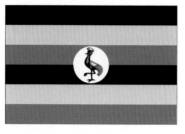

Uganda

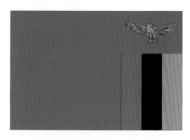

Zambia

Liberia

Rwanda

Burundi

Seychelles

Nigeria

South Africa

Flags of Revolution

Gran Colombia (variant)

Venezuela

Ecuador

Bolivia

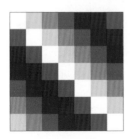

Wiphala

Mexico

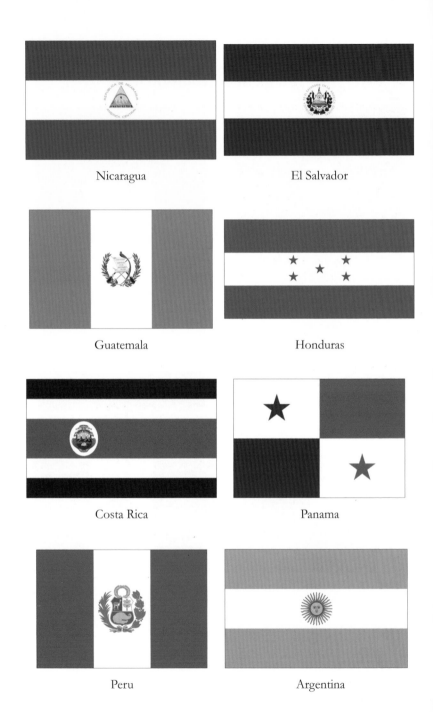

Nicaragua

El Salvador

Guatemala

Honduras

Costa Rica

Panama

Peru

Argentina

The Falkland Islands

Uruguay

Brazil

The Good, the Bad and the Ugly

Jolly Roger

Red Cross

Red Crescent

Red Crystal

NATO

Olympics

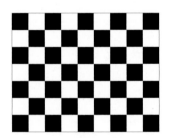

Checkered flag

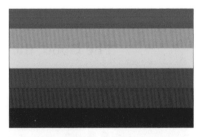

Rainbow flag

United Nations

International Flag of Planet Earth

CHAPTER 5

FLAGS OF FEAR

'I say that I am stronger than fear.'
Malala Yousafzai

Previous pages: A propaganda photograph released by Islamic State.

SOMETHING WICKED THIS WAY COMES. SOMETHING SO wicked, so beyond our ken, that we thought we had left it behind in the Middle Ages. Islamic State (IS) has seared itself into our collective consciousness. It goes to extreme lengths to kill people in a horrific way, in public, and then publicize their deaths, and its propaganda has been ruthlessly, mercilessly, terrifyingly efficient. It does this under a banner that is not its own, but which it is trying to make synonymous with its depraved actions. By so doing it damages the very religion in whose name it claims to act.

Most of this chapter is about the flags of non-state actors that are in the Middle East and therefore relate to Islam. This is not to single out Islam in a world full of armed revolutionary groups of different creeds. Rather, it provides an important focus: not only because so many of these groups are regularly in the news, and their symbolism speaks to so many people, but also because Islamist iconography is connected to deep undercurrents in Middle Eastern society that need to be understood. A chapter on the emblems of the Shining Path group in Peru or the Lord's Resistance Army from Uganda would throw up many a fascinating detail, but the former is a localized issue and the latter is plain mad, bad, exceptionally dangerous to know and going nowhere other than extinction, after which its 'ideas' will die with it. However, understanding the flags discussed in this chapter helps us to comprehend the events we witness on the evening news every day – events that will be with us for decades to come.

IS is in a league of its own when it comes to 'messaging'. We do not need to avail ourselves of the details of its depravity to understand its aim. Yes, it appears that members of the group enjoy their sadistic acts, but this madness is also completely, coldly, logical. It scares the hell out of us, and rightly so.

The best example of this can be seen in the group's June 2014 capture of Mosul, the second city of Iraq. Here was a city of 1.8 million souls, defended by around 30,000 Iraqi troops who ran away in the face of the crazy, burning, torturing, murdering fanatics of IS, who had gone to great lengths to publicize every weird and warped contortion of killing they had enacted in the run-up to advancing on the city. And borne aloft before them was the flag they have co-opted, which has become known as the flag of IS. In Mosul it flew without opposition for almost eighteen months before the Iraqi forces gathered the nerve and strength to begin the task of taking back the city, and only then with American firepower assisting.

We've grown used to seeing this flag in our media; the black background with a white circle containing Arabic script that reads 'Mohammed is the messenger of God', with another line at the top of the flag saying 'There is no god but God'. These two lines make up the *shahada*, the Muslim profession of faith. The style of the writing on the IS flag is deliberately rough and ready, in contrast to the calligraphy used for the *shahada* on the Saudi Arabian flag. This may be intended as a message that IS is ushering in a return to what it sees as the original form of Islam. In this, IS is in ideological competition with the Saudis: both adhere to an extreme Sunni version of the faith, Wahhabism, and both use this to claim the legitimacy to represent all of Islam. There are elements within Saudi Arabia who support IS, but at state level they remember how, having partially helped to create Al Qaeda, they were subsequently hit by a wave of terrorist attacks as AQ wanted to destabilize the kingdom and take it over.

IS announced the flag as its standard in 2007, but the use of black and the *shahada* are pan-Islamic symbols that should not necessarily be associated with terror; the cunning of IS is that it has made them so. According to the website of the Search for International Terrorist Entities (SITE) Institute, the IS media wing issued a statement back in 2007, when it was still called the Islamic State of Iraq, entitled 'The Legality of the Flag in Islam', which explained why the group used it. Drawing on traditional beliefs, it said: 'The flag of the Prophet, peace and blessings be upon him, is a black square made of striped wool.' In most instances the flags IS flies appear to be square. The white circle is supposed to represent the seal of the Prophet: there are letters on display in Istanbul's ancient Topkapi Palace that are said to be from Mohammed, and they bear this symbol. The statement also quotes a saying attributed to the Prophet: 'If you see the black banners coming, go to them immediately even if you must crawl over ice because indeed among them is the caliph.'

This is all very 'end of days', and it speaks to some younger Muslims of a certain mindset: the sort who, if they were Christians, say, might be found armed with a tambourine, having a rapture moment and insisting you repent before it's too late. Occasionally the tambourine brigade veers off into its own 'end of days' survivalist movements, often based in the Midwest of the USA. Alas, the teachings of this particular minority brand of Islam don't include tambourines; its adherents are more likely to have a sword and a balaclava.

IS also attaches huge significance to its proximity to the Syrian town of Dabiq, which is near Aleppo. In fact, its online magazine is named after the town. The IS 'Apocalypse Soon' theory repeats a prophecy allegedly made by Mohammed, which states that the armies of Rome (for which now read the West/ USA/Turkey/add enemy of choice) and the armies of Islam will meet in battle on the plain in front of Dabiq. The group loves a good quote – the statement also references another *hadith*, or saying of the Prophet: 'Black banners will appear from the east and they will kill you in a way that has never before been done by a nation', which is a little worrisome for IS's opponents, especially as it has indeed fulfilled that promise in a series of gruesome, well-documented murders that have furthered its aim of striking fear into all.

The banners referred to are those of the Mahdi, the Islamic messiah figure, so naturally in this story Islam wins at Dabiq and advances on Istanbul, all of which triggers the end times. At this point the Antichrist, or Dajjal, shows up and drives the Mahdi army back. A rump force retreats to Jerusalem and it's all looking a bit sticky until the Prophet Jesus descends from heaven, joins the Mahdi's side and the Dajjal is killed, which in turn ushers in the end of the world and the Day of Judgment. I'm afraid at this point infidels get some rough treatment, in the form of eternal punishment, which is not too different from the end of the fundamentalist Christian version of the tale.

I used to muse upon this story when reporting from Damascus in the first few years of the Syrian Civil War. At the end, it is said that Jesus will descend via the 'Jesus Minaret' in the eastern corner of the sensationally beautiful Umayyad Mosque in the capital. It is important to understand that, unlike in the mostly post-Christian West, many people of faith in the Middle East do take their scripture literally. Faced with the sight of the Jesus Minaret, the sound of distant explosions from the Damascus suburbs and the knowledge of the plethora of jihadist groups just a few miles away, it was vital to bear in mind that 'they really believe this stuff'. It is also understandable that amid the heat, dust, smoke and killing, the young brainwashed fighters of IS and other groups would see around them evidence that the prophecies were coming true.

When IS purportedly beheaded the American aid worker Peter Kassig in 2014, it issued a video in which the narrator said, 'Here we are, burying the first American crusader in Dabiq, and eagerly waiting for the remainder of your armies to arrive.' This was a direct reference to the story above and an example of how IS wants to draw in a foreign army in order to bring about the end of days. When IS took Dabiq, one of the first things its fighters did was to fly hundreds of black flags from the rooftops of the town, in their minds fulfilling that part of the prophecy in which black banners appear 'from the east'.

IS fighters and supporters tend to stay on-message. You can occasionally see photos of them with a yellow flag among the sea of black, and sometimes they add some rather fetching gold braid to the fringes of the black flag, but almost always they stick to that same stark image that, through its use and associations, has burnt itself into our imagination.

When most of us see this flag we see evil fanaticism. It is about as 'other' as a flag can be. But to its devotees it is a symbol of heroic courage to do God's work on earth, no matter the cost. That it is instantly recognizable is, in 'messaging' terms, a positive. But contrast it with another such flag: that of international Communism. The moment you see the Red Flag it conveys a message about the values of those holding it. The detail of those values, be they Maoist, Marxist-Leninist, or even Tooting Popular Front/People's Front of Judea, is secondary to the singular message of Communism, an ideology that is at least within our understanding, whether we agree with it or not. Conceptually, it embraces the universal brotherhood (and sisterhood) of mankind and justice for all, even if its associations and end product have been far from that. The IS flag, however, screams exclusivity and a narrow definition of what is acceptable, created by people who believe themselves to be carrying out the will of God. The Red Flag holds the possibility that if a supporter captured you, you might just come round to their way of thinking after a prolonged period in a re-education camp somewhere very cold. By contrast, the IS flag is the ultimate 'us and them' flag. It says: 'If you're not us, then you're a dirty kafir who deserves to die immediately, but not necessarily quickly.'

Where the two flags do have similarities is in the touching belief in the abilities of their proponents, and the belief that victory is assured, albeit at some cost. The lyrics to 'The Red Flag' anthem (1889) are interesting in that if you change some of the words, they could relate to the IS black flag – a few lines are given below:

> *The people's flag is deepest red,*
> *It shrouded oft our martyred dead . . .*
> *Then raise the scarlet standard high.*
> *Beneath its shade we'll live and die . . .*
> *With heads uncovered swear we all*
> *To bear it onward till we fall . . .*

True believers in each system consider it to be the answer to whatever question they are asked, and both systems have a basic, easily recognizable symbol around which to rally.

Organizations peddling their message might use a symbol in a variety of ways, but when it comes to merchandising, IS sticks to its austere worldview: you'd be hard-pressed to find an IS mug, pen or set of coasters down at Raqqa promoting the Islamic State of Iraq and the Levant. In English the name compresses down to ISIL, but because in Arabic the Levant is sometimes known as al Sham, or 'Land of the left hand', the group is also called ISIS, or just IS. The 'left hand' refers to the region to your left if you are facing east from Mecca. The other name for the group is Daesh, an acronym of 'al-Dawla al-Islamiya fil Iraq wa al-Sham'. Its Arab opponents enjoy using this term as it sounds similar to the Arabic word for an animal much derided in Arabic culture – the ass.

One of the jihadist rivals to IS in Syria is Jabhat Fateh al-Sham (Front for the Conquest of Syria/the Levant), formerly known as Jabhat al-Nusra or the Nusra Front, which until recently came under the Al Qaeda franchise. It has also used a black flag, an oblong one, with the *shahada* in classical Arabic script and the name of the group underneath. Jabhat Fateh al-Sham is a powerful group that was briefly the bogeyman of the Syrian Civil War when it came to the fore around 2012. However, it was soon surpassed by IS – not only on the battlefield, but also in the PR war, and that is a war which matters. The grotesque manner and scale of the murders carried out by IS and, equally importantly, the multimedia propagation of the images of those killings, are part of the reason why the world knows the IS banner but not that of Jabhat Fateh al-Sham. And with that name recognition comes potential support – both in the form of the young Muslims from around the world who serve as cannon fodder, and also from the wealthy would-be benefactors who help fuel global jihad.

The lists of 'designated terror organizations', as defined by the United States, the EU and many others, are long and they encompass the globe. All the groups on them seek to define themselves through symbols, usually flags. Elsewhere, Al-Shabaab in Somalia, Al-Tawhid wal-Jihad in Gaza, and at least one jihadi group in Chechnya have adopted black IS-style flags, as has Boko Haram in Nigeria, although it is unclear whether this is its 'official' emblem. The Al-Shabaab flag is black when used as a war symbol, but for 'administration' purposes it reverses the colours and has black inscriptions on a white background. This is simple messaging, a clear way to convey the time and place of conflict or of peace. Naturally the groups above might not see themselves as terror organizations, despite a continued propensity to bomb shopping malls, markets and schools, and torture and kill prisoners.

The similarities in the flags of IS, Jabhat Fateh al-Sham and other jihadist groups lie not in that each seeks to imitate the others; rather, each claims jurisdiction over Islam and therefore the right to fly the flag of the Prophet. The flag of the pan-Arab movement, which sought to overthrow Ottoman rule in the Middle East during the First World War, was designed with the colours white, black, green and red, all of which have significance in Islam, and it has since influenced many national flags in the region (see Chapter 4). The jihadist groups do not believe in the nation state, however, and so have been loath to borrow from the Arab Flag of Revolt. Other non-state groups in the Middle East have also gone for individual symbols that speak to their target audiences. Five good examples are Hezbollah in Lebanon, Hamas and the Izz ad-Din al-Qassam Brigades in Gaza, and Fatah and the Al-Aqsa Martyrs' Brigades in the West Bank.

Hezbollah is a Shia organization with close ties to Iran that is strongest in the south of Lebanon, in the Beqaa Valley, and in the south of the capital, Beirut. It emerged in response to Israel's invasion of Lebanon in 1982. It is deeply anti-Semitic, espousing the destruction of Israel and the occupation of Jerusalem, and seeks a Shia version of the caliphate. It is behind numerous bombings, especially of American targets, and the government of Argentina believes it is linked to the 1994 bombing of a Jewish Centre in Buenos Aires in which eighty-five people were killed. It has grown over the years to become the most powerful military force in multi-faith Lebanon, and is virtually a state within the state. Its militia would probably have the upper hand in any renewed civil war in Lebanon, and it increasingly has the ability to threaten Israel with tens of thousands of long-range rockets. Despite its involvement in schools, hospitals and charity work, Hezbollah is now seen as a sectarian movement concerned only with promoting the interests of Shia Islam. After Hezbollah's forces began operating in strength on the side of President Assad's army in Syria in 2012, many Sunni Muslims in the Middle East began to refer to it not as the Party of God, but as the Party of Satan: *Hizb al-shaytan.*

Its flag is displayed in different colours, but the most common combination is a yellow background with the Hezbollah motif across it, usually in green. According to local folklore, the yellow signifies Hezbollah's willingness to fight for the sake of Allah and the Shia. The logo depicts a globe (Hezbollah operates around the world), a seven-leafed branch, the Koran and a fist holding an AK assault rifle to show it is committed to using force to achieve its aims.

When Hezbollah was first formed in 1985 some of its ideological roots were socialist, and the AK is a familiar feature of the era's left-wing revolutionary iconography, similar to that previously used by militant groups such as the Red Brigades in Italy and the Baader-Meinhof Group (Red Army Faction) in Germany. Underneath the gun, you see that the fist holding it is at the end of an arm. The arm is actually the Arabic letter 'Alif' (which is the letter used for the first L in Allah). Reading right to left, the logo spells Hezbollah, with the fist at the top of the first Alif. At the bottom of the flag is written,

'The Islamic Resistance in Lebanon'. The flag is very similar to that of Hezbollah's main sponsor, Iran's Revolutionary Guard Corps. This unit was formed after the Iranian revolution in 1979, six years before Hezbollah, and the Lebanese group was clearly inspired by Iran's elite military organization. To this day they maintain close co-operation and have fought alongside one another in Syria.

At the heart of Beirut's Shia southern suburbs is the district of Al-Dahiya. This is a no-go area for state officials: here Hezbollah is the police, the army, the religious authority and the government all rolled into one. One of the things that strikes you about the neighbourhood is the sight of massive posters extolling Ayatollah Khomeini of Iran and the current Hezbollah leader, Hassan Nasrallah. There is also a sea of single-colour flags, including red, black and green for the traditional Islamic motifs alongside the yellow of Hezbollah. The yellow is sometimes tinged with gold, which is a colour often found at Shia shrines, but there is no conclusive evidence that this is why it is used.

When the Hezbollah militias march beneath their banner they can often be seen goose-stepping and giving the fascist salute. Apologists pretend there is no connection to fascism, but the ideologues at the top of the party are smart enough to know what they are doing and what message they are sending. If challenged, Hezbollah sympathizers will sometimes point to the use of the 'fascist salute' in Taiwan, ignoring the fact that there it is part of the 'Regulations for Taking Oaths'. They also ignore the fact that in Taiwan the salute does not have the same connotations as it does in a country bordering Israel, and that Lebanon has a major Christian political movement known as the Phalange, which was founded on fascist principles in 1936 and which uses the salute it adopted from the fascist parties of Europe.

In case anyone was confused about Hezbollah's ideology, Sheikh Nasrallah came up with a handy guide in a speech in 2002 (of which there is audio) when he said: 'The Jews will gather from all parts of the world into occupied Palestine, not in order to bring about the anti-Christ and the end of the world, but rather that Allah the Glorified and Most High wants to save you from having to go to the ends of the world, for they have gathered in one place – they have gathered in one place – and there the final and decisive battle will take place.' When you look at the Hezbollah flag you are seeing a message from an extremist revolutionary organization that demands loyalty from a nation within a nation state – the Shia in Lebanon – and is itself loyal to a religion inside a religion – Shi'ism in Islam.

With the Middle East in such turmoil, and identity politics seemingly dominant, Hezbollah has retained much popular support with the Lebanese Shia masses, but its heyday, when it was considered an Arab champion taking on the Israelis, appears to be over. The sectarian issues at the heart of the Syrian War resulted in Hezbollah fighting alongside President Assad's forces against what were primarily Sunni opposition groups. This did not go unnoticed in the Sunni-dominated Arab Middle East, in which most countries and people have sided with the opposition.

Across the border and down in the Gaza Strip, Hamas is clinging on to its reputation as the go-to organization if you want to inflict violence on the Israelis, and because it is 100 per cent Sunni Muslim it retains a degree of support among sections of the Arab Sunni populations. However, the upheavals in the Arab world this decade have drawn attention away from the Palestine/Israel conflict: people have seen that the scale of death and destruction elsewhere is much greater, and that solving the problem there will not necessarily solve that of the wider Middle East.

Hamas, founded in 1987, has as many difficulties as there are Palestinians trapped in the Gaza Strip – approaching 2 million, and growing fast. Its name in Arabic, in full, is Harakat al-Muqawamah al-Islamiyyah (which translates as 'The Islamic Resistance Movement'), from which we get the acronym Hamas, but the word *hamas* in Arabic also means 'zeal'. On the ideological front it has two challenges: the first is that it is not radical or violent enough for some, both inside and outside Palestine; the second is that it is too radical and violent for others. It risks losing support to even more extreme groups such as Islamic Jihad and even IS if it does not continue to take the war to the Israelis. However, it knows that when it does this, and Gaza is then smashed (with the consequent high death rate of urban warfare), it is often blamed for attracting the devastation visited upon the territory. Its imagery, messaging and iconography are at the heart of this difficult balancing act.

Its official flag simply features the *shahada* in white calligraphic writing on a green background. Green, as noted, is often seen as the colour of Islam; as such, it is not fair to call this 'the Hamas flag', as its components suggest that it is a flag for any Muslim; however, it does remain the emblem most often seen at Hamas' mass rallies in Gaza City and is one under which all, except for the few remaining Gazan Christians, can gather even if they also display the symbols of the other groups operating in the Strip, such as Islamic Jihad. Hamas is an offshoot of the now international Muslim Brotherhood organization, which originated in Egypt and with which it still has close ties. Unlike IS, it does not claim to be the only legitimate group representing Islam, but there is still sometimes resentment among Palestinians that Hamas uses a general Muslim flag to represent itself.

Another flag seen in Gaza is that of the Hamas military wing, the Izz ad-Din al-Qassam Brigades. The Brigades are named after Sheikh Izz ad-Din al-Qassam (1882–1935), who was a preacher and jihadi fighter against French and British colonialism. He was killed in a shoot-out with the British and is buried in the Muslim cemetery in Haifa, now part of Israel. The manner of his death turned him into a Palestinian hero, and his symbolism is such to Hamas that the Brigades have named the home-made missiles they fire into Israel 'Qassam rockets'. The flag features a man in a kaffiyeh headdress in front of the Dome of the Rock shrine in Jerusalem, clutching an M-16 rifle in one hand and a Koran in the other. To his left is a green flag with the *shahada* written on it.

The political wing of Hamas has a second flag with a design often used as its seal, but also on banners flown alongside the green version. At the top is a map that encompasses the State of Israel, the West Bank and the Gaza Strip, but without boundary markers, thus symbolizing the goal of one Islamic state for the whole territory, stretching from the River Jordan in the east to the shores of the Mediterranean in the west, an aim which remains in Hamas' charter. This concept is also summed up in the chant sometimes heard in English at pro-Hamas rallies in Europe: 'From the river to the sea, Palestine must be free.' Hamas flags are often present.

Beneath the map is a picture of the Dome of the Rock with two crossed swords over it, and on each side a Palestinian flag embracing it. The Dome covers a stone that is said to be the place from which the Prophet Mohammed ascended to heaven on his famous night journey from Mecca to Jerusalem, mounted on a winged horse. The building is the third most holy site in Islam. Scholars debate if the Dome of the Rock building is a mosque or not, and also whether it is the exact spot from where the leap to heaven took place, but for the faithful it is a simply a deeply holy place and to everyone it is the most visually stunning construction in the Al-Aqsa compound. In Judaism it is also a sacred site as it is considered to be the stone on which Abraham prepared to sacrifice Isaac, and also the foundation stone of the world.

To the right of the Dome is a flag that declares: 'There is no god but God', and to its left another saying: 'Mohammed is the messenger of God'. Underneath the shrine is the word 'Palestine' and beneath that a scroll reading 'Islamic Resistance Movement'. The symbolism of this Hamas flag is clear. It rejects a two-state solution and hints that a Palestinian victory will be achieved by force of arms. The Qassam Brigades openly vow to destroy Israel whereas the Hamas political wing, which claims it is separate, uses deliberately ambiguous language about whether it has or has not rewritten its charter to recognize the right of Israel to exist.

Hamas operates in all of the Palestinian territories but its stronghold is Gaza, where, in 2007, it took power during the violent overthrow of Fatah, the main group inside the Palestine Liberation Organization (PLO), which now only effectively operates in the West Bank. Well over 100 people died during five days of conflict in 2007 before hundreds of Fatah fighters fled towards Israel, leaving Hamas to finish off many of the prisoners it took by throwing them from the tops of tall buildings in Gaza City. The two factions have become partially reconciled in recent years, but their differences are huge and neither seems willing to share power. Hamas remains a party driven by religious zeal, and is far less prepared to compromise. Both parties treat their populations harshly, torture and executions being commonplace, but Fatah and the Palestinian Authority work with the Israeli government on a variety of issues in a manner Hamas will not contemplate. This ensures that the Palestinians remain divided, not just by the 25 miles between coastal Gaza and the landlocked West Bank, but politically and ideologically too.

Unlike Hamas, Fatah is officially secular, but it carries religious elements within it and its symbolism. Its full title refers to its original name when it was founded by the late Yasser Arafat in the 1950s. In Arabic this was 'Harakat al-tahrir al-watani al-Filastini' (Palestinian National Liberation Movement), which was reversed and turned into the acronym Fatah. The word *fatah* is also used among Arab Muslims, in a religious context, to refer to the rapid expansion of Islam after the death of the Prophet Mohammed.

The Fatah flag is usually yellow, but occasionally white. On it are two forearms in the colours of the Palestinian flag (black, white, red and green), and two hands, each holding an M16 rifle crossed over a map of the territory of the West Bank, Israel and Gaza, but with no border demarcations. Underneath the rifles is a grenade and across the centre of the image is the word 'Fatah'. At the top, in red, it says 'Al-Asifa' ('The Storm'), while underneath the symbol is the party name, and at the bottom of the flag is written 'Thawrah Hatta Al-Naser' – 'Revolution until Victory'.

Its main paramilitary wing is the Al-Aqsa Martyrs' Brigades, although it is unclear how much control Fatah has over it. The Brigades' emblem, to be found on yellow flags in the West Bank, is a picture of the Dome of the Rock shrine atop the Al-Aqsa compound in Jerusalem, with two long Palestinian flags wrapped around it. Above it are two crossed rifles and a grenade, and above that a Koranic inscription: 'Fight, Allah will punish them by your hand, he will smother them in humiliation, and help you rise above them, and heal the bosom of believers'. At the bottom is the group's name.

Many people believe that the mosque depicted is called the Al-Aqsa; however, a visit to one of Palestine's most eminent intellectuals, Dr Mahdi F. Abdul Hadi, clarified the issue. Dr Hadi is chairman of the Palestinian Academic Society for the Study of International Affairs (PASSIA), based in East Jerusalem. His offices are a treasure trove of old photographs, documents and symbols. He was kind enough to spend several hours with me. He spread out maps of Jerusalem's Old City on a huge desk and homed in on the Al-Aqsa compound, which sits above the Western Wall. 'The mosque in the Al-Aqsa [Brigade] flag is the Dome of the Rock. Everyone takes it for granted that it is the Al-Aqsa mosque, but no, the whole compound is Al-Aqsa, and on it are two mosques, the Qibla mosque and the Dome of the Rock and on the flags of both Al-Aqsa Brigades and the Qassam Brigades it is the Dome of the Rock shown', he said.

As both an intellectual and a Palestinian, Dr Hadi understands the importance of symbolism to political movements and he has been fighting symbolic legal battles for decades. In 1948, the Palestinian National Convention in Gaza had adopted the Arab Flag of Revolt as the flag of the Palestinian government. But then in 1964 the PLO took it over as its own flag. In 1967, citing numerous PLO attacks on Israelis, Israel denounced the PLO flag as a terrorist flag and so banned it. Dr Hadi did not accept this.

'I went to court to testify with many lawyers that this is not the PLO flag, it is the Palestine flag; but they continued to ban it, and it wasn't until the Oslo accords of 1993 that it became accepted. This is now deep-rooted in Palestinian consciousness and there are calls for only this flag to be in our demonstrations, not the other flags of the groups. But Fatah insist they must fly their yellow flag, I think because they are losing so much support.' He says the Fatah flag 'doesn't have roots. They don't have history; they are just a faction and they need it to establish their identity among others. They say they are the government and so can fly their flag, but not everyone likes this because the symbol of the Palestinians is the Palestinian flag.'

The Al-Aqsa Brigade motif is religious, and so gives the Brigades some distance from Fatah; this would allow them to carry on and operate alone if support for Fatah collapsed. All these, and more, are the subtle and sometimes less subtle messages transmitted by the pieces of cloth flying in the winds of change still blowing fiercely across the region.

The details matter. All cultures have symbols that speak to those who know how to decode them; this is one way, along with appreciating local humour, in which you can really begin to understand a place. Whereas in the UK a man wearing jeans with a rolled-up copy of the *Sun* newspaper sticking out of his back pocket might be assumed, rightly or wrongly, to be working-class, so in Muslim Middle Eastern culture a man's beard, or lack of it, suggests certain things about him. For example, being clean-shaven might mean the person is not particularly religious. In Egypt a full beard, but one that is groomed, betokens a moderate practising Muslim. A long, unkempt beard signifies that a person is probably a religious conservative, and having a beard but shaving the top lip is a sure sign that he is of a fundamentalist bent. If you meet a man with no moustache but a long unkempt beard, dyed orange, then you've usually hit the ultra-conservative jackpot.

All this conveys information that is meant to be understood; and, similarly, the Palestinians grasp the deeper messages these flags send. The Fatah flag, for example, is slightly at odds with the political position of the Palestinian Authority, of which Fatah is the leading member. The flag implies the use of violence to achieve its ends, and the borderless territory suggests that is the intended end. Official policy, however, is peacefully to negotiate a two-state solution. Fatah could remove the rifles and grenade from its emblem, but if it did so it would alienate those sections of Palestinian society that believe in the armed struggle, many of whom would abandon Fatah and join more militant groups.

The messages of Hamas, Fatah, the Al-Aqsa and the Qassam factions are localized, as to a lesser extent is that of Hezbollah. When we turn back to IS, however, we see not only a pan-Arab Islamist message, but a pan-Muslim signal to the global community known as the *umma*. It stands for the caliphate made real, nearly 100 years after the Ottoman Empire was dismembered. Its success in recreating the caliphate, albeit temporarily, has made it the go-to jihadi group, attracting fighters from all over the world. It achieved what Al Qaeda only theorized about, but as it goes the way of Al Qaeda and is diminished, it will be replaced by 'Son of IS', in the same way that Al Qaeda gave birth to IS in the first place. The battle for the symbols it uses, and what they mean, will continue.

In 2007 IS ended its announcement about 'its' flag with a prayer: 'We ask God, praised be He, to make this flag the sole flag for all Muslims.' The flag could indeed theoretically be that for all Muslims; thankfully, relatively few rally around it when it is intended to signal support for IS.

CHAPTER 6

EAST OF EDEN

---

*'You shall accomplish a long and
successful journey. A prosperous
wind shall blow in your flag.'*
Henning Haslund, *Men and Gods in Mongolia*

Previous pages: The daily flag ceremony held in Tiananmen Square, Beijing, in May 2008. The Chinese flag was designed for the Communist revolution but its symbolism has deep roots in the country's history; it now represents an increasingly strong and outward-looking post-Communist China.

EAST OF EDEN IS WHERE THE CRESCENT MOON OF Islam begins to fade, the stars of China rise, and we eventually reach the rising, and never setting, sun of Japan.

Most Bible analysts site Eden in the Ur region of Iraq. This is partially based on Genesis, 2:10–14, which refers to Eden and four rivers including the Tigris and Euphrates. Unless you are a literalist, the veracity of this is as important as that of King Angus of Scotland seeing the Cross of St Andrew in the sky in the ninth century. Which is to say, not very. The perception is more than the reality, and on occasion the perception becomes the reality.

Of more relevance is that this is considered to be the area from where the three great Abrahamic monotheistic faiths sprang. God had a quiet word with Abram, who lived in Ur of the Chaldees, and advised him that if he were to do a spot of wandering it would be in his favour. Via a circuitous route Abram ended up in what is now Israel and Palestine, by which time God had changed his name to Abraham and told him he would be the 'Father of many nations'. And lo, it came to pass that one of the nations, which knows him as Ibrahim, founded Islam, which, as we've seen, rapidly spread east and west.

We perceive the vague line of Islam's furthest reach in the west as we start to encounter the crosses in the flags and standards of Europe. Eastward the crescent and other Islamic symbols on state emblems stretch past Azerbaijan, as far as some of the 'Stans' of Central Asia, and on to Malaysia. After this they begin to peter out, although they still appear in outposts such as Brunei and on the regional flags of certain countries. The kaleidoscope of flags we encounter as we head east reflects the sweeping movements of ideas, peoples and religions across this vast continent. In many cases they represent a turning point in a nation's identity – a response to Communism, or imperialism, for example. Within them we also find clues to the rich breadth of culture and history that gives ancient roots to the flags of these modern nation states.

Of the flags of the five Central Asian 'Stans', only two feature the crescent, even though all have majority-Muslim populations, albeit with sizeable non-Muslim Russian minorities. All are ancient cultures but new states, formed out of the collapse of the Soviet Union in 1991. This required some pretty speedy nation-building, having been Soviet republics for so many decades. With the vast Soviet repression over, the elites quickly set about establishing their own regional repressions. As almost everywhere else, the myth that Soviet Man was immortal was wiped from the face of the culture. Local Man simply woke up from a long nightmare and carried on being what he always had been, but with the added complication that the Soviet years had introduced population movements that now can cause regional tensions within the borders of the new states. The most notable example of this is in the Ferghana Valley, where the borders of Tajikistan, Uzbekistan and Kyrgyzstan, drawn arbitrarily by the Soviets, meet in what can be a toxic mix. Here Turkic peoples bump up against Uzbeks, Tajiks and the Kyrgyz, with occasional outbreaks of ethnic fighting over land as well as water disputes.

The flag of Turkmenistan positively brims with symbolism and is almost a work of art. It is an affirmation of independence from Moscow in that it owes nothing to the Soviet era. It has a green background with a white crescent moon, five white stars towards its top left-hand corner and a red-patterned vertical stripe down the left-hand side.

The green and the crescent are obvious references to Islam, the dominant religion since the eighth century, but the white of the crescent and the stars is also supposed to convey serenity. The five stars represent the five main regions of Turkmenistan – Ahal, Balkan, Daşoguz, Lebap and Mary – and legend has it that the points of the stars symbolize the five states of matter: solid, liquid, gaseous, crystalline and plasmatic. As if that isn't cool enough, the red vertical stripe on the left-hand side has another five – this time five *guls*, which are symmetrical medallions used in traditional Turkmenistan carpet-making and which themselves speak to the people's nomadic ancestry. The carpet-weaving continues, but the population is now mostly sedentary, other than the large numbers who move abroad seeking work.

The country has a well-developed gas industry but the pipelines head north, meaning that the government is keen to keep on the right side of Russia. However, at the same time its location and ethnic make-up ensure that it maintains good relations with Iran and Turkey. At the bottom of the red stripe on the flag you see crossed olive branches. This reflects the policy of neutrality announced by the state in 1995 and enshrined in a law that declares: 'The State Flag of Turkmenistan is a symbol of the unity and independence of the nation and of the neutrality of the state.'

The United Nations recognizes this 'permanent neutrality', which is something the population is very proud of, although it's not always easy to ascertain as one of the government's definitions of neutrality seems to be to partially close the country to outsiders while simultaneously monitoring the activities of the people. Naturally, that aspect doesn't feature in the national anthem, but it does make play of its neutrality with the words, 'My land is sacred, my flag flies in the world' and ends with the memorable line, 'Live long and prosper Turkmenistan!', which is probably the only unwitting reference to *Star Trek* in any national anthem ever.

To the north-east, across the border, is landlocked Uzbekistan, whose flag gives Turkmenistan's a run for its money in terms of poetic symbolism. Uzbekistan has the largest population of the Central Asian 'Stans', at 30 million. It was the first of the republics to declare independence after the break-up of the Soviet Union, announcing a new state on 31 August 1991 and adopting a new flag two and a half months later.

At first glance it is a simple tricolour of three horizontal stripes, blue, white and green. In the left-hand corner are a white crescent and twelve white stars. The blue is because the Uzbeks, like their neighbours, are a Turkic people and this is their traditional colour. It was also the colour of the banner of the fourteenth-century Turkic-Mongol warrior Tamerlane, who was born near Samarkand, the country's second city. At the time the region was known as Transoxiana and covered territory which more or less corresponds to modern-day Uzbekistan. His nomadic armies dominated everywhere from India to Russia, ensuring that great riches were sent back to Samarkand, which now hosts Tamerlane's magnificent tomb, one of the gems of Islamic art.

Beneath the blue stripe is the white one, and beneath that the green. The white is for peace, and the green for nature and to acknowledge that the majority of the population are Muslim – predominantly mainstream Sunni practitioners whose faith outlasted the brutal Soviet attempts to destroy it. However, like its neighbours, the country has a simmering problem with Islamist extremists, some of whom have ventured abroad to join the likes of Al Qaeda and IS. The beauty of the flag is brought out by two thin red stripes (fimbriations), one at the top of the white stripe and one at the bottom. The red lines are to 'symbolize the current of the vital energy in any living body' and they connect the blue sky to the green earth through the peaceful white.

According to the Uzbek government, the moon can be seen as a link to Islam, but in this context it is officially a new moon, a 'symbol of the birth of the republic's independence'. Finally, the twelve stars are for the months of the year by the traditional Uzbek solar calendar. The months are named after the twelve constellations, a reference to the idea that the Uzbeks were pioneers in astronomical knowledge, dating back to ancient times, which is a good deal more romantic than the other official explanation – that they are also symbolic of the twelve principles of the foundation of state management.

The flags of the other 'Stans', Kazakh, Tajik and Kyrgyz, all repeat the poetic nature of the first two in various ways. For example, Kazakhstan has a steppe eagle flying underneath the sun, which to Kazakhs depicts freedom, and Kyrgyzstan has what to the uninitiated looks a bit like a tennis ball eclipsing the sun on a red background – the word 'Kyrgyz' means red. Closer inspection, and a call to the Kyrgyzstan information centre, reveals that it is in fact the sun with forty rays, which corresponds to the number of Kyrgyz tribes, and the lines across the sun are in the shape of the framework of a traditional Kyrgyz yurt. In recent years in the West the yurt has been used as a yuppified tent in posh camping grounds, but to the Kyrgyz people it symbolizes home, family, life and the unity of space and time. It also reminds the myriad tribes of their shared nationhood in a diverse neighbourhood.

These sentiments, and the symbols through which they are conveyed, appeal to the deep cultural currents that can unite a country in a time of change – or help politicians to establish power. Less appealing than the symbolism is the political climate across all the republics. There is no tradition of democracy and civil society is weak. Experiments with multi-party elections quickly resulted in the elites consolidating power. Often the former Soviet apparatchiks, who had spent a lifetime pretending to be Communists, simply switched to nationalism. A growing problem is also Islamist extremism, with groups such as IS recruiting in the region. A wake-up call was the bombing of Istanbul Airport in June 2016, where two of the perpetrators were said to be from Uzbekistan and Kyrgyzstan respectively. This was followed on the first day of 2017 with a massacre at an Istanbul nightclub in which at least thirty-nine people were killed. The police said the shooter was from Kyrgyzstan. The Turkish government blamed these incidents and others on part of a campaign by IS against Turkey for its role combating them in Syria. To the north, the Russians are concerned about the increasing influence of radical Islam in the 'Stans', knowing that the training and experience the fighters receive in Afghanistan and beyond may eventually be turned against them. Both countries know that as IS fighters are scattered by its defeats in Iraq and Syria, hundreds of them are seeking a way back to the Central Asian Republics, some with the intention of continuing their 'jihad' in what is becoming fertile territory for insurrection.

Afghanistan, like Iran (chapter 4), is another non-Arabic state whose national symbol resonates with the march of Islam out of Arabia. It is also thought to have made more changes to its national flag in the twentieth century than any other country, and it still hasn't finished. The current version dates from 2002 (although it was amended slightly in 2004), following

the overthrow of the Taliban. It has three vertical stripes –
black, red and green – with the Afghan national emblem in the
middle. The black is said to represent the past, as the colour
of previous versions of their flag; red is for the blood shed to
free the country from occupation; and green stands not only
for Islam but also hope for the future. In the middle sits the
white emblem depicting a mosque, symbolizing the country's
religion. The *shahada* is written above it, and under that are
the words *Allahu Akbar* – God is Great. Inscribed on the
flag is the year 1298, which is the Islamic date corresponding
to 1919, when Afghanistan won independence from Britain.
Underneath the mosque is written the word 'Afghanistan'. The
mosque is surrounded by sheaves of wheat, which represent
one of the main crops of the country. Another staple crop is
the poppy, but that might have sent out the wrong signal. As a
unifying flag it is having limited success. The country remains
fractured, and especially in the south significant proportions
of the population feel little allegiance to the flag, even if they
fear the white flag of the Taliban which flies over numerous
towns and villages.

In 2012 I spent a few weeks with British and Afghan forces
in Sangin in Helmand Province. On one patrol the Afghan
troops insisted on spending several hours getting to and then
pulling down a Taliban flag from a compound, at considerable
risk to themselves. It mattered because they could not coun-
tenance the symbol of another power. I noticed at the time
that many of them were from the north and spoke a different
language to the people in Helmand. It didn't augur well. With
the Brits (and Americans) gone, the Afghan army is struggling
and the locals have little faith in a government based hundreds
of miles away in Kabul. To an extent, the flag of Afghanistan is

the flag of the capital; no wonder, then, that the Taliban flag, and now that of IS, are up and fluttering in a wind which bodes ill. One last point about the Afghanistan flag is worth noting. In its 1974 flag code the government made provision for 'the use of the national flag in any space vehicle Afghanistan may launch'. It is a country that needs an optimistic spirit.

Heading down from Afghanistan, we reach the penultimate example of the crescent as a symbol of Islam in the east – the flag of Pakistan. It has a green background, a large white star and crescent in the centre, and a vertical white band on the hoist side. In its original 1906 form it was the flag of the All-India Muslim League, which even then was advocating a separate state for India's Muslims. It did not have the white band, which was added when Pakistan became independent in 1947 and represents the country's non-Muslim minorities. It sends the right message to the 5 per cent or so of people who are Sikh, Hindu or Christian, but at street level all the minorities, including the Shia Muslims, have been having a difficult time this century amid growing fundamentalism. The green with the star and crescent has the usual associations with Islam, but officially the crescent depicts progress, and the star light and knowledge; both get a mention in the third verse of the national anthem – 'This Flag of the Crescent and Star/Leads the way to progress and perfection'.

The Pakistani government provides a handy guide for would-be well-wishers (or terrorists) by listing the dignitaries who must fly the national flag at their official residences when they are at home. There's another list for those entitled to fly the flag from their car, but only if they are seated. This list appears to consist of most of the population of the country in the aftermath of a cricketing victory over India, when the cities are jammed bumper to bumper with horn-tooting, flag-bedecked cars.

Past the Indus Valley is another country with green in its flag: India, and therein lies a tale or ten.

The Indian flag is known as the 'Tiranga', which means tricolour. It has three horizontal bands: saffron at the top, white in the middle and green at the bottom. In the middle is a blue wheel with twenty-four spokes called a chakra. It is the same design as the wheel found on the abacus of the Sarnath Lion Capital of the third-century BCE Emperor Ashoka, which went on to become the national emblem of India.

The flag was adopted on 22 July 1947, shortly before independence, but not before Mahatma Gandhi had reminded the subcontinent just how important it was to get the symbolism right. He said:

> A flag is a necessity for all nations. Millions have died for it. It is no doubt a kind of idolatry which it would be a sin to destroy. For a flag represents an Ideal. The unfurling of the Union Jack evokes in the English breast sentiments whose strength it is difficult to measure. The Stars and Stripes mean a world to the Americans. The Star and the Crescent will call forth the best bravery in Islam. It will be necessary for us Indians, Muslims, Christians, Jews, Parsis and all others to whom India is their home to recognize a common flag to live and to die for.

Gandhi had come up with the prototype of the flag in 1921, by which time there had already been decades of debate about what a flag of India should look like. At a session of the All India

Congress Committee a young man showed Gandhi a flag he had designed of just two stripes – red and green – to represent the main communities, Hindus and Muslims.

Gandhi liked what he saw, but suggested including a white stripe for the myriad other Indian communities. He also added to the white strip a spinning wheel, a symbol the entire subcontinent would instantly recognize and one he felt would help Indians become self-reliant. In 1927 he argued that 'The spinning wheel is the thing which all must turn in the Indian clime for the transition stage at any rate and the vast majority must for all time.' This was linked to the belief that use of the spinning wheel would help create Indian goods, thereby improving her economy and ensuring that the practice of using cloth manufactured in Britain (often from Indian cotton) would cease, thus easing the way to independence. By 1931 the red at the top was changed to saffron, and now people were told that the colours had no sectarian associations but stood for courage and sacrifice, peace and truth, and faith and chivalry. Gandhi's spinning wheel remained.

However, when the time came for the flag of the new nation, although the colours remained the same, the spinning wheel had gone, replaced by the wheel of the dharma chakra. This circle represents the eternal cosmic law that upholds the order of the universe of cyclic reincarnation. Hinduism, Buddhism, Jainism and Sikhism all recognize the concept of dharma, and as such it speaks to huge numbers of the population even if not all are aware of the meaning of each spoke. For example, not everyone knows that, according to Buddhist interpretation, one spoke stands for *sparśa*, or contact – lovers consorting, kissing, or entwined – and another for *bhava*, a couple engaged in intercourse.

More prosaically, the wheel is also supposed to represent, for everyone, the idea of forward motion and progress. Gandhi is reported to have been not best pleased at losing his spinning wheel but, having meditated for a while, he accepted it. Besides, it was a safer bet than some of the symbols suggested during previous decades. These had included the Hindu god Ganesh which, given that he has an elephant's head, might have been seen as an unusual choice.

Officially the modern colours are no longer connected to religion, but everyone knows that green is for Islam and that saffron is significant to Hindus, Buddhist and Jains. It is supposed to convey detachment and a renunciation of the material world, and hence is the colour of choice for many a Buddhist monk, aspiring guru, and men and women dancing up and down city centres shaking tambourines and chanting 'Hare Krishna'. Unofficially, the white strip in the middle of the flag joins the saffron and the green in peace.

By law the flag can only be made from a type of hand-spun Indian cloth called *khadi*, which Gandhi had popularized, and destroying or desecrating it can be punishable by up to three years in prison. The Indian state learnt its bureaucratic lesson from the British Civil Service and rarely uses one regulation when three will do. From 1947 until 2002, among dozens of laws concerning the flag was one which stated that it could only be flown from official buildings and vehicles. The Indian civil service appears to have been inspired by Tennyson: 'Theirs not to reason why / Theirs but to write regulations in triplicate.'

One day in 2001 an industrialist called Naveen Jindal, who had been exposed to the pesky ideas of freedom prevalent in the United States, where he had studied, decided to fly the flag from his office building. The police arrived, took down the flag, confiscated it and threatened him with prosecution. Mr Jindal pre-empted them by filing a public interest case at the High Court in Delhi. He argued that it was against the rights of a private citizen to be restricted from expressing love of his country by flying the flag. The case went all the way to the Supreme Court, which ruled in his favour and asked the government to consider changing the law. In 2002 the flag laws were amended to allow private citizens to fly the flag on any day of the year they liked without fear of prosecution.

And they do like to fly it. The circle in the centre does appear to unite most Indians who inhabit 'this subcontinent of nationalities', as Mohammed Ali Jinnah, the founder of Pakistan, called the region. India does have problems, such as separatism, but this is both an ancient and modern country whose best years may still lie ahead of it. Born of one of the most powerful anti-colonial independence movements of the twentieth century, the story of India's flag reflects the religious, ethnic and political complexity that constitutes this powerful nation. India does not define itself in opposition to other countries, but as an increasingly important player on the global stage; its relationship and competition with China in both the economic and military spheres will be one of the defining geopolitical stories of this century.

We are about to cross the Himalayas into China, but it's worth pausing along the way to look at the world's only national flag which is not rectangular or square.

Nepal stands out for having a flag of two crimson triangles, one on top of the other, each with a deep-blue border. These represent the Himalaya Mountains and the country's two main religions, Hinduism and Buddhism. In the top triangle is a white crescent moon with half a sun appearing above it, in the bottom one a white twelve-rayed sun. These used to represent the royal family and the family of the prime minister, but now that Nepal is a secular republic they are supposed to symbolize the hope that the country will live as long as the celestial bodies.

It will probably survive longer than the last king and queen who, in 2001, along with eight other people, were shot dead by the crown prince; he then allegedly killed himself. After a remarkably short investigation, the king's brother, who had missed the massacre, took the crown. He was so unpopular that he helped fuel the Maoist insurgency which in turn persuaded him to end the monarchy altogether. So, new system, but same flag. Because of its unusual shape, the flag also has perhaps the most detailed manufacturing instructions. For example, to create the sun in the bottom triangle you must 'Bisect line AF at U and draw a line UV parallel to line AB touching line BE at V. With centre W, the point where HI and UV cut one another and radius MN draw a circle.' And it only took God a day.

Here we leave the divine behind and enter the world of the godless Communists of China. There are hundreds of millions of believers inside its now extended borders, but the current rulers of China prefer not to recognize this. However, the flag of the People's Republic of China contains symbolism going back thousands of years before the advent of Communism.

Many vexillologists believe that the Chinese were among the first people to use cloth flags as signals of identification and direction. Writing in *The Art of War* 2,600 years ago, Sun Tzu said: 'In battle all appears to be turmoil and confusion, but the flags and banners have prescribed arrangements; the sounds of the cymbals, fixed rules.' At least 2,000 years before this the Egyptians and the people in what is now Iran were carrying staffs with symbols attached to them, but as Dr Whitney

Smith puts it in his seminal 1975 book *Flags Through the Ages and Across the World*, 'The Chinese were probably the first to use silk flags. They have been used both at sea and on land for thousands of years, much longer than in the West.' Smith argues that we owe to the Chinese the focus on attaching cloth to a staff laterally, rather than fixing an object such as an animal carving to its top.

What is unclear is whether silk flags then spread to the Near East, or if it was just that the silk arrived through the trade routes and was fashioned into flags by people who were already using versions of them. What is more certain is that the Western world began copying the flags of the Arabs during the Crusades.

Several hundred years later, things came full-circle. The Chinese used a huge variety of flags for shipping and military purposes, but never bothered to come up with one to symbol-ize China and the Chinese. They had long had the sense of themselves as a nation – indeed a civilization – but it was obvi-ous to the inhabitants of the Middle Kingdom that they were what they were: a flag was not necessary. That changed when the Europeans and their nation-state flags showed up in force in the mid nineteenth century.

By 1863 the Europeans had 'persuaded' Emperor Tongzhi that he not only needed a navy (under European control, of course), but that it should have a flag. It helped that Tongzhi was only seven years old at the time. A yellow flag with a blue dragon was duly run up. Originally it was triangular, but the European bureaucrats felt that this would never do, and so had it changed to a rectangle.

As the push for independence grew in the early twentieth century, various cloth emblems of different iterations of a China controlled mostly by outsiders appeared, among them, in 1932, the Communist war flag of the 'Chinese Soviet Republic'. This 'Republic' was simply part of a province called Jiangxi and only lasted for two and a half years; nevertheless during that time a red flag with a yellow hammer and sickle in the centre and yellow five-pointed star in the top left-hand corner did fly over part of China. This was the prototype of the flag that would eventually represent the entire mainland.

The People's Republic of China was proclaimed on 1 October 1949 and, as so often happens, the new state, or indeed system, needed a new flag. It was designed by Zeng Liansong, a young member of the Communist Party who had won a competition that had received several thousand entries. The Party's requirements were that it must reflect Chinese geography, nationality, history and culture. It should also indicate government by a worker-peasant alliance.

Liansong, then working in Shanghai, sat in an attic during the night working on designs, influenced, it is thought, by the earlier Jiangxi version. It is said (and why spoil a good story) that he gazed at the heavens and thought of the ancient Chinese proverb, 'Longing for the moon and longing for the stars shows yearning'. Having sorted out the history bit, he hit on the idea that the Communist Party was the saviour of the nation and that a big star should represent it, with four smaller stars symbolizing Mao Zedong's idea of the four classes of Chinese people, set out in his essay 'On the People's Democratic Dictatorship'.

No surprise, then, that Mr Mao quite liked Zeng's ideas, although the final product did go through several versions, including one which removed the hammer and sickle from the design because it was too redolent of the Russian-dominated Soviet Union – at the time the concept of the international brotherhood of Communists was under a bit of strain in the

Sino-Russian relationship. It was then approved by the Party, which, as we also saw when the authorities considered the flag of the Islamic revolution in Iran, knew it had to blend collective memory with modern messaging.

So the Red Flag is for Communism, and the large, five-pointed yellow star in the top left-hand corner represents the Communist Party's leadership. However, there's a lot more going on as well. The four smaller five-pointed stars are Mao's 'united front' of the aforementioned different pre-Communist classes. They are the workers, the peasants, the petty bourgeoisie and the 'patriotic capitalists'. These classes were, of course, told that they were now united in building Communism. This last star was quite fortuitous, or even far-sighted, given that forty years later the Party realized it needed to move to 'capitalism with Chinese characteristics' and the majority of the 1.2 billion Chinese appeared to embrace what they had always been – which is to say, not Communist.

That the stars have five points is deliberate and speaks to the belief in the ancient meaning of the number. Pre-Communist Chinese philosophy spoke of Five Elements, an all-encompassing system that includes five virtues, five rulers, five phases and so on, and which signifies balance, strength and completeness. A more modern unofficial populist value is now also given to the five points: that they represent the majority Han Chinese and the other four traditional 'Chinese' peoples – the Mongols, the Manchus, the Tibetans and the Hui. Given the Hans' long history of colonizing their neighbours, the neighbours may not buy this idea. Officially this is not the meaning of the design, nevertheless there is in it an echo of a flag which flew from 1912 to 1928 called the 'Flag of the Five Nations', which had five colours representing the different Chinese peoples.

These days it symbolizes all the above. Zeng's adopted, and adapted, flag flew for the first time on a flagpole at Tiananmen Square in Beijing to officially announce the founding of the People's Republic of China.

Nowadays Chinese law stipulates that the provinces of the country are not supposed to have their own flags. This is partially because the Party knows it is one of the centrifugal forces holding what is a disparate country together. For example, there is such a thing as the East Turkestan Movement in the Muslim-majority Uighur region. The movement has a flag, light blue with a crescent and star, but allowing it to be flown would strengthen regional identity and thus the independence movement. The same is true in Tibet, where possession of the Tibetan flag is a serious criminal offence. This does not always dissuade some of those still agitating for greater autonomy; they run the risk in the desire to hold onto their culture, which reflects the depth of Tibetan identity. However, the Chinese grip appears to be tightening. Beijing hopes that through suppression of such symbols Tibetan culture and identity will gradually fade as the decades pass. In less volatile regions the law is not always observed, reflecting the balancing act the Party must perform in insisting on being the only power in the land while recognizing regional differences.

Zeng died in Shanghai in 1999 aged eighty-two. He was thus spared the indignity that upset the Party in 2011 when the Vietnamese government managed to produce thousands of Chinese flags with six stars instead of five. And, worse, they were waved during the visit to Hanoi of the then Chinese Vice-President, Xi Jinping. A similar thing happened when Chinese signatories visited Delhi in 2006. As anyone who knows anything about protocol knows, these things matter.

The 'Law of the People's Republic of China on the National Flag' (1990) makes for fascinating reading, if you are of a certain bent of mind. Even before we reach the bit which states that 'The four small five-pointed stars shall respectively have an angle pointing right at the centre of the big five-pointed star', we learn that as well as all the usual stuff about raising, lowering, raising, then lowering to half-mast, then raising to full-mast, before being lowered that most countries have, the flag can be lowered to half-mast not only on the death of the president and several lower ranks, but also 'persons who have made outstanding contributions to world peace or the cause of human progress'.

We also learn that, under Article 19, if you should foolishly burn the Chinese flag, perhaps while on a stag weekend in Beijing, you could face up to three years in prison. However, the good news is that if the offence is deemed relatively minor (meaning you have a good lawyer or some powerful relatives) you 'shall be detained for not more than fifteen days by the public security organ in reference to the provisions of the Regulations on Administrative Penalties for Public Security'. You have been warned.

This, then, is one of the world's best-known flags, having even been displayed on the moon by a Chinese space mission in December 2013. Placing the flag on the Jade Rabbit Moon Rover was a deeply symbolic and significant event. China became only the third country, after the USA and USSR, to display its national colours on the moon and signalled its intention to become a leader in space travel and technology. It was the first time a vehicle had made a soft landing on the moon since 1976, a source of enormous national pride, and proof of China's advances this century.

Their flag is increasingly seen on the oceans as China builds a blue-water navy with the intention of becoming a global sea power. It is visible around the world in far-flung places such as the Democratic Republic of Congo, from which China (and others) extracts precious metals, in Angola, where it built a highway to get the metals to port, and in Gwadar, Pakistan, where a port and highway are being built to ship goods up into China, thus avoiding the narrow and de facto American-controlled Malacca Straits between Malaysia and Indonesia. The symbol of the Middle Kingdom has now been seen in nearly every kingdom, republic and territory in the world, reinforcing its rapid expansion and growing influence over the past half-century.

It also flies above the artificial islands China has built in the South China Sea, which Beijing says now constitute sovereign Chinese territory. The neighbours – including Vietnam, Taiwan and the Philippines – are not convinced. Neither is the US navy, which ensures that the Stars and Stripes is seen fluttering above its warships, which pass close enough to the islands to make the point.

Somewhat harder to spot around the world than the Red Flag is the flag of Taiwan, or the Republic of China (ROC), as it also known. Having lost the civil war in the 1940s, the anti-Communist forces withdrew to the island off the mainland, which now has its own flag but wonders about its identity. The flag is known as the 'Blue Sky, White Sun and a Wholly Red Earth' and harks back to the flag of the defeated Kuomintang (Chinese Nationalist Party), which under Chiang Kai-shek retreated to Taiwan in 1949. The ROC says it is the rightful government of the whole of China, but across the water the People's Republic sees it differently. Beijing calls Taiwan a province which pretends to be independent.

Because the People's Republic is so powerful, and therefore so few countries recognize the ROC, Taiwan is not permitted to fly its flag when it participates in international meetings or at sporting events such as the Olympics. Instead the flag is replaced by that of 'Chinese Taipei', an acceptable compromise for both parties, albeit one they would both like to change if either could get their own way. From the Taiwanese point of view, as it has never declared independence from China, it is willing to accept this particular sacrifice of its national symbol in order not to provoke its much bigger brother.

In some ways the two national flags are symbolic of the disunity of the Chinese people. As such they mirror two flags that fly nearby.

One Korean peninsula, divided by two Koreas, equals two flags. It might have been different, and each could have used the pre-Second World War flag, which would have reflected that they are one people, but only South Korea, also known as the Republic of Korea (ROK), chose to keep it. The 'Flag of Great Extremes' or Taegukgi, as it's known in Korean, is not just a work of art; it is a deeply spiritual symbol. Therefore the godless Communists in the North were not going to have anything to do with what they considered religious mumbo jumbo – no, they would have their own political mumbo jumbo.

The Taegukgi takes its name from the red and blue yin-yang symbol in the middle of the flag, which is known as a *taeguk* circle. It is divided equally, with the red section for the positive force of yang and the blue for the negative force of yin. The traditional philosophy of the region says these two represent great cosmic forces which oppose each other, but which together achieve perfect harmony and balance.

In each corner of the flag is a trigram. These derive from

the ancient Chinese book the *I Ching*, known in English as the 'Book of Changes', which, according to legend, dates back well over 2,000 years. The trigrams surrounding the *taeguk* represent yin and yang going through a spiral of growth and change. The top-left symbolizes heaven and the bottom-right earth; the upper-right is for water and the lower-left fire. All four have other simultaneous meanings; for example the top-right one also represents water, the moon, intelligence and wisdom. All this is against a white background, which stands for purity and cleanliness. On special occasions Koreans often wear white, which has earned them the nickname 'the people in white'.

Taken as a whole, the flag symbolizes the ideal that the Korean people together will always develop in harmony with the universe. The complete opposite of this is division, but that was the political reality in 1947 and the leaders in the North wanted to underline it. The end of the Second World War saw the Japanese colonizers leave and the country split at the 38th parallel, with the Russians overseeing the North and the USA the South. The Russians subsequently left and China became the protector of the North.

North Korea's official title is the Democratic People's Republic of Korea or DPRK. As with most countries which include the words 'democratic' and 'republic' in their names, it is neither. It is arguably the most vicious, paranoid, murderous dictatorship left standing or, in the DPRK's case, staggering. In effect a royal family, members of the Kim dynasty have ruled it since day one and have provided political comedy for the world, but almost nothing for their subjects.

There's little concrete information about the story of the North Korean flag, but an essay by Fyodor Tertitskiy on DailyNK.com suggests that in 1947 the then de facto rulers of the North, the Soviet Union, dictated that as they were setting up a new state, a new flag was required. A fifty-six-year-old senior Party leader, Kim Tu-Bong, was summoned to the office of a Major-General Lebedev and made the case for the existing one: 'Kim started to explain, in detail, the meaning of the flag. However, from a Soviet military man's point of view, the Chinese philosophy upon which the design was based was little more than medieval superstition. After listening for some time to yins, yangs, trigrams of the Book of Changes and other oriental stuff, Lebedev interrupted Kim with a simple "Enough". A Soviet colonel present at the discussion grinned: "It sounds like a legend to me."'

A few months later instructions were issued and the flag of the DPRK came into being. It is a version of the standard Soviet-era flag, which, like standard Soviet architecture, has a directness to it. According to the government's website, the flag's predominant red represents revolutionary tradition. At the top and bottom are blue stripes for 'the desire to fight for the victory of the ideals of independence, peace and friendship in unity with the progressive peoples of the world'. The thinner white bands next to the blue 'represent the homogeneous Korean nation with a long and resplendent culture', while the large red star 'symbolizes forerunners and the fighting spirit of the Korean people'.

The following year Kim Tu-Bong published a book entitled *On the Establishing of the New National Flag and the Abolition of the Flag of the Great Extremes*. In it he explained that the New Flag was the symbol of a 'happy country developing in brilliance', whereas the Flag of Great Extremes was unscientific and superstitious. Its needless unintelligibility and multifariousness could cause disunity, and that would never do.

As the 1950s began, in classic dictatorial Communist fashion, the increasingly nationalistic North Korea airbrushed the Soviet influence out of the flag and Kim Tu-Bong out of any position of power. Now not only had the Great Leader Kim Il-sung smashed the Imperial Army of Japan (with a little help from Moscow), why, he had even designed the glorious flag of the People's Republic. As we now know there is no end to the brilliance of the Kim dynasty. Kim Il-sung's son, Kim Jong-il, was not only 'Guiding Star of the Twenty-First Century' and 'Eternal Bosom of Hot Love', he was also 'Bright Sun of Juche'. This last title was to underline the fact that the DPRK had developed its own political system, known as 'Juche' – a sort of hybrid Communist nationalist philosophy of self-reliance. After all, if you are self-reliant you don't need to let anyone into your country, and if it is such an amazing place why would anyone want to leave? As the national anthem declares, 'Breasting the raging waves with soaring strength, Let us glorify forever this Korea, limitlessly rich and strong'. The current leader, Kim Jong-un, also has to go through life burdened by hundreds more titles extolling his virtues.

One peninsula, one people, two very different flags – you'd think it would be hard to mix them up, but the organizers of the London 2012 Olympics managed it. The DPRK's women footballers were being introduced on a giant screen ahead of their game against Colombia, and each player's name and picture were flashed alongside a picture of . . . the flag of South Korea. This went on and on, passing from the defenders though midfield to the strikers, and on even to the substitutes. As each picture came up the North Koreans grew more and more angry and eventually walked off the pitch. They had a point: after all, technically North Korea is still in a state of war with the South – the 1953 Korean War ended in a truce, not a treaty.

The players insisted they would only return if the mistake was rectified. It took some frantic video-editing and profuse apologizing, but an hour later the team came back on, checked the screen, and went on to defeat Colombia 2–0.

Both Koreas are guilty of past transgression in the flag war. Ever since the North's flag first flew, the South has banned it from being displayed in their territory. It was therefore no surprise when, in 2008, a World Cup qualifying football game due to be played in the North's capital, Pyongyang, had to be moved to China when the DPRK refused to play the South Korean anthem or raise its flag.

Move on to the 2014 Asian Games in Incheon and the South insisted on upholding its law which bans the North's flag from being displayed in the street. It flew in the athletes' village, but nowhere else, despite Article 58 of the Olympic Council of Asia's rule book stating that 'In all the stadiums and in their neighbourhood the OCA Flag must be freely flown with the flags of the competing NOCs [countries attending].' If people were going to be prevented from seeing their flag, the North therefore decided that no one was going to see their 350 cheer-leaders, known as the 'Squad of Beauties'. The young women chosen to cheer on their athletes share two attributes: not only are they all drop-dead gorgeous but, we are told, they are all fanatically devoted to the regime of Kim Jong-un. When the South complained about the size of the flags the cheerleaders were going to bring, diplomats from the North stormed out of a meeting and cancelled the Beauties.

The two Koreas remain as far apart and as close together as they always have been. War is a constant potential threat;

everyone in the South's megacity of Seoul knows they are within range of the North's artillery, dug in along the 38th parallel, and the North's nuclear programme frightens the entire region.

Family quarrels can often be the most bitter, although in the case of both Koreas' relationship with Japan and its flag, it's sometimes hard to tell which goes deeper.

Japan raised its Imperial flag over Korea for thirty-five years in the twentieth century. That the flag now represents a stable, peaceful democracy and yet is similar to the standard of those barbaric years is . . . problematic. The years of misrule in Korea were brutal. This was partly symbolized by the imposition of the Japanese flag on a country then considered part of the Japanese Empire. It flew on official buildings, and schoolchildren sang the Japanese anthem as it was raised each morning.

The Pacific island nation is known as 'The Land of the Rising Sun', its name means 'sun origin' and the flag is officially called Nisshoki, or 'sun mark flag'. However, it is popularly known as Hinomaru, meaning sun disc. We all know it the moment we see it in its striking simplicity – a white background with a red circle. The other flag seared into our consciousness is the Japanese war flag, which portrays the sun on a white background but with sixteen rays radiating from it.

Versions of the Hinomaru had been used on the Japanese islands for centuries before it came to symbolize a nation state. The hundreds of Japanese islands are located at the eastern edge of the Eurasian land mass, and looking east from the islands there was nothing but water, above which each day the sun rose. The earliest reference to the sun as a symbol of Japan comes in 607 CE when a somewhat impertinent Japanese emperor sent a letter to his Chinese counterpart beginning with the words, 'From the Son of Heaven in the land of where the sun rises, to the Son of Heaven on the land where the sun sets'. The second Son of Heaven, where the sun sets, was not impressed.

Japanese tradition says that the sun goddess Amaterasu founded Japan 2,700 years ago. She is the chief deity of the Shinto religion, and the ancestor of one of the first emperors. The current Emperor is known as 'Son of the Sun' and is considered by believers to be a divinely appointed direct descendant of Amaterasu. However, like the Chinese, the Japanese felt they had no need to identify themselves and until recently there was no symbol representing the nation.

When Europeans began arriving in force in the mid nineteenth century, the early Meiji government realized it needed to engender a spirit of unity among the people. It decreed that the rising sun flag should be used as the flag of the navy, a force as important to the Japanese island race as that of the British, and from this grew the idea that it represented the country. The national anthem, the Kimigayo, followed.

After that, though, came a spirit of militarism, triggered in part by the fact that Japan became an industrial power but did not have any natural resources with which to fuel that process. Their neighbours to the west did have the materials, however, and Japan had the military might to steal them. Imperial Japan fought a number of wars, which culminated in the nation's most catastrophic experience in its long history.

First came the Sino-Japanese War (1894–5), then the Russo-Japanese War (1904–5), limited involvement in the First World War (1914–8), the Second Sino-Japanese War (1937–45) and then the Second World War, ending in total surrender following the nuclear bombing of the cities of Hiroshima and Nagasaki. During these years Japan occupied and brutalized several countries.

The flag the Japanese once thought 'would light the darkness of the world' had itself become a symbol of darkness. The Hinomaru was hauled down in Japan, Korea, China, Singapore, the Philippines and elsewhere, and as the scale of the Japanese atrocities became known in Japan itself the domestic media tried to help the nation come to terms with what had happened by examining the war record. That process continues today, as does the limited spirit of reconciliation we see in Japan's neighbours, notably the Koreas, but also China – so limited that there remains a generation who still can't bear to see this symbol of the war years that had such an impact on their lives.

The American administrators of Japan at first severely restricted both the national and war flags. However, in 1947 General Douglas MacArthur allowed the Hinomaru to be flown from several government buildings. The following year ordinary people were allowed to fly it on national holidays, and in 1949 all restrictions were lifted. The long process of reclaiming the national symbol was under way.

Nevertheless, it was difficult.

The thing about the modern Japanese flag is that it is the same as the old Japanese flag, the one flown during the Second World War. To some observers this is akin to the modern German flag being the swastika. This is not entirely fair given that the Nazi symbol is the epitome of evil, and that for all its disgraceful behaviour in the war the Japanese war machine did not, unlike the Nazis, set out to systematically destroy entire peoples using industrial methods for ideological reasons.

There is another difference. The Japanese flag predated the period in which the militarized nation rampaged its way across South-East Asia, whereas the Nazi flag was inaugurated by a party that took over the nation state and lasted just twelve years. The flag of war-era Germany refers to a party, an ideology and a specific period of time, whereas that of war-era Japan refers to the country. If you follow the argument that Japan should change its flag because of a certain period in its history, you could make the same claim about many states – colonial slave-trading Britain, perhaps. Conversely the theoretical argument can be made that if the flag had changed, it might have helped the post-war reconciliation as a recognition of the anger that this symbol could invoke.

When we come to the Japanese military flag, though, things become more complicated. This could have been altered more easily, but when, in 1954, the Japanese Self-Defence Forces were established, they all readopted the war flag of the rising sun with sixteen beams of light. It was an odd choice, and one which can still look strange to anyone with any knowledge or personal experience of the war years. Changing the military flag would have been part of an acceptance of what the Japanese military machine did in the 1930s and 1940s, whereas changing the national flag would have been more traumatic for the Japanese people, a loss of part of their national identity.

By the 1950s Japan was a democratic, peaceful nation. Some sections of the population remained traumatized by the behaviour of its armed forces in the 1930s and 1940s, which makes the decision about the forces flag even more puzzling, though it is worth bearing in mind that the 'intellectual demilitarization' of Japan was not as deep-rooted as that of Germany.

However, it did have lasting effects. For example, if we fast-forward to the 1970s, the left-leaning Japan Teachers' Union instructed its members not to bow to the national flag, nor to sing the national anthem. The flag had been flown since 1947, but it was never taken up with enthusiasm and was not on the statute books as the symbol of the country. The death in 1989 of Emperor Hirohito, who had reigned during the Second World War, allowed the space to debate the merits of flying the flag, and in 1999 parliament took the opportunity, when amending the flag's proportions, to officially recognize it as representing the nation state, although there was an emotional and bitter debate before the measure was passed.

From this, consequences would flow. In 1999 the Ministry of Education issued guidelines stating that at graduation ceremonies the flag was to be flown and the national anthem sung. This was partly justified by the statement that if Japanese students cannot respect their own symbols, then they will not be able to respect the symbols of other nations.

Not everyone agreed, among them a Hiroshima secondary school head teacher named Ishikawa. He was so conflicted about having to relay such instructions that he committed suicide. The story became a national cause célèbre and the debate was still so strong that even during the football 2002 World Cup finals in Japan there were still few flags flown in support of the home team.

With the passage of time, as the twentieth century's most cataclysmic moments fade into history, the Japanese flag is emerging from its wartime shadow. Nevertheless, even as late as 2016 the Japanese Prime Minister, Shinzo Abe, felt it necessary to issue advice 'strongly recommending' that the country's universities fly the flag on campus.

After all, the sun never sets in the east, and likewise its representation on a piece of cloth to symbolize the Land of the Rising Sun is not about to be lowered into history.

If we now head further east, we end up where we started, with the Stars and Stripes. So the time has come to look south – to the red, gold, black and green of Africa and the yellow, red and blue of Latin America.

CHAPTER 7

FLAGS OF FREEDOM

'The best way of learning to be an
independent sovereign state is to be
an independent sovereign state.'

Kwame Nkrumah, first Prime Minister of Ghana

Previous pages: Ghanaian football fans gather in Yeoville, Johannesburg, South Africa, to watch their team in an Africa Cup of Nations match, January 2012. The Ghanaian football team is often known as the 'Black Stars'; the black star in the centre of Ghana's flag and the red, gold and green colour scheme were inspired by the pan-African ideals of those who fought colonialism and looked forward to a more confident, modern Africa.

AFRICA HAS EXPORTED MANY THINGS OVER THE CENturies, not always by choice. Among those that have travelled with the continent's blessing is an idea based on symbolic colours – red, gold, green and black – and that idea is of African independence or, put another way, freedom.

The roots of these colours go back at least to the nineteenth century, probably much further, and are taken from the flag of Ethiopia, the only country on the continent not to have been colonized, despite the best efforts of Italy. Ethiopia's current flag proudly flies the red, gold and green of long tradition, but since 1996 has also featured a blue circle in the centre with a yellow star and five rays. The rays stand for the various peoples of the country, the star representing their equality and unity. It is also variously considered to be the Star of King Solomon and the Star of David, as the first Emperor Menelik was claimed to be the son of Solomon and the Queen of Sheba.

Italy was late to the 'Scramble for Africa'. By the early 1890s the British, French, Germans and Belgians had seized the majority of what was considered the most valuable territory and Italy was left with what is now Eritrea; it used its colony there as a launch pad to invade what was then Abyssinia – now Ethiopia. In 1895 heavy fighting broke out, and, to their surprise, the following year the Italians were driven back to Eritrea, having suffered the loss of at least 7,000 men. Africa now had a champion, and an inspirational example of what could be achieved.

Pennants using the single colours of red, gold or green had been flown in Ethiopia for decades before the military victory, often together; in what was a majority Christian country, tradition identified these colours with the rainbow that God showed to the world following the Flood, as told in the Book of Genesis. So, they were a natural choice when, in the wake of the defeat of the Italians, Emperor Menelik II commissioned the first official flag in 1897. This was to become the first African nation state flag. The imperial coat of arms showing the 'Conquering Lion of Judah' holding a staff flying the national colours was added, indicating the royal ancestry of the first Emperor Menelik. A symbol long associated with royalty, it remained on the flag until the Marxist revolution of 1974, after which it was removed, but lives on via the flag of the Rastafarian movement (more of which later).

The Italians came back for a second go in the 1930s during the fascist era of Mussolini. This time the machinery of modern warfare included mustard gas; the invasion succeeded and the country was occupied. However, Abyssinia/Ethiopia, a hitherto sovereign state, was also a member of the League of Nations, the forerunner of today's United Nations. As many (but not all) member states, as well as the USA, refused to recognize the annexation of the country, its five-year occupation by foreign forces is seen as an aberration and not a period of colonization as happened elsewhere.

The British and French, both League of Nations members, secretly agreed with the Italians that its act of aggression would stand, and the failure of the League to take action is seen as one of the major reasons why it failed as a peacekeeping body in the run-up to the Second World War. There's a famously sarcastic cartoon in *Punch* magazine from 1935 that draws on a popular nineteenth-century music hall song. In the original the lyrics are:

We don't want to fight, but by Jingo! if we do,
We've got the ships, we've got the men, we've got the money too.

Punch depicted the League as a music hall farce and rewrote the lyrics so that Britain and France sang to Mussolini:

We don't want you to fight, but by Jingo if you do,
We will probably issue a joint memorandum, suggesting a
mild disapproval of you.

By 1941 the Italians had been driven out again and Ethiopia resumed its status as a sovereign state. It was positioned to set an example to a continent in which, at the war's end, the winds of change began to blow.

During the tumultuous decades described above, something related and far-reaching was developing thousands of miles to the west of Ethiopia, in the USA.

The idea of black political consciousness has many parents in both America and Africa, among them the Jamaican-born Marcus Mosiah Garvey, an extraordinary man, who promoted racial separateness and was one of the founders of the concept of 'Back to Africa'. In 1916, having set up the Universal Negro Improvement Association (UNIA) in Jamaica, he took the movement to New York, where it flourished and quickly spread nationwide. While building a business empire, he was also advocating that African-Americans should not only be proud of their heritage, but that they should return to their ancestral homelands. To further this aim he set up a shipping company named the Black Star Line to provide transportation. The company failed, Garvey was arrested on charges of financial irregularity, sent to prison and then deported to Jamaica in 1927. However, before this he and the UNIA came up with what would be known around the world as the pan-African flag.

He and many others in America had been stung by a racist song from 1900, which was still being performed in 1920 when Garvey's flag was created. It was called 'Every Race Has a Flag but the Coon' and is one of three songs that the twentieth-century American writer and satirist H. L. Mencken attributes as being responsible for popularizing the offensive term. In response, Garvey commissioned the red, black and green flag of pan-Africanism, a movement to unite all people of African descent, strive to end colonialism and build economic opportunities in Africa and the African diaspora. The flag was unveiled at an international conference in New York in 1920, which was attended by representatives from twenty-five African countries, who knew that they needed a shared symbol to support their efforts. Several years later an edition of the *African Times and Orient Review*, where Garvey had once worked, quoted him as saying: 'Show me the race or the nation without a flag, and I will show you a race of people without any pride. Aye! In song and mimicry they have said, "Every race has a flag but the coon". How true! Aye! But that was said of us four years ago. They can't say it now . . .'

Article 39 of the 1920 UNIA 'Declaration of the Rights of the Negro Peoples of the World' states 'That the colors, Red, Black and Green, be the colors of the African race'. But why those colours? The following year the UNIA published the *Universal Negro Catechism*, which explained that 'Red is the color of the blood which men must shed for their redemption and liberty; black is the color of the noble and distinguished race to which we belong; green is the luxuriant vegetation of our Motherland'.

It has been widely speculated that Garvey, inspired by Ethiopian independence, mistakenly thought the Ethiopian tricolour was red, black and green, not red, yellow and green, as it is. There is a reference to this by the American journalist Charles Mowbray White, who interviewed Garvey. In the Marcus Garvey Papers he is quoted as saying: 'Garvey once described the meaning of the Ethiopian tricolour as follows: "The Red showed their sympathy with the Reds of the world, and the Green their sympathy for the Irish in their fight for freedom, and the Black – The Negro" . . . At another time, Garvey remarked that the Ethiopian flag of red, black and green showed "the Black race between blood and nature to win its rights".'

Whatever the truth, the influence of Ethiopia on Garvey is clear. The catechism for Garveyism states that what it calls the national anthem 'for our race' begins with the words 'Ethiopia, thou land of our father'. Earlier it quotes the 68th Psalm, the 39th verse of which is being fulfilled: 'Princes shall come out of Egypt. Ethiopia shall soon stretch out her hands unto God.' It goes on to say that this proves 'That Negroes will set up their own government in Africa with rulers of their own race'.

Mistake or not, the flag caught on, and it was too late to change it: the colours became associated with Africa, as did the red, green and yellow or gold on the Ethiopian flag. This is part of Garvey's legacy, as the American historian George Shepperson put it as early as 1960 in the *Journal of African Studies*: 'His massive propaganda for pride, not shame, in a black skin left an ineradicable mark on African nationalism everywhere.' Garvey died in London in 1940, never having set foot in Africa. He is buried in Jamaica where he is a national hero, and his influence is still felt around the world. It is not a coincidence that the colours of the Jamaican national flag are black, green and gold.

Garvey is considered to be a prophet by the Rastafarian movement, which originated in Jamaica in the early 1930s. In

1920 Garvey had said: 'Look to Africa, when a black king shall be crowned, for the day of deliverance is at hand', by which he meant the coming of the Messiah. Ten years later Ras Tafari Makonnen was crowned Haile Selassie I, Emperor of Ethiopia. Ras is Amharic for 'Head', or 'Prince', and Tafari means 'one who is revered'. Some took this and the idea that Haile Selassie was the 225th direct descendant of King David to be the fulfilment of the prophecy. It therefore followed that he was the second coming of Jesus, Son of Jah, or God. As such he was also the Lion of Judah, which explains why the Rasta flag is the same as the old flag of Ethiopia, with the Lion of Judah in the centre.

Garvey never bought into all this, nevertheless he remains revered by Rastas and his ideology infuses the movement, which has had a greater impact on the world than might have been expected given that there are only about one million adherents. This is mostly down to the popularity of the reggae music performed by artists such as Bob Marley, who frequently referred to Garvey and Haile Selassie. For example, he used a Garvey quote, 'Emancipate yourselves from mental slavery, none but ourselves can free our minds', in 'Redemption Song', and whole chunks of a 1963 Haile Selassie speech to the UN in his magnificent song, 'War': 'until the philosophy which holds one race superior and another inferior is finally and permanently discredited and abandoned . . . And until the ignoble and unhappy regimes that hold our brothers in Angola, in Mozambique and in South Africa in subhuman bondage have been toppled and destroyed . . . Until that day, the African continent will not know peace'.

Marcus Garvey may have been surprised if he had lived to see his speeches marked in popular culture around the world, but his influence on African politics is less surprising, albeit still remarkable. As young men, future African leaders such as Jomo Kenyatta of Kenya and Kwame Nkrumah of Ghana may not have believed in his doctrine of racial separateness, but his writings, speeches and works were part of their political education. They were both believers in the core pan-African tenet: that despite all the ethnic, linguistic and cultural differences between people from the continent and the diaspora, there was one thing that bound them together – Africa.

Nkrumah had read Garvey's works when he lived in the USA between 1935 and 1945 and had taken them to heart before going on to become Prime Minister of a newly independent Ghana – the first sub-Saharan country to break free from the shackles of colonialism. Formerly the British-controlled region known as the Gold Coast, Ghana became an independent state in 1957. The government in the capital, Accra, took the colours of the flag of Ethiopia, green, gold and red, but changed their order so that the red was at the top, gold in the middle and green at the bottom. Nkrumah also authorized a black star to be centred in the yellow band in homage to Marcus Garvey's Black Star Line shipping company, and because, as the flag's designer Theodosia Salome Okoh said, the five-pointed star had become 'the symbol of African emancipation and unity in the struggle against colonialism'. The icon is also why the Ghanaian football team is known to this day as 'the Black Stars'. Sadly, Nkrumah also went on to become one of the first of the new generation of African leaders to shackle their country under their own despotic rule – betraying the ideals of their fight for liberation and all that the new flags stood for.

During the 1960s, as more and more African countries freed themselves from colonialism, the influences of Ethiopia, Garvey, Ghana and Nkrumah led many of them also to use one of the two versions of what had become pan-African colours for their own national symbols. Several countries in the Caribbean followed suit but, as in Africa, often gave new meanings to each one. For example, Ghana maintains that the gold is for the mineral wealth found in the country, whereas the yellow central stripe in the flag of Gabon is said to reflect that the country is on the Equator.

The next five sub-Saharan countries to gain independence took red, gold and green as their colours: Guinea, Cameroon, the Togolese Republic, Mali and Senegal all had variations on the theme, but acknowledged that these were pan-African colours in a continent united in rejecting rule from abroad and seeking a better future. The variations spoke of the individuality of different places, but everyone recognized the common thread sewn into each flag. For example, Cameroon went for three vertical stripes, green on the left, red in the centre and yellow on the right. The yellow represents the sun, the green hope, the red unity, and the yellow star on the red stripe is the 'Star of Unity'. It is a unique design but, as the government says, it all adds up to the pan-African spirit.

Other countries chose to go with variations of Garvey's flag, using red, green and black. Malawi, for example, has a green horizontal stripe at the bottom, red in the middle and black at the top (representing the people), and on the black is superimposed a red rising sun symbolizing freedom and the hope of people across the continent. Kenya's first President, Jomo Kenyatta, authorized a flag that took the three Garvey colours, green at the bottom, red in the middle and black at the top, added thin white strips to separate them, and in a radical departure then put a Maasai warrior shield with two spears from top to bottom. The black represents the majority of the people, red the blood spilt for freedom, and green the natural resources. The white fimbriations stand for peace and honesty, and the shield and spears protect all these values.

The use of only one particular tribal symbol and not others in a highly ethnically diverse country is interesting and in other circumstances could be very problematic. However, the Maasai only constitute 1.8 per cent of Kenya's 44 million-strong population. As such they are not a threat to the major, often competing, power blocs in the country, such as the Kikuyu, the Luo and the Kalenjin. Therefore, using the shape of a shield, which is recognizable as a reference to traditional ways of life, and patterning it in the colours of one of the most famous tribes in Africa, was deemed acceptable. Swaziland also went for a traditional warrior shield. It was half black, half white, symbolizing the hope that the different peoples of the country would get on together. Mozambique went, shall we say, a little further.

Mozambique's flag is, at the very least, interesting. Depending on your point of view it might also be problematic, inspiring, worrying or perhaps justifiable. The single most interesting thing about it is the AK-47 assault rifle with a fixed bayonet on its left-hand side. This is the only national flag in the world with a modern weapon symbolized on it. The flag consists of five colours: red, yellow, green, black and white. In this case the yellow represents the mineral wealth of the nation. The red triangle on the left-hand side contains a yellow star which stands for the socialist creed of the government, and on it is a book denoting the importance of education, a hoe representing the peasants, and an AK-47 for the nation's determination to defend its freedom – by any means necessary.

The AK-47 was the assault rifle of choice used by the Mozambican Liberation Front, known as FRELIMO, during the war of independence against Portugal. FRELIMO was the main revolutionary force and duly took power in 1975, bringing to an end almost half a millennium of colonial Portuguese rule. In 1983 the current flag was inaugurated. It was similar to the old FRELIMO flag and FRELIMO remains the dominant force in Mozambique politics. The inclusion of the rifle troubles many ordinary people in the country, who find it difficult to see it as a symbol of national unity, not just because the flag as a whole reeks of party politics (FRELIMO is based on politics not tribe, though there is a tribal element to its leadership structure), but also because the rifle is felt to denote violence and civil war, which is not the image many want to project to the world. For more than a decade now there has been a fierce debate about removing the weapon, but the pressure to do so comes mostly from opposition parties, and as the government is not minded to give it up, there it remains, looking slightly odd when flown at international meetings alongside its sister flags from around the world.

At least eighteen sub-Saharan national flags are variations on the pan-African colours of red, gold, black and green, and many more are clearly influenced by them; the flags of the colonial powers have mostly been roundly rejected, with only the occasional nod to that period in Africa's history. The flags of Uganda and Zambia serve well as an example. Uganda's is a distinctive, multicoloured, striped affair only saved from looking like a Liquorice Allsort on acid by the addition of a white circle in the middle two stripes in which a rather splendid crowned grey crane stands majestically on one leg. The crane, regarded as a gentle creature, is the national symbol of the country; the grace of the bird is said to reflect that of the Ugandan people. Zambia chose an unusually designed emblem – predominantly green, but with red, black and orange in a block in the bottom right-hand corner. Above this flies an eagle, which is the national animal of the state and here symbolizes the Zambian people rising above the country's problems.

Liberia is an exception to the pattern of red, gold, green and black because of its unusual history. Its flag bears a strong resemblance to the Stars and Stripes because the country was partially founded by African-American former slaves. Liberia's name comes from the Latin *liber* – free. Abolitionists and freed slaves bought land from local tribes on the West African coast in the first few decades of the nineteenth century and this was then settled by thousands of African Americans. A US-style flag was used at first, but with a cross in the top left-hand field. In 1847 there was a call for a national flag, and the final result had eleven stripes, symbolizing the eleven men who had signed the Liberian Declaration of Independence, and the cross was replaced with a star.

There are other exceptions as well – these are not rejections of pan-Africanism, an idea that still has currency across the continent, but usually a response to specific events or circumstances within the country. For example, the region of central Africa has for years been plagued with conflict, most notably in the Democratic Republic of Congo, Rwanda and Burundi. Following the genocide in Rwanda in 1994 there was a general understanding of the need for national reconciliation. A part of this was the idea of a fresh start, and so in 2001 the country abandoned its red, gold and green flag, which had become associated with Hutu extremism, for a blue, yellow and green one. Green stands for prosperity through united effort, yellow for economic development and blue for peace. In the right-hand corner of the top blue band is the sun, which represents the gradual enlightenment of the people. For good measure Rwanda also changed its national emblem and its anthem to underline that this was a new beginning after the horrors of the mass killings.

More recently, ethnic violence has revisited Burundi, whose flag was designed to be inclusive of the major ethnicities of the country, but whose politics, alas, have struggled to be. It is another unusual flag: red and green with a large white circle in the middle with arms branching off to each corner, and in the middle of the circle are three red stars. The white represents peace and the three stars are emblematic of the national motto, 'Unity, Work, and Progress', but they also refer to the three main ethnic groups, the Tutsi, the Hutu and the Twa. As in neighbouring Rwanda, the former Belgian protectorate of Burundi has been wracked by terrible ethnic violence between Hutus and Tutsis. Almost 300,000 people were killed during the 1993–2006 civil war as the majority Hutu population clashed with the minority Tutsi-dominated armed forces. After that there were attempts to better integrate the military, and indeed the political parties, but the recent waves of violence beginning in the summer of 2015 show the limits of this effort at full reconciliation and the building of a genuinely united state.

Many African countries have been troubled by sectarianism and ethnic strife. This is partly due to the lines drawn on maps by the colonial powers in the nineteenth and twentieth centuries, which left many different peoples speaking different languages inside borders of newly created nation states. In some of these countries, although the flag was created in solidarity with the ideas of pan-Africanism, nothing was done to promote unity within the countries themselves. These 'national' flags were simply reinforcing the borders imposed upon the popula-tion. Some of the countries' governments, such as Burundi, recognized this, and tried to create a flag that would unite the peoples; others, for example that of the tiny island of the Seychelles, make no reference to a particular community but celebrate the multi-ethnicity of their countries. In 1996, to mark independence from Britain, the Seychelles came up with a beautiful five-colour fan effect. None of the bands of colour refer to race, but they do signify the major political parties, and as they become wider, radiating from left to right, they signify the multi-ethnic society and the birth of a new nation moving into a dynamic future.

Others chose to make no reference at all. A good example is Nigeria, a country constructed in 1914 by the British and made up of parts of what were once the Benin Empire, the Oyo Empire and the Sokoto Caliphate, among other entities. It has some 250 peoples, thirty-six regions and two main religions, Islam and Christianity. Over its almost sixty-year independent history there have been troubling times, including military coups, ethnic clashes, separatist wars and most recently the emergence of the IS-related Boko Haram Islamist terrorist group. The flag has three vertical bands – green-white-green – the green signifying the abundant forests and agriculture of the country, while the white is for peace.

It was designed in 1959 by a twenty-three-year-old student named Michael Taiwo Akinkunmi, who was studying engineer-ing in London. He saw a newspaper advertisement calling for submissions for the design of a flag for the new sovereign state due to become independent from the UK the following year. He set to work and mailed his design back home, where it was one of more than 2,000 entries. His family still has the letter sent to him from Lagos by a Colonel Hefford in the 'Independence Celebrations Office' dated 14 February 1959, which reads: 'Thank you for your suggestion regarding the National Flag. It will receive full consideration by the Judging Committee in due course.'

It did, and the following year he was invited to the London office of the Commissioner for Nigeria, where he was told the good news and the bad news. The bad news was that the judges didn't like his red sun with rays on the white vertical band in the green-white-green design he had sent in, and so had removed it. The good news was that they did like what remained and so his design had been selected. He won a prize of £100 and should have been guaranteed a position in Nigeria's history books, but that would take time and the perseverance of a Nigerian student more than forty years later.

By 2006 Mr Akinkunmi was a retired civil servant living in a poor part of Ibadan about 70 miles north of Lagos. He was unrecognized and virtually unknown. A student at the University of Ibadan, Sunday Olawale Olaniran, researching Nigerian history, came across the name of the flag designer, whom he later called 'the hero without honour'.

Olaniran got in touch with the national *Daily Sun* newspaper and together they tracked down Akinkunmi, discovering that his memory was failing him, he was in poor health and living in poverty. His pension payments were so irregular that they were not enough to feed him. The story resulted in ordinary Nigerians donating food and clothes to him, but Olaniran hadn't finished. He began a campaign to get Mr Akinkunmi recognized for his contribution to the country. It took several years, but in 2010, during the independence golden jubilee celebrations, the government named him a 'Distinguished

Nigerian' – his first honour. The publicity helped him become known as 'Mr Flag Man' and in 2014, now blind, he travelled to the capital Abuja where the then President, Goodluck Jonathan, made him an Officer of the Federal Republic (OFR) and awarded him the lifetime salary of a Presidential Special Assistant.

Mr Akinkunmi's original design, with the red sun, was more striking, and without it the flag is one of the less noticeable in the world, but the green-white-green is now the recognized, if not particularly recognizable, symbol of the state. It is not without its critics. Writing on Nigeria's highbrow 'Village Square (Marketplace for Ideas)' website in 2012, Farooq A. Kperogi felt that his country's flag was 'undoubtedly one of the world's worst-designed flags. It is unimaginative, aesthetically unpleasant, and sterile in imagery and symbolism. It is one of only few national flags I know that repeat one bland color twice.' This is harsh stuff; however, as Mr Kperogi says: 'it may seem like a trivial subject matter . . . but recent events in Nigeria should cause us all to question our representational images and the relation of those images to our experiential realities . . . I have never been able to wrap my head around the justification for the repetition of the color green in our national colors. You would think the color green was in danger of going out of circulation and needed to be captured and curated on a flag.'

It is worth quoting Mr Kperogi at length as he gets to the heart of the matter in a debate which is constant but not at a level where the flag is about to be changed. 'Are colors the only symbolic representations we can invoke to depict our culture, peculiarities and history? What about the awe-inspiring, time-honored rivers that course through the length and breadth of our country's landscape; the rich, labyrinthine tapestry of our history; our uniquely sumptuous culinary treats; our valiant pre-colonial empires . . . ? Why is none of these captured representationally on our national flag? . . . [W]e have been "independent" from British colonial rule for 52 years now. Isn't it about time we rethought the colors and design of our national flag? For one, it is a holdover from colonialism; it wasn't a product of a post-independence effort . . . We have no business having a green-white-green national flag.'

Ouch. But these things are emotive and very subjective, and Mr Kperogi is just one voice on the matter.

Fred Brownell was acutely aware of this emotional aspect when he sat down and thought long and hard when asked to design the flag for a post-apartheid South Africa, a country that had been wracked with conflict, struggling to adjust to an entirely new status quo, and with a population that was still extremely divided and wary of one another. They were in desperate need of a symbol to inspire unity. Here was a moment in history, a moment made up of a thousand collective decisions adding up to the future of a nation, to life and death. One of those decisions was made by Fred.

He is a quiet, unassuming man, not prone to flights of fancy or hyperbole, which is perhaps why, when the challenge came, he rose to it. His moment began when the phone rang at his home in Pretoria on a Saturday night in February 1994. President de Klerk was on his way out, Nelson Mandela was already out of prison and about to rise to the highest office in the land, and the new South Africa needed a new flag. The existing one had been based on the Dutch flag and was so identified with both colonialism and the apartheid government that it had to go.

The phone call came after 7,000 designs had been rejected

and the ideas of graphic design studios had failed to come up with the answer. These were heady days, and it was proving impossible to please everyone. The question now put to Fred by the authorities overseeing the transition of power was: 'What should our new flag look like?' He was given a week.

The retired seventy-four-year-old had been a state herald at the South African Heraldic Authority whose function was to register flags, badges and seals for the state. Happily, as such he had already given the matter some thought. The previous summer he had been attending an international flag conference in Zurich. During a particularly dull speech he began to sketch some ideas for the new South African reality based on the repeated plea by Mr Mandela that the many different 'colours' of South Africa must stay, and work, together.

In an interview for this book Fred explained his thinking: 'The idea that had been in the back of my mind, and I had been scratching my head about it, was that we were looking for something new, something to represent convergence and representation. I knew we needed something which from every side would be viewed as acceptable.'

He came up with a Y-pronged shape, the predominant colour being green, but with red at the top and blue at the bottom, then added black and gold, colours which featured on the flags of the African National Congress (ANC), the Zulus' Inkatha Freedom Party and other political groupings. 'The red, gold and green were existing political realities and I thought if I put all these together in the design there would be a convergence, a convergence of colour, of people, of languages. There was also our former national flag, predominantly orange, white and blue. Instead of orange my choice was to go for chilli-red, which is halfway between red and orange, and a lovely colour. I was accused of sitting on the line between red and orange, but no, it was a meeting of the two.'

Fred was aware that chilli-red was also midway between the colours of the Dutch and British colonial-era flags, but says that none of the colours used are necessarily symbolic of anything – as in, green for vegetation – but that together they are a synopsis of the country's flag history, and that the design, particularly the Y shape, reflects the convergence of the past and the present and all the different peoples.

He took the advice of a friend and fellow flag expert, Olof Eriksson: 'He'd told me if you can't get your design down to the size of a postage stamp without it losing detail then you've got a bad design. Well, this one can be reduced to 6 millimetres by 4, and you can get sixteen of them onto an inch square and still see what it is. If you look at so many of the world flags, especially those in three colours, even I have to go to a book to check which one it is, but ours – well, it jumps out and hits you.'

Two of his variations on the design caught the eye of the commission; it came down to those two and another three submissions from other entrants, which were presented to President de Klerk. Acutely aware of the sensitivities of the decision, he felt it was not one he could take on his own, and so showed them to a hastily convened Cabinet meeting, which chose the version we now know. This was then sent to the chief ANC negotiator, Cyril Ramaphosa. He, understanding that the decision on what would be the symbolic embodiment of the new nation needed to have the blessing of the physical embodiment of the new era, in turn faxed it to Nelson Mandela.

At this point one of those fascinating details of history enters the story. This was before emails were in widespread use and faxes were in black and white. Fred chuckled as he retold what happened next, although at the time he was oblivious to it. 'Mr Mandela was up in the north-east when the fax came through. Someone there had to run down to the local shop, buy some colouring pencils, then come back and colour in the fax. I'm told he studied it and said, "Fine, let's go for it".'

With that the race was on to get the new flag ready for the beginning of the general election, which would effectively mark the handover of power on 27 April. They had just over five weeks. The Transitional Executive Council adopted the design within hours of Mandela's go-ahead but hit an immediate problem. There were about 100,000 flagpoles in the country, all of which would require the new flag to be flown on the day of the changeover, but the country could only produce 5,000 a week, which would leave three-quarters of the flagpoles embarrassingly naked. Dutch factories stepped in and saved the day, but not before using up Europe's stock of flag-making materials.

And the result? 'There was initially a muted reaction from the public', says the designer, but in the weeks between polling day and Nelson Mandela's inauguration as President, the design and the colours began to seep into the collective consciousness: 'Within a matter of two or three weeks attitudes changed, and in many cases people began to have a fond attachment to it. Now people have bought into it – after all, colours are a psychological component of life, part of the essence of life.'

And is he proud of this? 'Well, I was doing what I considered to be my job. It was my responsibility to do what I could, I feel happy to have contributed in some small way.'

It was more than a small way – indeed, Fred played his part in the whole difficult post-apartheid reconciliation process. However, although the flag was considered a success, the unity of the Rainbow Nation has proved less so, and looks destined to be a work in progress for some time to come. The ideals symbolized in the bringing together of the colours are struggling in the face of continuing national divisions, which are now being exacerbated by immigration and a struggling economy.

Another work in progress is the development of what are, mostly, relatively new African nation states. Red, gold, green and black will always help promote the idea of unity across the continent, but within that huge land mass is the reality of thousands of peoples now forging the identities of dozens of nations, and amid the interplays of power, politics and ethnicity the symbolism of each flag plays an important role. The challenge is in cementing these emblems of nationhood; the new flags give people something around which to coalesce, but older identities can and will remain strong.

CHAPTER 8

FLAGS
OF REVOLUTION

---

*'Ironically, Latin American countries,
in their instability, give writers and
intellectuals the hope that they are needed.'*
Manuel Puig

Previous pages: The Bolivian and Wiphala flags. The Wiphala has recently become a symbol of the rights of indigenous peoples throughout the Andean region. In 2009, Bolivian President Evo Morales controversially stipulated that public buildings fly both the multicoloured Wiphala and the Bolivian tricolour.

GONDWANA NEVER HAD A FLAG. THERE ARE SOUND scientific reasons for this, the most important being that there were no humans around to make it, and Tyrannosaurus Rex, lacking an opposable thumb, never got round to it. This is just as well: it would now be redundant, given that the world's last great supercontinent fell apart about 180 million years ago and instead of Gondwana we have, among other regions, the continents of Africa and South America.

It wasn't until the 1620s, when detailed maps of the coastlines of western Africa and eastern South America became available, that people first noticed that they would actually fit into each other like pieces in a jigsaw puzzle; but the conjecture, supported by tectonic plate theory, only became widely accepted in the 1960s.

Once separated, the two continents had little to do with each other right up until the beginnings of the colonial and slavery era. Then they both began to be dominated by the Europeans, followed by an immense amount of human trafficking from West Africa to South America. However, as each threw off the shackles of colonialism, when it came to the matter of national symbols they chose different paths.

In South America there are regional groupings of colours relevant to shared regional history, but there is no pan-South American or Latin American colour scheme. Also, proportionally more European-style flags, such as tricolours, exist in Latin America than in Africa. References to the ancient cultures and peoples are visible, notably in the Mexican flag, but they are few and far between; this may be due to the different eras in which the continents were colonized and later became independent. In Africa the periods of full-scale occupation and colonization were mostly shorter than in the Americas, in many cases less than 100 years. In that time much of the native culture, and indeed people, survived. As such it was natural that in the post-colonial era the emblems of the occupiers would be rejected.

By contrast the indigenous populations of Latin America – the Aztecs, Mayas, Incas and so on – were almost wiped out by war and the diseases brought by the Europeans. Many of the survivors retreated into remote areas and thus had less impact on their societies over the course of almost three centuries of Spanish, Portuguese and, to a much lesser extent, British and French colonization. Now they make up less than 10 per cent of the continent's 626 million people.

Therefore, when the populations of Latin America began to clamour for independence, many of the people were of the same origin, culturally and linguistically, as their colonial masters. As such there would have been less of a psychological incentive to throw off the symbols of the old order. Few drew inspiration from the cultures they had done so much to suppress. The American Revolution had demonstrated that the descendants of European settlers could separate themselves from the European powers and establish their own, new, identities. In the first years of the nineteenth century, the French Revolution was recent history and, as mostly the descendants of Europeans, Latin American revolutionaries embraced the ideas of liberty that the French tricolour had come to embody; they also profited from the instability wrought by the march of Napoleon across Europe as the Spanish and, later, Portuguese monarchies weakened.

Definitions of Latin America vary, but for the purpose of simplicity I'll stick to the contiguous land mass beginning in Mexico in the north and stretching 5,500 miles south down to the tip of Argentina, in which most inhabitants speak Spanish or Portuguese.

In 1498 Columbus landed in what we now know as Venezuela and was very impressed by the huge offshore current of fresh water in the sea off the coast. He wrote to his patrons, the Spanish King Ferdinand and Queen Isabella, that he had found heaven on earth:

> I have never read or heard of such a large quantity of fresh water being inside and in such close proximity to salt water; the very mild temperateness also corroborates this; and if the water of which I speak does not proceed from Paradise then it is an even greater marvel, because I do not believe such a large and deep river has ever been known to exist in this world.

The Spanish quite fancied this, and the prospect of the rest of the continent as a second home; within a couple of decades they were arriving in droves. By 1717 the whole region around where Columbus landed was part of the Spanish Empire and called New Granada. It corresponded roughly to what we now know as Venezuela, Colombia, Panama and Ecuador.

Almost another century later, enter Simón Bolívar, born in the province of Venezuela, mad as hell and not going to take Spanish colonialism and its New Granada any longer. In 1810 he and a military junta expelled the Spanish governor of the province and the following year declared Venezuela's independence. There followed a tumultuous couple of decades with Bolívar at the centre; by 1819, after some astonishing battles, he entered Bogotá and declared the Republic of Colombia, which covered modern-day Colombia, Panama, Ecuador, Venezuela and a little bit of Peru and Brazil.

Barely pausing for breath, and by now known as the

Liberator, he set about expelling the Spanish not just from Colombia but from the whole region. By 1822 his Republic was a reality. To avoid confusion with modern-day Colombia, it is known by historians as Gran Colombia.

He took as his flag a tricolour with yellow, blue and red horizontal stripes. Tradition has it that the yellow at the top stands for the wealth of the country, the blue for the ocean now separating the Republic from Spain, and the red for the courage and blood of those who had fought to overthrow Spanish rule. It had been designed as early as 1806 by one of Bolívar's fellow revolutionaries, Francisco de Miranda, who credited two things for his inspiration. He remembered a fresco he had seen in Italy in which Christopher Columbus was unfurling a yellow, blue and red flag as he came ashore at Venezuela; he also recalled a conversation he had had with the great German writer Johann Wolfgang von Goethe several decades earlier.

De Miranda claimed that Goethe, upon hearing of his adventures in the Americas, had told him: 'Your destiny is to create in your land a place where primary colours are not distorted.' Goethe had thought long and hard about colour and de Miranda says he proved to him '[why] yellow is the most warm, noble and closest to light, why blue is that mix of excitement and serenity, a distance that evokes shadows; and why red is the exaltation of yellow and blue, the synthesis, the vanishing of light into shadow'. He went on to say: 'A country starts out from a name and a flag, and it then becomes them, just as a man fulfils his destiny.'

The peoples of Gran Colombia had a go at being proud of their flag, but regional differences and the ambition of leaders proved obstructive, and without the bond of long-formed, strong state institutions, the regions began to go their own separate ways. While Bolívar was off revolutionizing in Peru, one of his Venezuelan colleagues led a revolution against him. There were similar stirrings in Ecuador and by 1830, following an assassination attempt, an exhausted and increasingly ill Bolívar called it a day and set off for retirement in Europe. He got as far as the Atlantic coast of Colombia, where he succumbed to tuberculosis.

Gran Colombia was dissolved, and the new sovereign states of Colombia, Venezuela and Ecuador were established. All three took as their flags what were almost carbon copies of the Gran Colombia version: yellow at the top, blue in the middle, red at the bottom. They are now very different countries, but there remains a general understanding of a shared regional history.

Venezuela's flag has seven white stars on the middle blue stripe to represent the seven provinces that took part in the fight against Spain. Bolívar remains such a hero that in the 1990s President Hugo Chávez renamed the country the Bolívarian Republic of Venezuela. In 2006 Chavez even introduced a new flag featuring a bow and arrow to symbolize the country's tiny indigenous minority. It never caught on but it did reflect the fact that, despite Bolívar's paternalistic attitude towards the indigenous population, this century has seen a growing awareness of the place of native peoples in the modern societies of Latin America.

Ecuador's flag features a large coat of arms in the middle topped by a condor, the national emblem. In 1860 it added four signs of the Zodiac – Aries, Taurus, Gemini and Cancer – to commemorate the revolutionary months in 1845 – March, April, May and June – when General Juan José Flores was overthrown, an event that typifies the history of the republics, which were born in violence and continually misruled by political gangsters.

228 WORTH DYING FOR

Replacing one tyranny with another was not Simon Bolívar's original intention, although he developed some dictatorial tendencies himself, along with a taste for locking up former friends and granting himself supreme powers. Along with Columbus, Bolívar is one of the very few people in history who have had countries named after them, which is more than the famous twentieth-century Mexican revolutionary Emiliano Zapata managed. Outside Mexico he is now known more for a style of moustache than for changing history. This is only marginally better than the fate which befell the Italian revolutionary Garibaldi, who went on to become a biscuit.

The flag of Bolívar's namesake is standard fare: a red, yellow and green horizontal tricolour saved from ordinariness only by an excellent coat of arms in the middle yellow band. This features an array of weapons, a condor at the top, and what looks to the untrained eye like a llama in the centre, but is in fact an alpaca, which, as everyone knows, is considerably smaller than a llama.

Perhaps of more interest, other than the alpaca, are two other flags flown in Bolivia. The first is that of the Bolivian navy – not so much because of its design, but because the navy operates at 12,000 feet up in the Andes in landlocked Bolivia and most of the sailors have never seen the sea. This is due to the 1884 treaty signed to end the War of the Pacific, in which Bolivia ceded 240 miles of coastline to Chile and thus lost access to the ocean.

Bolivia wants it back, not just to put an end to Chilean jokes about inviting their neighbours to the beach for the weekend, but because of the boost in trade revenue and national pride it would bring. Hence Bolivian presidents sometimes make speeches in front of antique maps showing the original borders, and the navy flag has a large yellow star which is symbolic of the country's diplomatic position: that it has a right to sovereign access to the sea, not just the access it currently enjoys thank to Chilean largesse. Holding your breath might be a useful skill in the navy, but the 5,000 Bolivian sailors need not bother as it is unlikely the borders will change in the foreseeable future. Besides, they are kept busy patrolling Lake Titicaca and 5,000 miles of navigable river.

The other flag of interest here is the Wiphala, which has become a second national emblem and also a symbol of indigenous peoples right across the Andes in Ecuador, Peru, Bolivia and Chile. It is a square flag containing forty-nine squares in the seven colours of the rainbow. The word Wiphala comes from the local language, Aymara, and simply means 'flag'. There is much debate about the heritage of the flag and whether the colours relate to the Incan Empire, but the bottom line is that variations of it now represent the native peoples, and it has grown increasingly popular over the last few decades as those people have become more politically organized.

In 2009 President Evo Morales, who is from an Aymaran-speaking family, decreed that the Wiphala should be flown alongside the red, yellow and green national flag in all public areas and buildings, including schools. This did not go down too well in some parts of eastern Bolivia, where the majority of the population are from non-indigenous backgrounds and where in some places the decree has been ignored. Those against the Wiphala fear that it is intended eventually to replace the tricolour as the national flag, and/or that it encourages division between ethnic and class groups. Critics say that it only represents a minority of the dozens of different cultures in the country and that those differences were recognized when

Morales changed the name of the country to the Plurinational State of Bolivia.

For the Aymarans the flag not only acknowledges their troubled history, but its colours are symbolic: the yellow is for energy, white for time, green for nature, blue for the sky, orange is an expression of society and culture, violet is a pan-Andean colour and red is for the planet earth. Archaeologists suspect that the modern multicoloured flag is derived from ancient symbols, but there is no solid evidence for this. Either way it is now established right across the region.

The only national flag to draw on the iconography of indigenous peoples is found further north, in Mexico. It is often said that Mexico's flag looks like the Italian flag. However, this is a little unfair as the origins of the vertical green, white and red stripes of Mexico predate the formation of Italy by several decades. Nevertheless, the current official version was introduced in 1968 because Mexico was due to host the Olympic Games that year, wanted to avoid any confusion between the two, and so ordered that the Mexican flag should always have an eagle in the central white stripe, as opposed to it being a matter of choice (which traditionally it had been). The eagle is standing on a cactus plant which is in a lake. In its mouth is a snake. And behind that is one of those great 'birth of a nation' tales.

The name Mexico comes from the Aztec or Nahua word *metzlixcictlico* (usual pronunciation). The Aztecs, who also called themselves the Mexihcah, arrived in what we know now as the Valley of Mexico region in the thirteenth century. According to legend the Aztec priests said that their god had told them to search for a new place to live. They would know when they had reached it because they would see a giant eagle, standing on a cactus. Lo and behold – there it was, on a cactus, on a rock, on an island, in a lake.

Here it gets a bit complicated, but the locals called the lake Metztli iapan, or 'Moon Lake'. The island, it is surmised by etymologists, would therefore have been called Metztli iapan ixic which, to cut a long word and story short, may have come down to 'Mexic-co'. It's a fairly big 'may', apparently, but either way you can't imagine that when the Spanish showed up 300 years later they would have gone for the original version.

They certainly didn't go for the eagle and cactus story, which irked their Catholic tastes – so much so that they set about destroying much of the Aztec iconography featuring it. The papers of the Spanish Viceroy in 1642, Dr Juan de Palafox y Mendoza, reveal him writing irate letters to the great and good of Mexico City demanding that images showing the eagle be removed and replaced with Christian ones. Despite this, that the eagle landed on some of the Mexican revolutionary flags of the early 1800s is testament to the power of the legend and its symbol. Its place in the national iconography is testament to the new hybrid culture formed in this part of the New World, as Mexicans cast back to the history of the region as a means of separating from the Spanish. The people it originally represented may have faded into history (although there are still Nahuatl speakers in the region), but there, right in the centre of the national flag, is the ancient Aztec symbol. There's no doubt the indigenous cultures were both suppressed and diluted, but colonialists cannot help but pick up elements of the local cultures.

Mexico's War of Independence from Spain (1810–21) was waged by several groups under different banners, but they came together as the Army of the Three Guarantees and fought under a green, white and red tricolour. This became the basis of the national flag, designed in 1821, which, when first flown in 1822, featured the eagle. The Supreme Provisional Governing Junta had issued a proclamation stipulating that the flag 'should be tricoloured, adopting perpetually the colours green, white and red in vertical stripes and representing on the white a crowned eagle'. The top military man, Agustín de Iturbide, took the 'crowned' bit so seriously that in May 1822 he proclaimed himself Agustín I, Emperor of Mexico, and set about creating an empire.

However, in these turbulent and revolutionary times his 'empire' lasted all of ten months, at which point he ran away to Europe, the empire was dissolved, and therefore the eagle's crown had to go as well. By the time Agustín got back from England in 1824, the eagle was bald, but had acquired a snake in its right talon. Sadly for Agustín, he hadn't got the memo that he had been sentenced to death in his absence and upon his return he was promptly put against a wall and shot by a firing squad.

The flag lived on, though, in green, white and red, but went through several iterations – for example, a laurel wreath and ribbons in the national colours were added, and the eagle appeared vaguely imperial or neo-imperial depending on which imperious leader was in charge. However, it rarely looked as if it would vote for a democratic republic, which was what Mexico was supposed to be. That changed in 1916 when, following yet another revolution, President Venustiano Carranza asked for a flag which might seem less like something on the top of an imperial Roman centurion staff. He chose 'the Aztec eagle', which is seen from the side, with its head down and attacking the snake that it holds in its talons: a symbol that was clearly defending the nation against evil. Admittedly the bird was still somewhat fearsome, but that was OK because it was no longer, as under the previous president, staring haughtily at everyone as if to say 'I'm in charge'.

As for the colours of what is known as the Bandera de México, there have been many claims at different times as to what each represents, but the doyen of vexillologists the world over, Dr Whitney Smith, wrote in 1975 that 'traditionally green is said to stand for independence, white for the purity of religion, and red (the Spanish national colour) for union'.

In many ways it no longer matters, because with the coat of arms it all adds up to the symbol of a modern Mexico, a growing country of about 125 million people which, together with Portuguese-speaking Brazil, dominates Latin America. The state remains weak and poverty is widespread, but nevertheless the economy has been strengthening for years now, partly fuelled by a low-wage manufacturing base which sometimes even undercuts that of China. Despite its myriad problems, not least the reach of the drug gangs into the state institutions, Mexico is an increasingly confident country with a fiercely proud population. In Mexico, and throughout Latin America, colonial independence remains an essential founding story and the revolution against Spain is an enormous source of national pride, with green, white and red displayed widely for Independence Day.

Beneath Mexico are the seven far smaller nations of Central America, and here we find our second set of pan-regional colours. Blue and white were the colours of the short-lived Federal Republic of Central America, consisting of what is now Guatemala, Honduras, El Salvador, Costa Rica and Nicaragua. Having declared independence from the Spanish Empire in 1821, the Republic was not too keen on becoming part of the

First Mexican Empire, which had been proclaimed in the same year, and so some states took up arms.

Following the unfortunate end of Agustín de Iturbide, the empire did not strike back and Mexico allowed the region to go its own way; accordingly a sovereign state known as the 'United Provinces of Central America' was formed in 1823. It took as its flag horizontal stripes in blue-white-blue with a coat of arms in the middle white strip consisting of a circle bearing the words *Provincias Unidas del Centro de América*. Inside the circle were five mountains representing the five regions making up the state. The following year, upon becoming a republic, the wording was changed to *República Federal de Centro América*.

The inspiration for the blue and white flag seems to have come from Argentina, where revolutionaries were flying similar colours from as early as 1810; some of them, it is said, presented one of their flags to militia from the El Salvador region who were being formed to fight the Mexicans. In time, though, the white strip was said to represent the land, with the Atlantic and Pacific oceans on each side of it.

The only common cause to bond the five regions was opposition first to Spanish and then to Mexican rule. Without that necessity for unity the political and geographical differences between them, and between factions within each state, began to show. In 1838, after years of instability, Nicaragua was the first to leave and by 1840 the Federation had fallen apart, effectively resulting in five independent but unstable and poverty-stricken sovereign states, each requiring a flag. All drew on a shared history and hinted at the possibility of future reunion.

Nicaragua's flag, for example, is almost a carbon copy of that of the Federal Republic except that the top and bottom horizontal stripes are of a deeper shade of blue. The coat of arms in the middle white stripe features the five mountains and is surrounded by the words *República de Nicaragua América Central*. El Salvador's flag is similar but its coat of arms has a triangle containing the five mountains, behind which are five blue and white flags. Honduras has horizontal blue and white but five stars on the white instead of the five mountains of the others. Guatemala's is also blue and white, but this time in vertical stripes with crossed swords and fixed bayonets in the centre of the middle white stripe. Initially Costa Rica went with blue-white-blue as well, but in 1848, inspired by the republican revolutions in France and many other European countries that year, redesigned the national symbol, adding a red horizontal stripe but giving the flag five stripes as a reference to the former five provinces. At the very top of the coat of arms are the words *América Central*, yet another sign of the hope that all five countries may reunite one day.

Various attempts were made to do just that in the nineteenth and early twentieth centuries. These always ended without success, and sometimes with firing squads. Throughout their 200 years of independence, the Central American states have endured numerous dictatorships, wars, revolutions, coups d'état, illiberal democracies and breathtaking levels of corruption. In this, especially the latter, they share their experience with the whole of Latin America. Many of the 626 million-strong population simply shrug their shoulders until the levels of corruption reach breaking point. The Brazilians even have a phrase – *Rouba, mas faz* – which means 'he steals but he acts'.

Nevertheless, in the present century some of the democratic ideals of the original revolutionary years have been strengthened in Central America and the countries to its north and south. The generals are mostly in their barracks, and the judiciary is in a constant battle to check and balance the political class. The current relative stability has allowed the formation of several regional multinational associations: for example, there is a free trade zone, an economic 'integration' system, a Central American Parliament (with its own familiar-looking flag) and even a borderless travel area, all of which involve some or all of the members of the former Federal Republic and in some cases include neighbours. There does not appear to be any need to dust down the old flags of 1823 and 1824, but the idea is still there and is on display for all to see in the flags of each former member.

Just to the south of the five is a flag that is massively popular all over the world, which is convenient for a number of reasons – well, at least with people who own large ships, for whom the very appropriate phrase 'Flag of Convenience' might have been coined. Despite having a population of slightly under 4 million people, Panama boasts the largest shipping fleet in the world. In fact, the Panama government itself says that 'approximately 23 per cent of the world's fleet is under the Panamanian flag'. This is partly because Panama is home to the famous 48-mile-long canal, which provides a fantastic shortcut between the Atlantic and Pacific oceans; in 2016 the authorities unveiled a $5 billion upgrade to the waterway featuring longer and deeper locks to accommodate larger, heavier ships. This was partially to meet the demands of modern shipping, but also to head off the stop–start Chinese project to build a rival canal across Nicaragua. And the shiny new and improved product continues to be just as attractive to the average shipping magnate as it still has some of the least stringent shipping laws in the world.

As advertised by the Panamanian government, 'There are

no requirements under Panamanian legislation for the owner, whether a natural or legal person, to be Panamanian.' Nor are there any restrictions in registering or manning your vessel, and this is a case where size doesn't matter – big, small, there's no minimum tonnage required. Better still, if you register between five and fifteen vessels you get a 20 per cent discount. There's more: not only can you register your ship in a period of eight hours, but 'the revenues generated from international maritime commerce of merchant ships registered in Panama are exempt from taxation . . . Furthermore, the proceeds of the sale or transfer of a vessel registered in Panama are not subject to capital gains tax even when the transaction is executed in Panama.' To top it all, Panama approves the use of private armed security personnel on board, and (the icing on the cake) in accordance with Panamanian law No. 57 of 6 August 2008, captains on board can celebrate civil marriages of any nationality while on open sea.

All this and more; and to get the paperwork done you don't even have to go to Panama. No wonder that well over 8,000 ships around the world fly the proud red, white and blue of Panama. That is more than are registered in the USA and China combined and as such they are worth hundreds of millions of dollars annually to Panama's economy. While the world knows that at sea this questionable laxity can cover a multitude of sins, big business and governments accept that the system helps trade flow.

The system is called 'Open Registry' or, more pejoratively, 'Flags of Convenience'. Ships began to transfer to Panama just six years after the canal opened in 1914 when some enterprising Americans realized they might be able to get around Prohibition laws.

The Americans had history in the country. From 1821 to 1903 Panama had been part of Colombia in its various guises, but in 1903 it was also the part of Colombia which said to the USA, 'A canal? What a good idea.' However, the Colombian government had said no, and so the Americans engineered a revolution in Panama, which quickly gained independence, and construction work on the passageway began almost immediately, financed by the USA, which stood to benefit from the trade waterway to the Pacific.

Panama had been looking to break free from Colombia for most of the previous century and so relations with the USA were good. There's no evidence to suggest that this is why there is a vague nod to the Stars and Stripes in Panama's flag, but I wouldn't rule it out. With its four squares and two stars it is designed like no other national flag in Latin America. It was sketched by the revolutionary leader Manuel Amador Guerrero, who went on to become the newly independent country's first president in 1904. It was stitched together in secret by his wife María Ossa de Amador while Panama was still part of Colombia.

Top-left, as we look at it, is a white square with a blue five-pointed star. Next to that is a plain red square, beneath it a white square with a red star, and to the left of that a plain blue square. The blue and red correspond to the two traditional political parties, the conservatives and liberals. The white is for peaceful relations between them. The blue also symbolizes the oceans on each side of the country and the red the blood of patriots. It was designed and adopted in 1903, and indeed baptized in a religious ceremony on 20 December that year, and has remained unchanged ever since.

So Panama was now a sovereign state, but the actual canal and the land five miles each side of it became an 'unincorporated territory' of the USA – controlled by the USA but not part of it. Panama granted it this status 'in perpetuity'. However, by the 1950s what were regarded increasingly as imperialistic 'Yankees' were significantly less popular, and flags, as the representation of sovereignty, became central to what became a battlefield.

In May 1958 nine people died during anti-American rioting. The following year nationalists threatened a 'peaceful invasion' of the Canal Zone in order to raise the flag of Panama alongside the Stars and Stripes, to proclaim its sovereignty over the territory. Several hundred people forced their way past barbed-wire barriers into the Zone and clashed with security forces. A second attempt was countered by the National Guard and US troops. US government buildings were then attacked and the American flag torn down from the Ambassador's residence.

A fierce debate broke out back in Washington after the State Department let it be known that it favoured making concessions and allowing the Panamanian flag to be flown. In a private letter to President Eisenhower in December 1959, Congressman Daniel J. Flood of Pennsylvania framed the matter in almost apocalyptic terms:

Furthermore, if the Panama flag ever flies officially in the Canal Zone, this will open up a veritable Pandora's box of controversy, conflict and chaos. The extremists who have been inciting Panamanian mobs to violence and have thus been establishing the foreign policy of Panama have as their immediate aim a duality of control which the great leaders at the start of the century thought had been forever prevented. The ultimate aim is Panamanian Nationalization.

Whether his motivation was right or wrong, he may have had a point, especially about duality and nationalization.

In 1960 tensions were still high and the USA had built a fence marking the border of the Zone. Another 'invasion' was planned, but the State Department won the argument and it was called off after Washington let it be known that it would allow a single Panamanian flag to be hoisted at a special site alongside the US flag.

The ceremony in September that year did not go well. President Ernesto de la Guardia officially asked if he could personally raise the flag, thus marking Panama's 'titular' sovereignty over the zone. The Americans officially refused. He boycotted the event and excluded all American officials from the subsequent presidential reception except the US Ambassador and his senior aides. No Canal Zone representatives were invited. The message sent was that this was far from over.

Four years later, on 9 January 1964, a group of about 200 high-school students marched into the Zone carrying a Panamanian flag. They confronted some American teenagers who were trying to raise the Stars and Stripes in a school yard. Several hundred more Americans from among the 36,000-strong US population arrived at the scene and in the ensuing scuffles the Panamanian flag was torn.

That was the spark. Thousands of Panamanians began to gather at the border fence and eventually stormed it. The rioting lasted three days, left more than twenty people dead, hundreds injured, and caused more than $2 million worth of damage to property. Diplomatic relations were broken for three months before being restored, and the controversy led, over several years, to a renegotiation of the sovereignty issue. In 1979 the Canal Zone was abolished and the canal jointly administered until 31 December 1999, when it was fully turned over to Panama. Congressman Daniel J. Flood had been right. In Panama, 9 January is known as Martyrs' Day.

A flag that is somewhat less interesting graphically is that of Peru. As it consists of fairly standard red-white-red vertical stripes, the only reason to bring it up is to mention that possibly the coolest ever national football team strip was the one Peru wore for the 1970 World Cup Finals in Mexico. Based on the flag, it had gleaming white shorts and socks, a brilliant white short-sleeve shirt and across the front a bright-red diagonal band, almost like a banana republic dictator's sash. It was worthy of a winners' medal even without anyone in it.

Another reason to mention it is in debates about the rights and wrongs, the tribute or tawdriness, of sitting on your country's flag when naked and using it as a saddle for a horse. Without meaning to, the Peruvian glamour model Leysi Suárez tested Peru's flag laws in 2008 by doing just that for a magazine shoot. Cue degrees of Peruvian outrage, possibly matched by degrees of Peruvian perving, before the Defence Minister got up on his own high horse, worked himself up into a lather and said she would face charges of flag desecration, which carried a potential four-year jail sentence. The case dragged on for two years before being closed in 2010, but not before adding to the gaiety of the nation. Peru is not special in taking umbrage at perceived desecrations of the national flag, however this was a particularly entertaining episode, turning as it did on a glamour model, a horse and a careerist politician.

So let us raise our eyes from the gutter to the heavens and the flag of Argentina. The first name to conjure with here is one familiar to readers in both Argentina and Britain, but perhaps not elsewhere – Manuel Belgrano. Whereas Bolívar had a country named after him, 'General Belgrano' ended up being the name of an Argentine navy light cruiser which was sunk by a British submarine during the Falklands/Malvinas War of 1982.

Back in 1810, though, Belgrano was leading mass demonstrations against the Spanish in Buenos Aires. Many demonstrators were wearing a light-blue and white cockade in their hats. These were the colours of a militia force called the Legion Patricia, which had been formed to fight the British invasion a few years earlier and had done so successfully without any help from the Spanish Viceroy, who had run away.

Why blue and white? The romantic explanation is that the blue is for the sky and the River Plate, while the white represents silver. The early conquistadors had named the area Argentina after the Latin word for silver, *argentum*, thinking that the region contained vast amounts of the metal. As far as Bolivia and Peru were concerned they were right, but apart from some spectacular finds, notably in Potosí, they were to be mostly disappointed in Argentina, whose silver-mining industry only really took off this century. True or not, either way supporters of the demonstration did need colours to differentiate themselves from the Spanish red and yellow.

Legend has it that it during a demonstration in May the sun suddenly broke through the clouds on what had been an overcast day. This was taken to be a good sign – indeed, it later became the national symbol – and the demonstrations were in fact destined to be successful. The Spanish Viceroy had to accept that a local government could be formed, and the uprising finally culminated in the end of Spanish sovereignty in the region then known as the Viceroyalty of the River Plate, an area covering present-day Argentina, Uruguay, Paraguay and Bolivia.

In 1812, when designing the new flag of what would become Argentina, Belgrano took as his inspiration the light (celestial) blue and the white of the cockades in a horizontal blue-white-blue format. By 1816 full independence had been declared and in 1818 the 'Sun of May' (*Sol de Mayo*) with a human face was added to the middle band. The sun's face is rather enigmatic: to some it may look serene, to others emotionless. I think it looks like Thomas the Tank Engine. Argentina celebrates Flag Week each June, culminating in events on the 20th, the anniversary of Belgrano's death in 1820.

The Argentinians take both the British and the Falklands flags almost as seriously as they do their own. This is almost entirely down to the dispute between the two countries over the Falklands/Malvinas Islands. Having fought a short war over British rule in 1982, tensions still simmer. The Falklands flag (which includes the Union Jack) is now used by Argentina as a political and economic weapon. In 2011, Argentina persuaded its South American neighbours to close their ports to ships flying the Falklands flag, and threatened not to do business with any company involved in British exploration for oil off the coast of the islands.

You may have noticed that the flag of Uruguay, which features blue and white stripes, also has a Sun of May in a design very similar to that of Argentina; this reflects their shared history. What is now Uruguay had been part of the Spanish-ruled River Plate region and participated in the uprisings of 1810 and subsequent years but then broke free. It wasn't until 1828 that it was recognized as a sovereign state by its giant neighbours Brazil and Argentina, but by then there were already variants of the flag which became the one we see today. The Sun of May refers back to the original uprisings but also signifies the birth of a new nation, and the nine blue and white stripes are for the original nine provinces of Uruguay.

Finally, on to what is the probably the most recognizable and globally popular flag of the continent – that of Brazil. Its vibrant green and yellow have been adopted as a fashionable design by millions via the Brazilian national football team's shirt. That and the team's often exuberant style of play have endeared it, and its colours, to hundreds of millions of people around the world.

The design of the flag we see now is not the original one that was in use when Brazil fought and won its independence from Portugal in 1822, but it is similar. The run-up to independence holds clues as to the reasons for the colours in the flag. In 1807 Portugal's Prince Regent, Dom João (later King Dom João VI), had fled to Brazil to escape Napoleon's invasion of that year and to set up government in Rio de Janeiro. João was of the Braganza dynasty and was married to Queen Carlota Joaquina, who was descended from the Habsburgs, a detail which would become important in the story of the flag.

João returned to Portugal in 1821 to try to deal with a political crisis. By this time Brazil was part of the 'United Kingdom of Portugal, Brazil, and the Algarves' and as such was equal to Portugal in status. João left behind his son and heir, Dom Pedro, to rule Brazil as Prince Regent.

Due to various political machinations back in Lisbon, the Portuguese 'Cortes', a sort of embryonic parliament which was getting a bit uppity with the royals, downgraded Brazil's status back to a colony, which left Dom Pedro pretty much the Governor of Rio de Janeiro province and not a great deal else. The Cortes also ordered him to come home in case he reacted by heading an independence movement. Which of course he did.

There followed a series of epoch-making events and speeches which are as well known in Brazil as, say, the Gettysburg Address or Churchill's 'We shall never surrender' speech are in the USA and UK respectively. In September 1822 Pedro rejected an ultimatum from Portugal and set out on the path to independence. One of his companions, Father Belchior Pinheiro de Oliveira, wrote later about the exact moment:

D. Pedro silently walked toward our horses at the side of the road. Suddenly, he halted in the middle of the road and said to me, 'Father Belchior, they asked for it and they will get it . . . From today on our relations with them are finished. I want nothing more from the Portuguese government, and I proclaim Brazil for evermore separated from Portugal.'

With enthusiasm we immediately answered, 'Long live liberty! Long live an independent Brazil! Long live D. Pedro!'

The Prince turned to his adjutant and said, 'Tell my guard that I have just declared the complete independence of Brazil. We are free from Portugal.'

He then addressed his Guard of Honour and, pulling off his blue-white armband that symbolized Portugal, ordered his men to do the same. He ended with the suitably heroic cry of '*Independência ou Morte!*' – 'Independence or Death!'

There is a stirring painting by Pedro Américo at the Museu Paulista in São Paulo depicting the event, which is only diminished slightly by the knowledge, imparted by the historian Neill Macaulay in his book on Dom Pedro, that at the time the prince was suffering from a severe bout of diarrhoea. Such are the vagaries of epoch-making moments in history.

The story is worth telling for many reasons, primarily because it is so colourful. Pedro and the Brazilians may have gone on to have a brief war with Portugal, but they always recognized their connections to the old world. The blue and white in the Brazilian flag is considered to be a reflection of that, while the green and yellow were colours of the royal Houses of Braganza and Habsburg.

Pedro was named Emperor of Brazil in 1822. The first Brazilian flag had the familiar green background with a yellow diamond, but in the centre of the diamond was a royal coat of arms that featured twenty stars representing the regions of the country. When the Empire of Brazil became a republic in 1889, the flag was changed. Out went the coat of arms, in came the blue globe, a white strip curved across it, the national motto *Ordem e Progresso* (Order and Progress) and the stars, now in a pattern across the globe with one added to reflect a territorial change. The blue globe allows the stars to be shown clearly. In 1889 they represented the twenty-one federal states of the new sovereign country, but there are now twenty-seven.

The flag was designed by Raimundo Teixeira Mendes, a Brazilian philosopher and mathematician. The stars on the flag are a replica of the position in the constellations they would have occupied on the day Brazil became a republic and they include the Southern Cross. Vexillologists and astronomers enjoy arguing about exactly what time the stars were in this position – whether it was the evening, when people might have been able to see them, or in the morning, for which there is some documentary evidence. They even argue whether it was 08.37 or 08.30, because 08.30 was, according to the Brazilian astronomer Professor Paulo Araújo Duarte, 'the moment at which the constellation of the Southern Cross was on the meridian of Rio de Janeiro and the longer arm [of the cross] was vertical'.

The white curved band across the globe is said to denote Brazil's position on the Equator. There's not a great deal to prove this, but given that Mendes was a mathematician it makes sense. Mendes was deeply influenced by Auguste Comte, the early-nineteenth-century philosopher who created the secular 'Religion of Humanity' and who, when trying to distil his philosophy of Positivism, wrote, 'Love as a principle and order as the basis', thus inspiring 'Order and Progress'. Mendes went on to lead the Positivist Church of Brazil in 1903. He died in 1927 aged seventy-two.

In the modern era the green is considered to be symbolic of the tropical rainforests and the yellow of the gold of the nation, but anyone delving deeper will soon come across the country's history. There are divisions, notably between the rich and poor, but also along racial lines. Brazil has had periods of violence and its share of corrupt leaders, as indeed we see again now, but compared to other Latin American countries Brazil has enjoyed more order and more progress. The country also has a strong identity, partly because its national language helps define it in relation to its Spanish-speaking neighbours.

The green and yellow now carry that message around the world, and there is something global about the flag as a whole which reinforces Brazil's attempts at soft power. The globe and the stars are common to us all, the green and yellow echo the vibrancy of humanity, and people are captivated by Brazil in a unique way that few countries have achieved. Any retailer knows that having instantly recognizable packaging helps sell the brand. Brazil wraps itself in a flag we are all familiar with and seem to love.

As we know, the modern Republic has many problems in its politics, its economy and its favelas, and yet its essence still seems to captivate us through its football, its music and its people. The French philosopher Albert Camus wrote: 'Alas, after a certain age every man is responsible for his face.' Their joyful flag is one of the faces the 200 million Brazilians present to the world and it suits them.

Latin America was part of the New World, but these nations are, compared to many around the world, no longer young. A new culture has emerged on the continent. These nations have forged solid identities over the past two centuries and their flags display this fusion of the old and the new. The symbols now seem anchored in this fusion culture, which helps create stability in what has, at times, been a turbulent region.

CHAPTER 9

THE GOOD, THE BAD AND THE UGLY

'We are a people, a tribe if you will. And flags are about proclaiming power.'

Gilbert Baker, designer of the Pride Flag

Previous pages: Flags of the world line the approach to the United Nations' Palais des Nations, Geneva, Switzerland; the UN flag flies from the top of the building.

WHY ARE PIRATES CALLED PIRATES? BECAUSE THEY *arrr*. Why is the 'Jolly Roger' called the Jolly Roger? No one knows for sure. It's possible that neither of those sentences is funny and certainly pirates were, and are, no joke. Nasty, thieving murderers are rarely amusing, and yet over the centuries the skull and crossbones flag, the eye patch, the peg leg and the swashbuckling 'Yo ho ho' have become almost romantic and, in the form of Johnny Depp's pirate in the Caribbean, cartoonish.

The Jolly Roger is, like other flags in this chapter, recognized around the world; it is one of those that transcends borders. Flags do not need to represent a nation or a political idea to engender emotion and convey a message. It might be a symbol of peace; a sign of solidarity for an international community to rally behind; or even just a successful form of branding. These flags represent diverse ideas, but what they share is the recognition factor, albeit through varying ways and means. There are also those, such as the Jolly Roger, that convey a different message depending on the context in which they are used; at an outdoor music festival it suggests the person flying it might be a bit 'rock 'n' roll', but seen from a merchant ship off the coast of Somalia it would be taken a lot more seriously.

Pirates are as old as seafaring and exist the world over, but the association with the skull and crossbones flag seems to originate in the twelfth century, when it was flown by the ships of the Knights Templar, which at the time formed the world's biggest fleet, deployed to protect the Templars' business empire. Why they used the image is beyond morbid. It stems from the legend of the 'Skull of Sidon', as told by one Walter Map in the twelfth century concerning some troubling events in the mid 1100s:

A great lady of Maraclea was loved by a Templar, a Lord of Sidon; but she died in her youth, and on the night of her burial this wicked lover crept to the grave, dug up her body and violated it. Then a voice from the void bade him return in nine months' time for he would find a son. He obeyed the injunction and at the appointed time he opened the grave again and found a head on the leg bones of the skeleton (skull and cross-bones). The same voice bade him guard it well, for it would be the giver of all good things, and so he carried it away with him. It became his protecting genius, and he was able to defeat his enemies by merely showing them the magic head. In due course, it passed to the possession of the order.

The Knights Templar rather fancied themselves as being on God's side, as opposed to being pirates, but their behaviour at sea was frequently piratical. These incredibly rich 'poor knights' were not above stopping lesser vessels and relieving them of any valuables, and their emblem may well have been the inspiration for later 'buccaneers' – or to say it another way, 'thieves'.

Our classic image of pirates begins in the early 1700s. One of the first recorded sightings of the Jolly Roger (as it became known) as a symbol of piracy is in the log of Captain John Cranby of the British navy ship HMS *Poole*, now held in the UK's National Archives in Kew. Under the (daily) heading 'Remarkable Observations and Accidents', amid the 'this 24 hours' fair weather and small gales' comes the tale of giving chase to a French pirate vessel off the Cape Verde Islands in July 1700. The pirates escaped, but the captain noted in his log that their black flag had 'cross bones, a death's head and an hourglass'.

The practice swept the pirate world in the first few decades of the eighteenth century and caught the public's imagination. For pirates black was the new black and on it they emblazoned the classic images, adding a few bloodcurdling extras as caught their fancy. The hourglass was to inform those on the ship they were approaching that their time had run out; sometimes a full skeleton would be added in case the message wasn't clear enough, while daggers and other weapons would remind the victims of the manner of their impending demise. The pirates developed a system known as the 'Pirates' code', which, in a time when most people were illiterate, still managed to convey volumes of information. The skull and crossbones told the ship being approached what they were dealing with. If the pirates also flew a black flag, this signalled that surrender without a fight would result in the lives of the crew being spared. If there was resistance, or if the ship attempted to flee, a red flag would be raised to say that no quarter would be given.

As a PR exercise it was excellent marketing. It provided a clear statement of intent, was instantly recognizable and associated with terrible deeds, and encouraged the opposition to give in without a fight – which they often would. It helped if the captain was known as 'Blackbeard', 'Black Bart', 'Blood' or some such. Spotting the fearsome flag a mile away through your eyeglass would have made your blood run cold. Quick calculations would have to be made. Could they be outrun; could they be outfought? Were you really prepared to die horribly for your cargo?

These questions are as relevant today as 1,000 years ago, as the pirates off Somalia, Nigeria, Indonesia and other hotspots know full well. There are even a few instances of flags bearing a skull and crossed AK-47s being flown. The intention, then as now, and as we saw with the IS flag, is to engender such fear in your enemy that they run or surrender.

Despite, or perhaps because of, the outlaw image, eighteenth-century pirates captured the public imagination. Daniel Defoe was among the writers, poets and dramatists who romanticized their lives, just as later screenwriters would do in Hollywood accounts of their exploits. The 1935 film *Captain Blood*, starring Errol Flynn, is a prime example, showing Blood's vessel flying a white flag with the skull and crossbones motif on it.

In the film the flag is not referred to as the Jolly Roger, although by that time the name was firmly embedded in the English language. The first references to it appear early in the eighteenth century. In his *A General History of the Pyrates* of 1724, Charles Johnson writes that two pirates had both named their flags the Jolly Roger, despite them having differing appearances. Some historians take this to mean that the term was therefore in widespread use for pirate flags of various designs.

As for why – there are three explanations. One of the names for the devil at the time was 'Old Roger', and putting a grinning skull on the flag may have led to the association. Another, more popular, theory is that in earlier centuries some pirates flew plain red flags which in French were called the *Jolie rouge*, and this may have caught on. Lastly, and equally plausibly, is that because the word 'roger' at the time meant 'wandering vagabond', so the symbol of these wandering vagabonds of the high seas was given the name Jolly Roger.

Finally to the 'arrr', which, while not related to the flag, is certainly worth relating. Our perception of 'pirate speak' is almost entirely down to the 1950s actor Robert Newton, who, whether he played Long John Silver or Blackbeard, 'arrred' his way through the roles. His greatest moment may have been in *Long John Silver's Return to Treasure Island* when, after a saying a prayer over a dead sailor's body, he managed to drawl 'Arrrrrmen'.

In order to avoid an unfortunate end at the hands of the pirates, many sailors will have run up the white flag of surrender. This is a symbol going back thousands of years and is present across cultures. Roman chroniclers mention it as a flag of truce in the Second Punic War (218–201 BCE) and again as a flag of surrender at the Second Battle of Cremona in 69 CE. The Chinese were also using white as the colour of surrender at the same time. Vexillologists speculate that, as it was the colour of death and mourning for the Chinese, it may also have signified grief at defeat.

The white flag is another example of the communication of vital information from a distance, or amid the confusion of a battlefield, via an easily seen and understood signal. It was held aloft millennia before most people could write, but they could all read what the flag was saying. It is now a globally recognized symbol that crosses international, cultural and linguistic barriers for battlefield negotiations, safe passage, ceasefires and surrender. Its use has been codified in the Hague and Geneva Conventions regarding conduct in war. The relevant passages state, among other things, that 'making improper use of a flag of truce constitutes a war crime in international armed conflicts when it results in death or serious personal injury', and 'improper use refers to any use other than that for which the flag of truce was intended, namely a request to communicate, for example, in order to negotiate a cease-fire or to surrender;

any other use, for example, to gain a military advantage over the enemy, is improper and unlawful.'

Most states have written advice on interpretation, protocol and best practice when dealing with white-flag situations. For example, the British military's 2004 publication *Joint Service Manual of the Law of Armed Conflict* states:

> The display of a white flag means only that one party is asked whether it will receive a communication from the other. In some cases, it may also mean that the party that displays it wishes to make an arrangement for a temporary suspension of hostilities for a purpose, such as the evacuation of the wounded, but in other cases it may mean that the party wishes to negotiate for surrender. Everything depends on the circumstances and conditions of the particular case. For instance, in practice, the white flag has come to indicate surrender if displayed by individual soldiers or a small party in the course of an action.
>
> 10.5.2. Those who display a white flag should cease firing until the invitation has been answered. Any abuse of a white flag is likely to be a war crime. Great vigilance must, however, always be displayed in dealing with enemy forces.

Alas, there are many allegations of misuse of the white flag to trick the enemy: the British accused the Boers of so doing in the Boer War, for example. And there are several instances where people have been accused of ignoring the flag – in 2009 there was an international outcry over an alleged case during the Sri

Lankan Civil War, known as 'the white flag incident', in which it was claimed three Tamil Tiger leaders were shot on official orders when trying to surrender, unarmed and carrying white flags. However, definitive proof of misuse is more rare. Either way, that such allegations are so emotionally incendiary is an indication that deep in our hearts, amid the logical madness and brutality of war, we still seek some semblance of order, of rules, of something which when all else fails can appeal to our common humanity. In some ways it is more than an appeal: it is a demand for mercy, and it is based on trust. The very fact that it still exists shows the recognition and respect for the trust and faith placed in this symbol around the world.

The Conventions also cover the use of the flag of the International Committee of the Red Cross. The ICRC allows state military forces to use its emblem of a red cross with arms of equal length on a white background and in return it monitors unauthorized use or misuse. There are strict rules about its use and these differ in times of peace or war. For example, which buildings can display the symbol, and how large it can be vary according to certain conditions. In wartime, 'a deliberate attack on a person, equipment or a building carrying a protective emblem is a war crime under international law.'

The Red Cross symbol was adopted in 1863 and officially recognized at the First Geneva Convention in 1864. They chose the reverse of the flag of neutral Switzerland, partly because of the idea of neutrality but also because the colours and design were easily recognizable at a distance. The flag is supposed to be non-religious and universal, but there was no getting away from the fact that it had a cross on it and looked very similar to some of the banners flown by the Christians during the Crusades. Thirteen years later, when the Russo-Turkish War broke out, the Ottoman Empire replaced the cross with a crescent. Other Muslim-majority countries later followed suit.

The ICRC has long been concerned that the true meaning of the symbols is sometimes overlooked in conflict, and that despite not being a symbol for any one side the cross and the crescent might be taken as such in difficult conditions with passions running high. There were other issues: the two existing symbols may not have been intended to convey religious identity, but could be seen as such in, for example, Jewish-majority Israel or in China, with a population that might be secular, Buddhist or Tao, for example.

In 1992 the then president of the Red Cross said that a third symbol was required, but it took until 2005 before governments signed up to an alternative flag that we are still getting used to – the Red Crystal. This is a red diamond on a white background which has begun to appear both on official buildings and occasionally in the field. It has no intended political, religious or geographical symbolism and allows any states which considered the first two flags problematic to join the Movement. The crystal, sometimes called a diamond, has equal status, meaning and legality to its better-known sister flags, although it perhaps doesn't yet have quite the same level of global recognition.

Another flag that seems to be not as well known internationally is that of the North Atlantic Treaty Organization (NATO), despite being a fairly straightforward affair: a dark-blue field has what is described as a 'white compass rose emblem' on it, although were it not for the official description the casual viewer might think it was simply a circle with a star. There is a white line radiating from each of the points of the star.

NATO was established in 1949, with twelve nations signing up to form a military alliance to counter what was regarded as the threat from the Soviet Union and thereby keep the peace. The flag was not introduced until 1953. Its designers in the NATO Council working group were given the task of coming up with something that had to be 'simple and striking' and simultaneously represent the 'peaceful purpose' of the Alliance.

The first proposals, in 1952, were based around a silver shield bearing fourteen stars and two blue stripes. The shield was to represent the defensive nature of NATO, the stripes the Atlantic Ocean, and the stars the, by then, fourteen members. It looked like something dating from the sixteenth century. The members couldn't agree on the design and noted that if, as expected, more states joined, the motif would have to be altered each time. The following year the Council approved the flag we now see. NATO's first Secretary-General, General Hastings Ismay (1st Baron Ismay, KG GCB CH DSO PC DL), explained its symbolism: 'The blue background was for the Atlantic, the four-pointed star represented the compass that keeps us on the right road, the path of peace, and a circle represented the unity that binds together the fourteen countries of NATO.'

There are now twenty-eight members, which suggests not only that the organization has been a popular success, but that its founding fathers were right to reject putting another star on the flag each time a new member joined.

Things were complicated enough in the 1950s when, despite having only fourteen members, low-level flag-squabbling broke out at NATO's Supreme Headquarters Allied Powers Europe (SHAPE), which was at the time located on the outskirts of Paris. SHAPE's commander, General Eisenhower, had approved a system whereby the flags of the member states would be flown outside the building in a semicircular row, with the flag of the host nation at the front of the semicircle. Thereafter the flag of each nation would be flown alphabetically in French, but every day each one would be moved one position further round. Thus, as it was a 'circle' with no beginning or end, and as the flags moved, none would be ever be last. Who could possibly complain?

The Dutch quickly objected to the French version of their name, 'Pays Bas', and demanded they be called the 'Netherlands'. The flag duly took its place between Luxembourg and Norvège, where it felt a lot more comfortable. A couple of years later a NATO lawyer with some spare time on his or her hands took the view that the official name for the United Kingdom in French was not 'Grande Bretagne' but 'Royaume-Uni'. So not G, but R. 'Oh,' said the British as the flag was hauled down and moved a few places along. 'Ah,' said the French, 'well in that case, as we told you earlier, the correct name for the Netherlands in this country is "Pays Bas".' 'Are you taking the P?' those tasked with lowering and raising the flags might have asked, to which the answer was 'Yes'. The Dutch flag was moved back to its original position.

In 1959, a few years after joining NATO, Turkey complained about being 'last' in the order and suggested scrapping the rotation system and using English names so that, for example, 'États-Unis d'Amérique' would become the United States of America. The French were hardly going to accept that.

France left the Military Command Structure of NATO in 1966 and the following year SHAPE moved to Casteau in Belgium. In time-honoured fashion the squabbling continued, and we have had fifty years of bright ideas about whose flag should be called what and positioned where. To date, the host nation is the furthest forward, the French alphabet remains in use, and every Sunday at midnight each flag is moved one position further around, thus intentionally symbolizing the never-ending circle, and unintentionally symbolizing a never-ending argument. The member states have no issue with the NATO flag itself, but are very concerned about their proximity to it. After all, for the French it would never do to have, let's say, the British flag closer to the main event than theirs. And vice versa.

So for a flag that's meant to represent unity, there's an awful lot of disunity going on behind the scenes. One flag that does seem to inspire a great deal of unity between rival nations, however, is that of the Olympics; an event where countries of the world display their own banners with great enthusiasm and no real animosity towards their neighbours.

If you leave aside the corruption, cheating, drug-taking, commerciality and those irritating sprinters making stupid hand gestures to the cameras, it's possible to have warm feelings about the Olympic flag and all it stands for.

The Olympic motto *Citius, Altius, Fortius,* 'Faster, Higher, Stronger', does not refer to drug dosage but to the idea enshrined in the Olympic Creed that the most important thing in life is not the triumph, but the fight. In sporting terms it is indeed a noble thought, but whether it was applicable to, say, landing on the D-Day Normandy beaches is debatable.

Either way, the motto and creed complement the symbol of the five rings on a white background. The design was introduced to the world by the founder of the modern Games, Baron Pierre de Coubertin. As a young boy he had taken the 1871 defeat of France by Bismarck's Prussia rather badly. He believed that a lack of French physical prowess, due to a lack of sport, had contributed to the loss. Later he became convinced that competitive sport could be a way of bringing nations together and in 1892 began lobbying for the creation of a modern Olympic Games. Two years later, seventy-nine delegates from twelve nations formed the first International Olympic Committee, and in 1896 the first modern Summer Olympic Games were held in Athens.

At the time there was still no symbol for the Movement. The five rings first appear as a sketch at the top of a letter from Coubertin in 1913; he then presented them as the idea for a flag the following year and the design was duly adopted. Due to the First World War the next Games were not held until 1920 in Antwerp, where the new flag had its debut in an Olympic stadium. At the opening ceremony the flag was unfurled, five doves of peace were released, and the Olympic Oath was taken for the first time by an athlete holding the flag.

The rings represent the five continents of the world and are interlaced to signify unity (put to one side the fact that by some reckonings there are seven continents). The white background of the flag symbolizes peace. The rings are in five colours: the top three circles are (left) blue, (centre) black and (right) red. The bottom two are (left) yellow and (right) green. There is a misconception that each colour represents a continent, and indeed this assertion used to be in the handbook of the Olympic Movement but it was removed in the 1950s as there is no evidence for it. In 1931 Mr Coubertin wrote: 'This design is symbolic; it represents the five continents of the world, united by Olympism, while the six colours [including white] are those that appear on all the national flags of the world at the present time.'

Given that the flag was designed just prior to the catastrophic war and flown soon after it, its symbolism cannot have escaped those present. Twenty-nine countries were represented, from as far afield as Argentina and Egypt. However, the spirit of world unity and peace was somewhat undermined by the fact that Germany was not invited, a decision made again in 1948 after the Second World War. Austria, Hungary, Bulgaria and Turkey were also excluded in 1920.

That first flag mysteriously disappeared at the end of the Games only to show up seventy-seven years later. In 1997, towards the end of a remarkable life as a Keystone Cop in Hollywood films, a banjo player and juggler, 100-year-old Harry Prieste was attending a dinner hosted by the US Olympic Committee. A reporter told the story of the mysterious disappearance of the Antwerp flag. 'I can help you with that,' said Harry. 'It's in my suitcase.' He then revealed that in 1920, after winning a bronze medal in the diving competition, he also won a dare offered to him by a colleague when he climbed up the 15-foot flagpole and stole the flag. Three years after confessing all, aged 103, he gave the flag back to the IOC at the 2000 Olympics in Sydney. In return they gave him a plaque thanking him for his 'donation'. The flag is now on display in the Olympic Museum in Lausanne, Switzerland.

Naturally, flags are a prominent feature during each Games. At the beginning of the tournament the Olympic flag is raised in the main stadium and remains aloft throughout the entire duration of activities. Flags are mentioned in the second verse of the Olympic anthem, as they have been since the 'hymn' was first performed at the first modern Games in 1896:

> *As now we come across the world*
> *To share these Games of old*
> *Let all the flags of every land*
> *In brotherhood unfold.*

This is indeed a noble sentiment, although it is an interesting point that national flags feature so prominently at the Olympics, with spectators there to support their nation's colours and to celebrate their nation's victories, when in fact the Olympics aren't intended as a display of national sporting prowess exactly. The focus of the Games is meant to be on the individuals, and not on the countries' overall performance and medal tally. In fact, the Olympic charter even states that they 'shall not draw up any global ranking per country, instead honoring individual medal winners . . . the Olympic Games are competitions between athletes in individual or team events and not between countries'. Nevertheless, that doesn't stop countries focusing and competing on the medal count, using the event as a way to boost their national pride, celebrate their apparent superiority and justify their often-massive investments in the sports sector.

The Olympics is not alone in this display; sports and national pride often go hand-in-hand. At international events of all kinds, flags are enthusiastically displayed on clothing, painted on faces and incorporated into all sorts of promotional items and memorabilia. Most of the time it is a harmless celebration of national identity and achievement, but in some extreme cases, it can turn nasty. As passions run high, sporting events are often perceived as the modern replacement for warfare, with opposing forces still flocking behind their respective banners, just as the armies of old might have done.

The 2016 European Championship saw hordes of young (and not so young) men running around the streets of France attacking opposing fans. When it came to the English and, most of all, the Russians, those initiating the fighting clearly felt they were representing their countries. In a sinister nexus of sport and politics the Russian authorities then made things worse by seemingly taking a perverse pride in their street thugs, and even calling in the French Ambassador to Moscow after a group were thrown out of France for their actions. This is a world away from the spirit of the spectators at the Olympics, however.

During the opening ceremony each national team parades its flag. That of Greece is always the first to enter the stadium, followed by the other participating nations in alphabetical order according to the language of the host country. The flag and team of the host country close the parade. Upon the lowering of the Olympic flag the Games are officially at an end. The flag is then folded and presented to a representative of the city hosting the event in four years' time, and a Greek flag is raised in honour and memory of the original Games.

There is one more tale about the Olympic flag, and it is a reminder to check facts and check again. It is possible that some myths have slipped through in this book, but one that has not is that of Baron Coubertin taking inspiration for his five-ringed design from a stone found in the ancient Greek city of Delphi which bore the same symbol. This has been widely reaffirmed, but according to other sources, including the Archaeological Institute of America, there's a more prosaic, less romantic, but possibly better story.

In the lead-up to the 1936 Berlin Olympics the then President of the Olympic Organizing Committee, Carl Diem, wanted to hold a ceremony in the stadium at Delphi, where similar athletic competitions had been held in antiquity. He commissioned the construction of a stone with the Olympic rings carved on it. The idea was that a runner would leave the site carrying the Olympic torch to begin its journey to Berlin. This duly happened, but the stone was left behind.

Two decades later two American popular science writers,

Lynn and Gray Poole, were in Delphi researching information for their book *A History of the Ancient Olympic Games*. They came across the stone and, mistaking it for an ancient Greek monument, wrote that it was a symbol of the original Games which Coubertin had resurrected for the flag. This was repeated in subsequent books, and is still repeated today. In reality the stone has become known as the 'Carl Diem Stone'.

It is a tradition during the Olympics opening ceremony for participating teams to briefly dip their national flags as they pass the leader of the host nation. Most do. The Americans are among those who do not. The US tradition has its roots in the 1908 Olympics during the first ever team parade when the Americans failed to lower their flag on the grounds that 'This flag dips for no earthly king'. However, Penn State University historian Mark Dyreson argues that this was not an official decision and that in 1912, 1924 and 1932 the flag was lowered. In his book *Crafting Patriotism for Global Dominance: America at the Olympics*, he says the decision in 1928 by the head of the US delegation to the Olympic Games, General Douglas MacArthur, not to dip the flag set the precedent for making this official policy but that it was only at the Berlin Games in 1936 that it became accepted practice and was a political act supported by the US government.

The Berlin Olympics are memorable for many reasons, not least for the black American athlete Jesse Owens winning four gold medals in front of a regime that believed in Aryan mental and physical superiority, but also for the many teams giving the Nazi salute to Hitler. The Americans marched past with a respectful 'eyes right' but did not dip the flag. The German authorities, including Hitler, were enraged. In 1936 this was indeed a sign of disrespect, although normally it is not the intention: it is more a sign of respect for the flag itself insofar as the Americans think so much of it and what it represents that they do not dip it to anyone.

Signalling the finishing line, and thus bringing to a close our tour of flags in the sporting world, is the black-and-white checkered flag, which took just a few decades to gain global recognition and now stands not only for the end of a race, but also for excitement. Its origins are somewhat prosaic, but almost all the research into its history ends up with a folk tale. In this one the flag originates in the American Midwest in the 1800s. It is claimed that towards the end of a horse-racing competition a tablecloth would be waved to signal that food was now available and so the racing should come to an end. The tablecloths of the time were usually checkered, either black and white or red and white, and gradually these became used at the end of each race. Folk tales can often have their basis in some form of truth, but alas in this case there is no primary-source evidence to back it up and the story simply seems to have been repeated because it seems plausible.

However, a book written by a specialist in Midwestern history, Fred R. Egloff, appears to solve the mystery. His 2006 publication *Origin of the Checker Flag: A Search for Racing's Holy Grail* came after years of research. Fred, originally from Illinois, has spent a lifetime seeking the stories which made legends out of lives such as that of Jesse James and testing them against evidence. I tracked him down to Texas, where he now lives, and found he'd used the same skills for *Racing's Holy Grail*. Fred is a racing car fan, indeed a racing car owner, and in his sixties was the proud winner of the 1997 Vintage Sports Car Competition in a 1930s BMW 328. Not just any BMW 328, mind, but one which its original Dutch owner had hidden from the Nazis during the Second World War by burying it under hundreds of old chairs in the basement of a museum.

So Fred knows a thing or two about history, and about cars. His story begins with a visit to the USA by René Dreyfus, a Frenchman who was one of the greatest Grand Prix drivers of the 1930s. Fred recounts how, on a visit to the Midwest, René asked, 'Where and when did the use of the checker flag originate, and what exactly did it mean?' but no one could ever tell him. He says: 'That got me thinking and a few years later I began to look into it. You know, I thought it would be easy, I knew a lot of old timers – took me ten years!'

He researched horse racing because of the myth of the tablecloths but got nowhere, and so got back in the saddle and moved on to cycling. A trawl of the archives of the League of American Wheelmen, the Bicycle Museum of America and numerous other bike-related minutiae failed to throw up a single checkered flag. As he says, 'I was at another dead end and the search returned to square one. All the stuff about it being from horse races and tablecloths was just guesses, as most people admit. I looked for it in Europe but it didn't start there. It started here.'

The USA's first automobile race had been held in Chicago on Thanksgiving Day 1895, and so Fred visited the University of Chicago's library (which by coincidence is close to where the race had begun). 'There was a magazine called *The Automobile* which was published every other week. They brought out their collection and I went through copy after copy after copy, looking for either a photograph or a description of a checkered flag.' In the 1902 July edition he found a photograph of a white flag with one black square at its centre being used at the end of a race, and then another from 1906 showing a checkered flag hanging among a collection of patterned flags at a New York car exhibition.

This was interesting – not the proof he was looking for, but he was getting closer. He began to read up on an early version of distance road races, 'Glidden Tours'. These were a sort of rally which grew out of long-distance car 'reliability and endurance' tests sometimes staged over distances of up to 1,000 miles. Manufacturers began to compete to win the tours in order to better market their models and the events were supported by the American Automobile Association:

In a different issue I found the story of a man called Sidney Walden who did the PR for the Packard Motor Company. At the time they were involved with the Glidden Tours. Sidney Walden came up with the idea that in order to better decide the winner, the course should be divided up and there should be time limits. They put people at certain distances to check the time and these people were called 'checkers'. To show where they were, and who they were, they used checkered flags.

Eventually, in an issue from May 1906 there was a photograph of a car and in front of it a man with a checkered flag; it was from the Glidden Tour of earlier that year. I believe that it is the first photograph of a checkered flag used in a race. The car still exists, it's a 1906 Darracq model and it's in New Zealand, but that's another story.

It's obvious, really. But the sort of obvious which becomes apparent only after years spent running down blind alleys in horse racing, dead ends in cycling, and then the many open roads of sports car racing. Fred R. Egloff may have taken his time getting to the truth, but he stands on the victor's podium.

It is ironic that this icon of the sports car world has become associated with speed given that its original design was to signal a driver to slow down. Nevertheless, it is now painted on the side of cars, printed on T-shirts and used in advertising as a symbol of speed and victory. Go to a Formula 1 race now and you will see people flying the checkered flag for fun alongside the national flag of their favourite driver or team.

Flag-flying is part of a global phenomenon both ancient and modern. As we've seen, the Chinese have been flying these silk emblems for thousands of years, the Arabs since before the time of Mohammed, the Europeans since at least the Crusades. Flags have been used as battle standards, as symbols of nations – and as a way of staking a territorial claim.

For example, in 2007 the Russians didn't plant their national flag on the ocean floor of the geographic North Pole because it looked good, they did it to say, 'Ours – not yours'. The validity of that, and the subsequent right to drill for oil and gas, is to be negotiated but it helps, albeit in a purely propaganda manner, to mark 'your' territory. That can be increasingly tricky in contested areas like the Arctic; those areas without a flag – ie, without a controlling nation – might still be seen as up for grabs. The Arctic isn't represented by a single flag as different parts of it have been claimed by a number of countries, including Denmark, Canada, Russia, and the USA, all of which reserve the right to drill in certain areas. This is an issue which will require careful negotiation to avoid an economic/diplomatic dispute sliding towards a military one.

Likewise, at the bottom of the world is another contested area that is yet to be claimed – Antarctica. It has an official flag which has been agreed by the dozens of countries involved in the Antarctic Treaty System, which stipulates that there shall be no military presence, no mining, and no nuclear explosions there. Seven states have (sometimes overlapping) claims to wedge shaped sections of Antarctica, but only for scientific studies and not for traditional territorial sovereignty purposes. Some of these states do fly their national flags to represent the territory they claim, others have unique flags for example the flag of British Antarctica, but none have ownership of the land. The USA, which was a signatory to the 1959 treaty, neither claims any of it nor recognizes any other countries claim; it does however, keep a scientific base there which flies the Stars and Stripes. After all, you never know . . .

Although flags can still very much be seen as the preserve of nation states, this is the age of the banner. Now it seems there are flags displayed for everything, from local sports teams to global movements and organisations, such as the LGBT rainbow flag and the universal blue of the United Nations. Admittedly you will not find either flown in the remaining pockets of territory under the control of IS, nor are they in abundance in North Korea, but the latter is the symbol of the idea of the world united, and the former is an emblem recognized throughout the developed world which speaks of a concept of freedom applicable to all people.

In scientific terms a rainbow is merely an arc-shaped spectrum of light appearing in the sky, caused by reflection, refraction and dispersion of light in water droplets – but what a phenomenon! It has captured our imaginations for as long as we've been on the planet and able to register natural beauty.

In Judeo-Christian civilizations, the rainbow is a sign that God will not send the Flood again. To the pre-Christian Norse it was a bridge which connected earth to the home of the gods, but only the virtuous could use it. To the Sumerians, according to the Epic of Gilgamesh, it was a symbol sanctioning war. The Fang people in Gabon prohibit children from looking at the rainbow as it is used in the initiation to their religion during a transcendental experience. The Karen in Burma believe it to be a symbol of evil.

Popular legend has it now that some Native Americans consider the rainbow around the sun to be a sign from God, marking a time of great change, and it is in this tradition that the LGBT communities have inherited the symbol, albeit mostly unknowingly. We are in a time of change, more rapid than in previous centuries, and the shift in attitudes towards LGBT people has been remarkable compared with the past millennium.

The original rainbow flag is now on display in the Museum of Modern Art (MOMA) in New York City. Credit for its design and popularization goes mostly to an American named Gilbert Baker who died in spring 2017. He said he began thinking through the need for a gay flag during the USA's bicentennial celebration in 1976 when the Stars and Stripes was even more omnipresent than usual. The rainbow was one of the first symbols he came up with, as to him it symbolized the diversity of nature – just as gay people were of all different colours, genders and ages.

In the early 1970s Baker had settled in San Francisco after service in the army, and was earning a living as a drag queen and making banners for gay rallies and events. He was friends with Harvey Milk, who in 1977 became the first openly gay public official in California. Milk wanted a symbol for the 1978 Gay Parade in San Francisco and asked Baker to come up with ideas. In a 2015 interview with MOMA the designer explained his thought process:

> [Harvey Milk] carried a really important message about how important it was to be visible . . . A flag really fit that mission, because that's a way of proclaiming your visibility, or saying, 'This is who I am!' . . . It's not a painting, it's not just cloth, it is not just a logo – it functions in so many different ways. I thought that we needed that kind of symbol, that we needed as a people something that everyone instantly understands. [The Rainbow Flag] doesn't say the word 'Gay', and it doesn't say 'the United States' on the American flag but everyone knows visually what they mean. And that influence really came to me when I decided that we should have a flag, that a flag fit us as a symbol, that we are a people, a tribe if you will. And flags are about proclaiming power, so it's very appropriate.

The first two flags, 30 feet by 60 and with eight stripes, were made by a team of thirty volunteers at the Gay Community Center in the city. In June 1978 they were unfurled in the United Nations Plaza in San Francisco during the Parade. Five months later Harvey Milk was assassinated along with Mayor George Moscone by a former politician angered by what he felt was the growing tolerance of homosexuality.

Milk died, but the flag survived – indeed demand rose dramatically as people wanted to express solidarity with Milk's legacy and the LGBT communities. It then rapidly spread around the world, representing another of the globe's transnational tribes.

The original design had eight colours. Pink represented sex and was deliberately included to claim it from the Nazis' use of the pink triangle which homosexuals were made to wear. Red represented life, orange healing, yellow sunlight, green nature, turquoise art, blue harmony and purple the human spirit. Pink was dropped fairly quickly as it was such an unusual colour for a flag and made manufacture expensive, and in 1979 turquoise was taken out so that the flag would have an even six stripes.

Now those six stripes, in a variety of forms, express many things. Gay people travelling around the world see it and know that the shop, hotel, restaurant or building where it is displayed is an inclusive place in which they are safe to do what other people do. It has also been flown from the Canadian Embassy in Tunisia and the UK's Cabinet Office in Whitehall. The six-striped image has been projected onto the Eiffel Tower and the White House.

In the summer of 2016, following the massacre of LGBT people at the nightclub Pulse in Orlando, the flag was almost immediately displayed in countless locations around the world. Social media was ablaze with the rainbow icon, which was attached to millions of Twitter and other accounts. Thousands of rainbow symbols flew at rallies and vigils. Flags were hung from windows in towns and cities in the parts of the world which have developed enough to allow people to express their sexuality and/or their solidarity with the victims. This was identity politics, but more. The flag was used not only to identify a person as LGBT, but also as being with LGBT. The rainbow flag is in a way a battle standard, but in an ongoing culture war. It has made huge advances, especially in the urban parts of the

Western world, but even there a risk remains in flying it. In huge swathes of the rest of the world, notably in Africa and the Middle East, its display can lead to jail or worse.

In 2016 the flag was also flown from the headquarters of the British intelligence agency MI6. The agency's chief, 'C', was signalling in an immediately recognizable manner that not only does MI6 support gay rights, but that it welcomes recruits from all backgrounds. It was one flag with six stripes, and flown with multiple layers of meaning. James Bond will not have been shaken, but may have been stirred.

And finally to the flag of the United Nations. It is a global flag; it has pretensions to being the flag of the world, but somehow falls short. Perhaps this is because of the Byzantine politics of the UN; perhaps because it represents nation states and yet within those nation states, as we have seen, are so many people who do not pay allegiance to the national flag. Perhaps simply because it's not a particularly inspiring flag and is out of date, although naturally that is a subjective judgement.

There is a putative 'International Flag of the Planet Earth', designed with the idea that, should we boldly go further than we've gone before, we could plant it on faraway planets or at least show it to their inhabitants who, if they know anything about our history, might take a dim view of our intentions. It was designed by Oskar Pernefeldt of Beckmans College of Design in Stockholm and has drawn a lot of attention but no official recognition.

It has an ocean-blue background with seven interlocking rings which, according to the flag's website, 'form a flower – a symbol of the life on earth. The rings are linked to each other, which represents how everything on our planet, directly or indirectly, is linked.' This, we are told, reminds people that 'we share this planet, no matter of national boundaries. That we should take care of each other and the planet we live on.' Fair enough, but that could be said of the UN, and indeed has been in a million communiqués in dozens of languages often printed out on thousands of dead trees.

The UN flag was first hoisted at the General Assembly in New York in October 1947. It was based on an original design by Donal McLaughlin for a UN badge in 1945 for the conference in San Francisco to draw up the UN Charter. It was a hastily concocted affair related in his *Origin of the Emblem and Other Recollections of the 1945 UN Conference*, which he published in 1995. Under pressure to get something out rapidly, he drew several designs, quickly discarded them, then came up with a round emblem showing the continents against circular lines of latitude and vertical lines of longitude, framed by two overlapping olive branches. This badge, with slight modifications, became the official United Nations seal and emblem.

In 1947 it was further adapted by the UN cartographer Leo Drozdoff to become the design for the UN flag. Against a blue background it features a map of the world in white with five continents and the North Pole at its centre. There are five concentric circles over the continents. At the time the view was that there were only five continents, although this has subsequently changed to six or seven, depending on whom you ask. Either way, the five is a reminder that the structure of the UN, especially the Security Council, reflects the world of 1945 and not the world as it is today. The five remind us of the countries that triumphed at the end of the Second World War (Russia, the USA, the UK, France and China) and then built the world order to suit them, including making themselves the only states with permanent membership of the Security Council, who have a veto. Brazil, Mexico, Indonesia, India, Germany and other nations could, and sometimes do, make a case for a UN Security Council that reflects the twenty-first century. That is a row older than this century, though, and for the foreseeable future we are stuck with the structure, and the flag.

The concentric circles in it can, if you are of a certain disposition, look alarmingly as if the world is caught in the crosshairs of an alien race. As far as those of us who do not wear tin foil hats are aware, that is not the case, but naturally the flag's design has attracted the interest of various sectors of the conspiracy theory world. For example, you may have noticed that on the flag the world is . . . flat! Furthermore, it is well known in these circles that the lizard people/Freemasons/Illuminati/insert weirdness of choice hide their symbols in plain sight. Explanations about the difficulties of drawing a 3D object onto a flat surface need not dent their belief as it is much more fun to see thirty-three segments in the concentric circles, remember that thirty-three is a number of significance to the Illuminati, and . . . Q.E.D. Happily, for the rest of us these theoreticians spend more time arguing with each other about which of their truths is the truth and thus leave the 'mainstream' alone.

At the weekends the only flag flying outside the UN headquarters is that of the Organization itself unless an important meeting is taking place. That they rarely do take place at weekends will not be a surprise to anyone who has tried to contact the UN at these times. It remains a Monday to mid-afternoon-Friday kind of place.

The member state flags are raised each day at 08.00 (except at weekends) and lowered at 16.00 by a team of ten or so staff. The process takes half an hour. Each flag is, by order, of equal size – 4 feet by 6 at a height-to-width ratio of two to three. This is just as well, as you would otherwise invariably get outbreaks of 'My flag is bigger than yours' syndrome. However, the conformity itself has caused problems. Many flags have different height-to-width ratios, causing various ambassadors, dignitaries and even leaders to complain that their country's flag looks stretched or just a little odd.

The order of the flags runs from north to south along New York's First Avenue and they are assigned according to the English alphabet. When there is a breeze, not unusual along the East River, they make quite a sight. What that sight conveys is complicated. Britain's leading vexillologist, Graham Bartram, is sanguine: 'Over the last few years I've come to the conclusion that it doesn't actually matter what's on the flag. One of the mistakes we make is assuming that what's on the flag is what makes it powerful . . . it's what it means to someone, and that it belongs to them, and say perhaps to ten million other people, which gives it the power.'

The UN flag is supposed to speak to, and for, all 7 billion of us – after all, we are the nations, and it does say United. Inevitably, as a mixed human enterprise the UN has mixed opinions within in it and, outside, mixed emotions about it. Its myriad committees are riven with the politics not just of member states, but of regional and religious blocs too. It's hard to love the flag, but it's the only one we've got. And if we didn't already have a flag – and an organization – that supposedly represented all 7 billion of us, someone would invent them. It's what we do.

The International Flag of the Planet Earth is a lovely idea, and a decent design, but if it were ever officially adopted as 'our' flag it would quickly become politicized. After all, who gets to choose it, who runs the committee? Who speaks for it and therefore for all of us? As a planet, we are not united. As soon as we see some people or groups in charge with whom we might not agree, we might not agree with the flag. And so it goes.

Usually flags mean identity; they identify what people are, but by the same token they also identify what they are not. This is why a national or religious flag can have such a hold on our imaginations and passions. But the UN flag doesn't stand in opposition to an external enemy, which makes it more difficult for us to unite behind it. Perhaps we lack the imagination to see ourselves as one united entity with a common purpose and must wait until Mars attacks to truly understand that.

But let's end with a more positive view. What we have, while waiting for our Red Planet cousins to visit, are, running the full length of the UN headquarters complex, the flags of the world's nation states. They are lined up, one after the other – representations of the groupings of peoples in every internationally recognized state in the world. It is a visually clear and bold affirmation of our diversity in colour, language and culture, political and otherwise, and simultaneously a reminder that we can come together – and that for all our flaws, and all our flags, we are one family.

BIBLIOGRAPHY

General References

The following sources were those I found to be invaluable in my research for this book. More specific sources are listed afterwards by chapter.

Complete Flags of the World (London: Dorling Kindersley, 2002)

Devereux, Eve, *Flags: The New Compact Study Guide And Identifier* (London: Apple Press, 1994)

Eriksen, Thomas Hylland and Jenkins, Richard (eds), *Flag, Nation and Symbolism in Europe and America* (Abingdon: Routledge, 2007)

Marshall, Alex, *Republic or Death! Travels in Search of National Anthems* (London: Random House 2015)

Smith, Whitney, *Flags Through The Ages And Across The World* (New York: McGraw-Hill, 1976)

Tappan, Eva March, *The Little Book of the Flag* (Redditch: Read Books Ltd, 2015)

Znamierowski, Alfred *The World Encyclopedia of Flags* (Wigston: Lorenz Books, 1999)

The Flag Research Centre website, http://www.crwflags.com/fotw/flags/vex-frc.htm

Introduction

'Guns, Drones and Burning Flags: The Real Story of Serbia vs
Albania', YouTube. 17 October 2015, https://www.youtube.
com/watch?v=WuUUGIn8QuE

The Stars and the Stripes

Hughes, Robert, *American Visions: The Epic History of Art in
America* (New York: Knopf Publishing Group, 1999)

Luckey, John R., 'The United States Flag: Federal Law Relating to
Display and Associated Questions', CRS Report for Congress,
14 April 2008, http://www.senate.gov/reference/resources/
pdf/RL30243.pdf

'Every race has a flag…' Notated Music, Library of Congress,
(Jos. W. Stern & Co., New York, 1900) https://www.loc.gov/
item/ihas.100005733/

Sunday Spartanberg Herald, 4 August 1935

http://nomoretatteredflags.org

The Union and the Jack

Lister, David, 'Union Flag or Union Jack', Flag Institute
Guide (2014)

Bartram, Graham, 'Flying flags In The United Kingdom', Flag
Institute Guide (2010)

Groom, Nick, *The Union Jack: The Story Of The British Flag*
(London: Atlantic Books, 2006)

The Cross and the Crusades

Buckley, Richard, *Flags of Europe: Understanding Global Issues*
(Cheltenham: European Schoolbooks, 2001)

Schulberg, Jessica, 'Video: The Ridiculous Meaning of Europe's
Flag, Explained', New Republic, 29 September 2014.
https://newrepublic.com/article/119601/european-flag
-doesnt-have-anything-do-europe

Walton, Charles, *Policing Public Opinion in the French Revolution* (Oxford: Oxford University Press, 2009)

'The European Flag', Council of Europe http://www.coe.int/en/web/about-us/the-european-flag

http://www.radiomarconi.com/marconi/carducci/napoleone.html

http://www.portugal.gov.pt/en/portuguese-democracy/simbolos-nacionais/decreto-que-aprova-a-bandeira-nacional.aspx

Colours of Arabia

Guinness World Records 2015 (Vancouver: Guinness World Records, 2014)

'Muslims World Cup Flag Anger', *Burton Mail*, 7 June 2006 http://www.burtonmail.co.uk/muslims-world-cup-flag-anger/story-21485018-detail/story.html#ixzz41ZDlrhWL

Flags of Fear

McCants, William, 'How ISIS Got Its Flag', Atlantic Magazine, 22 September 2015

SITE Intelligence Group, https://ent.siteintelgroup.com/

East of Eden

Bruaset, Marit, 'The legalization of Hinomaru and Kimigayo as Japan's national flag and anthem and its connections to the political campaign of "healthy nationalism and internationalism"', Department of East European and Oriental Studies, University of Oslo (Spring, 2003)

'Constitution of the Peoples Republic of China' (1982) http://www.npc.gov.cn/englishnpc/Constitution/node_2825.htm

'Chinese National Flag: Five-starred Red Flag', http://cn.hujiang.com/new/p478857/

Daily NK.com Kim Tu Bong and the Flag of Great Extremes [Fyodor Tertitskiy Column]

Sun Tzu, *The Art of War* (London: Penguin Classis, 2002)

Flags of Freedom

Barrett, A. Igoni, 'I remember the day . . . I designed the Nigerian
Flag', Al Jazeera, 3 September 2015
http://www.aljazeera.com/programmes/my-nigeria/2015/
09/nigerian-flag-150901092231928.html

Hill, Robert A. (ed.) *The Marcus Garvey and Universal Negro
Improvement Association Papers*, Vol. IX, Africa for the Africans
1921–1922 (Berkeley: University of California Press, 1995)

Official Website of the Universal Negro Improvement Association And
African Communities League, http://www.theunia-acl.com/

Shepperson, George, 'Notes On Negro American Influences On
The Emergence Of African Nationalism', *Journal Of African
History*, 1, 2, (1960), 299–312

'Taiwo Akinkunmi: An Hero Without Honour', Online Nigeria,
15 January 2007 http://article.onlinenigeria.com/
ad.asp?blurb=478#ixzz41fRsUZGe

Flags of Revolution

Flood, Daniel J., official correspondence, 1959
http://www.foia.cia.gov/sites/default/files/document_
conversions/5829/CIA-RDP80B01676R000900030089-5.pdf

'Advantages of the Panamanian Registry', Consulate General of
Panama in London Website, http://www.panamaconsul.
co.uk/?page_id=115

Carrasco, David and Sessions, Scott, *Daily Life of the Aztecs: People
of the Sun and Earth* (Westport, CT: Greenwood Publishing
Group, 1998)

von Goethe, Johann Wolfgang, *Goethe's Theory of Colours: Translated
From The German, With Notes* (Cambridge: Cambridge
University Press, 2014)

Jensen, Anthony K., 'Johann Wolfgang von Goethe (1749–1832)',
Internet Encyclopedia of Philosophy, http://www.iep.utm
.edu/goethe/

'Latin America Has Achieved Progress in Health, Education and Political Participation of Indigenous Peoples in the Last Decade', Economic Commission for Latin America and the Caribbean, Press Release, 22 October 2014 http://www.cepal.org/en/pressreleases/latin-america-has-achieved-progress-health-education-and-political-participation

Macaulay, Neill, *Dom Pedro: The Struggle for Liberty in Brazil and Portugal, 1798–1834* (Durham, NC: Duke University Press, 1986)

'Panama Canal Riots – 9–12 January 1964', GlobalSecurity.org http://www.globalsecurity.org/military/ops/panama-riots.htm

The Good, the Bad and the Ugly

Ship's Log, British Navy Ship HMS *Poole*, July 1700. From records held at The National Archives.

Antonelli, Paola and Fisher, Michelle Millar, 'MoMA Acquires the Rainbow Flag', Inside/Out, Museum of Modern Art website, 17 June 2015, http://www.moma.org/explore/inside_out/2015/06/17/moma-acquires-the-rainbow-flag/

Dryeson, Mark, *Crafting Patriotism for Global Dominance: America at the Olympics* (Abingdon: 2015, Routledge)

Egloff, Fred R., *Origin of the Checker Flag: A Search for Racing's Holy Grail* (Watkins Glen: International Motor Racing Research Centre, 2006)

'Geneva Conventions 1949 And Additional Protocols, and their Commentaries', International Committee of the Red Cross website, https://www.icrc.org/applic/ihl/ihl.nsf/vwTreaties1949.xsp

'Joint Service Manual of the Law of Armed Conflict', UK Ministry of Defence, 2004 https://www.gov.uk/government/uploads/system/uploads/attachment_data/file/27874/JSP3832004Edition.pdf

Leigh, Richard, Baigent, Michael and Lincoln, Henry, *The Holy Blood and the Holy Grail* (London: Arrow Books, 2006)

McLaughlin, Donal, 'Origin of the Emblem and Other Recollections of the 1945 UN Conference', 1995 https://www.cia.gov/news-information/blog/2015/images/McLaughlinMonograph.pdf

Olympic Games website http://www.olympic.org/documents/reports/en/en_report_1303.pdf

Rawsthorn, Alice, 'Skull and Crossbones As Branding Tool', *New York Times*, 1 May 2011

Shirer, William L., *The Rise and Fall of the Third Reich* (New York: Simon & Shuster, 1990

Young, David C., 'Myths About the Olympic Games', Archaeology online, 6 April 2004 http://archive.archaeology.org/online/features/olympics/games.html

ACKNOWLEDGEMENTS

Thanks to Graham Bartram, David Waywell, Samir Bambaz, Mina Al-Oraibi, Zein Jafar, Ollie Dewis, Sarah Ader, Fred R. Egloff, Fred Brownell, Sunday Olawale Olaniran and Dr Mahdi F. Abdul Hadi.

Thanks also to my publishers Elliott and Thompson, especially editors Jennie Condell and Pippa Crane from the Bad Joke Prevention Unit who made it immensely challenging to sneak any such examples into the final edit. I bear full responsibility for any poor jokes contained herein.

Flags are an emotive subject and the story of any given flag is often subject to various versions of history. I've done my best to make clear where the historical evidence is sketchy and am responsible for any errors.

INDEX

BOOKS BY TIM MARSHALL

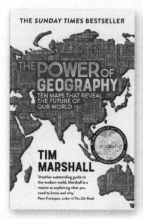

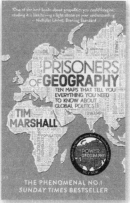

The Power of Geography
978-1-78396-602-8
£9.99

Prisoners of Geography
978-1-78396-243-3
£9.99

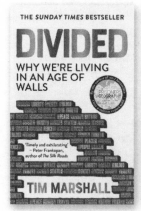

Divided
978-1-78396-397-3
£9.99

Worth Dying For
978-1-78396-303-4
£9.99

Shadowplay
978-1-78396-445-1
£9.99